MEN & WOMEN
OF THE **BIBLE**

NEED-TO-KNOW
DETAILS ON
EVERY PERSON
NAMED IN SCRIPTURE

MEN & WOMEN
OF THE BIBLE

PAMELA L. MCQUADE

BARBOUR
PUBLISHING

Our mission is to publish and distribute inspirational products offering exceptional value and biblical encouragement to the masses.

Member of the
Evangelical Christian
Publishers Association

Introduction

We have based *Men and Women of the Bible* on the King James Version of the Bible and *Strong's Expanded Exhaustive Concordance of the Bible* (Nashville / Thomas Nelson, 2001). The King James Version is the standard text for many Christians, and James Strong based his widely used concordance on it—so instead of reworking our entire volume to another, perhaps passing, translation, we have used these favorite and familiar volumes as the starting place for our work.

For the 2,026 proper names in scripture, covering some 3,400 people, the *Men and Women of the Bible* provides readers with concise information in the following categories:

Number of Times Mentioned—providing the number of times references to this person are found in the King James Version. This number appears in parentheses following the individual name entries. For those mentioned only one to three times, separate listings are provided at the end of the section for their letter of the alphabet.

Men and Women—since, as today, some names can be used by both men and women, women have been indicated by an asterisk (*) after their names. Where more than one person in scripture shares the same name, that is indicated by a plus sign (+) after the name. If readers find only one person of a name with a plus sign in the biography section, other references may appear in the lists at the end of each alphabetical section, which include the people who are referred only one to three times in scripture. Please note that we have not included titles or the names of spirit beings in this dictionary.

Meaning—where possible, a name translation based on *Strong's Hebrew and Aramaic Dictionary* and *The New Strong's Expanded Dictionary of the Words in the Greek New Testament* is provided.

Biography—an outline of the history of each person who is mentioned in four or more places in the Bible. For those mentioned only one to three times, listings are provided at the end of the section for their letter of the alphabet. Each name is followed by the first reference to that person in scripture. Within the biographies, when a reference has been made to a name held by more than one person in scripture, the first reference to that person has been included in parentheses after the name.

References—for each person who is mentioned four or more times in scripture, the first and last times the name appears in scripture is listed after the biography. Where many references describe one person, some key references for that biography have also been provided.

Where a person who is frequently mentioned in scipture had more than one name or where scripture provides us with variations of the name, some alternative names or spellings are listed at the end of the biography section. For example, Abijah's biography includes the information "Same as Abia (1 Chr 3:10)," referring readers to the first listing for the name *Abia* and the first reference to him in scripture.

In a few cases, readers will find differences here from what is shown in *Strong's*. One man, working manually on such a large project, was bound, perhaps, to make some minor errors. On top of that, scholarship through the ages has given us varying answers to questions about confusing references. Scholars of any age may differ on whether, for example, a person mentioned in one of the biblical name lists is the same as one mentioned in another place. Where a name is listed multiple times and references are not clear, we have made use of existing scholarship to determine one logical solution. In some cases, where references to a person were out of scriptural order in *Strong's*, the reference has been replaced into the order it would be in the Bible.

For the many hundreds of people recorded in scripture, *Men and Women of the Bible* will provide the concise information you need to quickly understand each individual's background, prominence, and contribution to history. We hope it will spur you on to further study of scripture.

Abbreviations for Bible Books

Acts: Acts

Am: Amos

1 Chr: 1 Chronicles

2 Chr: 2 Chronicles

Col: Colossians

1 Cor: 1 Corinthians

2 Cor: 2 Corinthians

Dn: Daniel

Dt: Deuteronomy

Eccl: Ecclesiastes

Eph: Ephesians

Est: Esther

Ex: Exodus

Ez: Ezekiel

Ezr: Ezra

Gal: Galatians

Gn: Genesis

Hb: Habakkuk

Heb: Hebrews

Hg: Haggai

Hos: Hosea

Is: Isaiah

Jas: James

Jb: Job

Jer: Jeremiah

Jgs: Judges

Jl: Joel

Jn: John

1 Jn: 1 John

2 Jn: 2 John

3 Jn: 3 John

Jo: Joshua

Jon: Jonah

Jude: Jude

1 Kgs: 1 Kings

2 Kgs: 2 Kings

Lam: Lamentations

Lk: Luke

Lv: Leviticus

Mal: Malachi

Mi: Micah

Mk: Mark

Mt: Matthew

Na: Nahum

Neh: Nehemiah

Nm: Numbers

Ob: Obadiah

Phil: Philippians

Phlm: Philemon

Prv: Proverbs

Ps: Psalm

1 Pt: 1 Peter

A

Aaron [350]

Meaning uncertain

The older brother of Moses, Aaron was called into God's service when Moses balked at confronting Pharaoh about his enslavement of the people of Israel. "I know that he can speak well," God said of Aaron (Ex 4:14), who became God's spokesman and supported Moses' leadership for nearly forty years. He was the first priest of Israel and headed a familial line of priests that continued for more than a thousand years. But Aaron made three memorable mistakes: He created a golden calf idol for the people of Israel when Moses stayed long on Mount Sinai receiving God's Ten Commandments (Ex 32), which started a cycle of idolatry that would plague the Israelites for centuries. He and his sister, Miriam, complained about Moses' Ethiopian wife, and Miriam contracted a temporary case of leprosy as punishment (Nm 12). And Aaron and Moses both incurred God's judgment—banishment from the Promised Land—when they disobeyed the Lord by striking, rather than speaking to, a rock that would provide miraculous water for the people at Kadesh (Nm 20). Aaron died at age 123 on Mount Hor (Nm 33:39), with his brother at his side.

First reference Ex 4:14
Last reference Heb 9:4
Key references Ex 4:30;
    32:2–4; Lv 9:7

Abed-nego (15)

The Babylonian name for Azariah, one of Daniel's companions in exile. Daniel had King Nebuchadnezzar make Abed-nego a ruler in Babylon. When some Chaldeans accused Abed-nego and his fellow Jews and corulers, Shadrach and Meshach, of not worshipping the king's golden idol, the three faithful Jews were thrown into a furnace. God protected His men, who were not even singed. Recognizing the power of their God, the king promoted them in his service.

First reference Dn 1:7
Last reference Dn 3:30
Key reference Dn 3:16–18

Abel (12)

Emptiness or vanity

Humanity's fourth member, the second son of Adam and Eve. Abel was murdered by his jealous brother, Cain, because the shepherd Abel's meat offering pleased God more than Cain's "fruit of the ground." When God asked Cain the whereabouts of his murdered brother, Cain replied, "I know not: Am I my brother's keeper?" (Gn 4:9). Jesus called Abel "righteous" in His denunciation of the scribes and Pharisees for persecuting the prophets.

First reference Gn 4:2
Last reference Heb 12:24
Key reference Gn 4:4

Abiathar (31)
Father of abundance

The only priest of Nob who escaped when King Saul ordered this enclave of priests killed because they supported David, Abiathar became one of David's trusted counselors and the high priest of Israel. But at the end of David's life, Abiathar supported David's son Adonijah as king and drew King Solomon's displeasure down on him. He was banished to his home, though he kept the title of high priest.

First reference 1 Sm 22:20
Last reference Mk 2:26
Key references 1 Sm 22:21–
    22; 1 Kgs 1:7

Abidan (5)
Judge

A prince of Benjamin who helped Moses take a census of his tribe.

First reference Nm 1:11
Last reference Nm 10:24

Abigail*+ (14)
Source of joy

A wife of King David. She provided food for David and his men after her first husband, Nabal, refused to help these warriors who defended his land from harm while King Saul and David fought. Nabal died after his wife told him what she had done. Because David appreciated Abigail, he married her.

First reference 1 Sm 25:3
Last reference 1 Chr 3:1

Abihu [12]

Worshipper of God

A son of Aaron who, along with his brother Nadab, offered strange fire before the Lord. God sent fire from His presence to consume them, and they died. Abihu had no children.

First reference Ex 6:23
Last reference 1 Chr 24:2
Key reference Lv 10:1

Abijah+ [14]

Worshipper of God

A son of King Rehoboam of Judah. Abijah inherited the throne from his father and went to war against Jeroboam of Israel, claiming that God had given Israel to David and his heirs. Triumphant because his troops had called on the Lord in desperation, he gained some cities from Israel and "waxed mighty" (2 Chr 13:21). Same as Abia (1 Chr 3:10) and Abijam.

First reference 2 Chr 11:20
Last reference 2 Chr 14:1
Key reference 2 Chr 13:1–5

Abijam [5]

Seaman

Son of Rehoboam, king of Judah. He inherited his father's throne and did evil for the three years of his reign, during which he fought with King Jeroboam of Israel. Same as Abijah.

First reference 1 Kgs 14:31
Last reference 1 Kgs 15:8

Abimelech+ [23]

Father of the king

The Philistine king of Gerar who took Abraham's wife, Sarah, as his concubine because Abraham introduced her as his sister. God warned Abimelech, and the king returned Sarah to her husband. Later Abraham made a covenant with Abimelech. Isaac repeated his father, Abraham's, lie when he moved to Gerar during a famine, but the king discovered it and protected him and his wife, Rebekah. God so blessed Isaac that Abimelech asked him and his family to leave. But eventually the two men made a covenant.

First reference Gn 20:2
Last reference Gn 26:26
Key references Gn 20:3–18; 26:8–11

Abimelech+ [40]

Father of the king

A son of Gideon, by his concubine. He killed all but one of his brothers and was made king of Shechem. Three years later the Shechemites rebelled, and he destroyed the city. He moved on to attack Thebez, and there he was killed when a woman dropped part of a millstone on his head.

First reference Jgs 8:31
Last reference 2 Sm 11:21
Key references Jgs 9:5–6, 45, 50–53

Abinadab+ [5]

Liberal or generous

A Levite who lived in Gibeah and housed the ark of the covenant for twenty years.

First reference I Sm 7:1
Last reference I Chr 13:7

Abinadab⁺ (4)

Liberal or generous

One of three sons of Israel's king Saul. Abinadab and his brothers died with Saul in a battle against the Philistines on Mount Gilboa (1 Sm 31:1–2). Same as Ishui.

First reference I Sm 31:2
Last reference I Chr 10:2

Abinoam (4)

Gracious

Father of Barak, who led Israel's army under Deborah.

First reference Jgs 4:6
Last reference Jgs 5:12

Abiram⁺ (10)

Lofty

One of the Reubenites who, with Korah the Levite, conspired against Moses. Because they wrongly claimed that all of Israel was holy, God had the earth swallow the rebellious Reubenites.

First reference Nm 16:1
Last reference Ps 106:17

Abishag* (5)

Blundering

A beautiful young woman called to serve the dying King David by lying with him to keep him warm. After David died, his son Adonijah wanted to marry Abishag, but Adonijah was put to death by his half brother Solomon, who feared his brother was trying to usurp the kingship.

First reference I Kgs 1:3
Last reference I Kgs 2:22

Abishai (25)

Generous

The brother of David's commander, Joab, Abishai accompanied David to King Saul's camp on a spying mission in which David chose to spare Saul's life. Abishai became a military leader under his brother and supported David in his fight with his son Absalom. Abishai killed the Philistine Ishbi-benob, who sought to kill David, and became a respected captain of the king's troops.

First reference I Sm 26:6
Last reference I Chr 19:15
Key reference I Sm 26:6–12

Abishua⁺ (4)

Prosperous

A descendant of Abraham through Jacob's son Levi and a priest through the line of Aaron.

First reference I Chr 6:4
Last reference Ezr 7:5

Abner (63)

Enlightening

The son of Ner, Abner was the uncle of King Saul of Israel and captain of his army. David confronted Abner for not protecting Saul when David crept into Israel's camp and removed Saul's spear and water jar. After Saul's death, Abner declared Saul's son Ishbosheth king of Israel. But when Ishbosheth wrongly accused Abner of taking one of his father's concubines, Abner went over to David's side and began encouraging all Israel to support him as king. David's commander, Joab, objected to David's accepting Abner as a friend, because Abner had killed the commander's brother Asahel. After Joab and his brother Abishai killed Abner, David mourned at his funeral. Solomon declared that Abner was more righteous than his killer (1 Kgs 2:32).

First reference 1 Sm 14:50
Last reference 1 Chr 27:21
Key reference 2 Sm 3:12

Abraham (250)

Father of a multitude

A new name for Abram, whom God called out of Ur of the Chaldees and into the Promised Land. This new name was a symbol of the covenant between God and Abraham. The Lord promised to build a nation through Abraham and his wife, Sarai (whom He renamed Sarah), though she was too old to have children. God refused to accept Ishmael, son of Abraham and Sarah's maid, Hagar, as the child of promise.

In time, God gave Sarah and Abraham a son, Isaac, who would found the nation God promised. When God asked Abraham to sacrifice his son on an altar, Abraham took Isaac and set out toward Moriah. There he prepared the altar and laid his son on it. But the angel of the Lord intervened, and God gave Abraham a ram to sacrifice in Isaac's place.

God knew the depth of Abraham's faith from his willingness to sacrifice his son. He promised to bless Abraham and his seed.

In his old age, after Sarah's death, Abraham arranged a marriage for Isaac, ensuring God's promise. Then the old man married Keturah. But her sons and the sons of his concubines were not to disturb Isaac's inheritance. Abraham gave them gifts and sent them away from his land.

Abraham lived to be 175. He was buried with Sarah in the cave of Machpelah, in Hebron. Same as Abram.

First reference Gn 17:5
Last reference 1 Pt 3:6
Key references Gn 17:2–8; 22:8

Abram (58)

High father

A man from Ur of the Chaldees, married to Sarai. God called him to the Promised Land and promised to bless him. At age seventy-five, Abram left with Sarai, his nephew Lot, and all their goods and servants. As he entered Canaan, God promised to give the land to Abram and his descendants.

God blessed Abram. When his flocks and Lot's were too large, they separated, and Lot headed for the area around Sodom. When Lot ran into trouble there, Abram prayed for him and rescued him, and God removed Lot's family from the wicked city.

God promised Abram a son, but he and Sarai waited many years. Sarai gave him her maid, Hagar, to bear him a child, but the promised child did not come. When Abram was ninety years old, God made a covenant with him and changed his name to Abraham. Same as Abraham.

First reference Gn 11:26
Last reference Neh 9:7
Key references Gn 12:1–4;
  17:1–5

Absalom (102)

Friendly

King David's son by his wife Maacah. When Absalom's sister Tamar was raped by their brother Amnon, Absalom hated him and commanded his servants to kill Amnon. When this was accomplished, Absalom fled Jerusalem for three years.

Joab, the head of David's army, tried to reconcile father and son. Though David allowed Absalom to return to Jerusalem, he would not see his son. But as David ignored him, Absalom won over the hearts of Israel's people, including David's counselor Ahithophel.

When David left Jerusalem, Absalom took over the city and a battle began in the wood of Ephraim. As Absalom rode under an oak tree, he was caught in it and his mule ran out from under him.

Joab heard of this, went to Absalom, and thrust three spears into his heart. Yet Absalom lived, so Joab's armor bearers killed him and threw his body into a pit. They covered his body with a pile of stones, and the battle ended.

First reference 2 Sm 3:3
Last reference 2 Chr 11:21
Key references 2 Sm 13:22;
15:10; 18:9

Achan (6)

Troublesome

An Israelite who ignored
Joshua's command that
nothing in Jericho should
live or be taken from the
city. He stole a mantle,
200 shekels of silver, and
50 shekels of gold and
hid them under his tent.
Because of his sin, Israel
could not stand at the first
battle of Ai. When Joshua
discovered Achan's sin,
he asked, "Why has thou
troubled us?" and prom-
ised that the Lord would
trouble Achan that day
(Jo 7:25). The sinner and
his family were taken to
the Valley of Achor and
stoned.

First reference Jo 7:1
Last reference Jo 22:20

Achish+ (19)

The Philistine king of
Gath before whom David,
who feared him, pretended
madness. Later David
sought refuge in Ach-
ish's land and received the
town of Ziklag from him.
Though Achish wanted
David to fight with him
against Israel, when the
king's troops objected, he
sent David home.

First reference 1 Sm 21:10
Last reference 1 Sm 29:9
Key references 1 Sm 21:10–
15; 29:6–7

Achsah (4)

Anklet

Caleb's daughter, whom
he promised in marriage

to the man who could capture the city of Kirjath-sepher. Caleb's brother Othniel captured the city and won Achsah as his wife. Afterward Caleb gave her land that held springs, since the lands of her dowry were dry. Same as Achsa.

First reference Jo 15:16
Last reference Jgs 1:13

Adah*+ (5)

Ornament

A wife of Esau, "of the daughters of Canaan." Possibly same as Bashemath (Gn 36:3).

First reference Gn 36:2
Last reference Gn 36:16

Adam (30)

Ruddy

The first man, who was created by God to have dominion over the earth. Adam's first act was to name the animals; then God created Adam's wife, Eve, as "an help meet for him" (Gn 2:18). God gave this couple the beautiful Garden of Eden to care for. There Satan, in the form of a serpent, tempted Eve. Though God had banned them from eating the fruit of the tree of the knowledge of good and evil, under Satan's influence Eve picked it, ate it, and offered it to Adam, who also ate. Aware of their sin, they attempted to avoid God. He banned them from the garden and cursed the earth's ground so Adam would have to work hard to grow food. As a result of their sin, they would die. Following their banishment, the couple had two children, Cain and Abel. When Cain killed his brother, God gave Adam another son, Seth. Adam lived to be 930.

First reference Gn 2:19
Last reference Jude 1:4
Key references Gn 2:7, 21–23;
  3:6

Adonijah⁺ (24)
Worshipper of God

A son of King David, born in Hebron. When David was old, Adonijah attempted to take Israel's throne, though David had promised it to Solomon. Nathan the prophet and Bath-sheba, Solomon's mother, reported this to David, who immediately had Solomon anointed king. When Adonijah heard this, he went to the temple and grasped the horns of the altar, in fear of his life. Solomon promised he would not be killed if he showed himself a worthy man. But when Adonijah wanted David's concubine Abishag as his wife, Solomon saw it as another threat to his throne and had Adonijah executed.

First reference 2 Sm 3:4
Last reference 1 Chr 3:2
Key references 1 Kgs 1:5, 50

Agag⁺ (7)
Flame

A king of the Amalekites whom King Saul of Israel spared in defiance of God's command. Obeying

God, the prophet Samuel killed Agag.

First reference I Sm 15:8
Last reference I Sm 15:33

Agrippa (12)

Wild horse tamer

Herod Agrippa II, great-grandson of Herod the Great, became king of the tetrarchy of Philip and Lysanias. Porcius Festus asked for Agrippa's advice on Paul's legal case, so he heard Paul's testimony, which almost persuaded him to become a Christian. Same as Herod (Acts 25:13).

First reference Acts 25:13
Last reference Acts 26:32
Key reference Acts 26:28

Ahab⁺ (90)

Friend of his father

A king of Israel, Ahab did great evil. He married Jezebel, daughter of the king of Zidon, and fell into Baal worship. God sent Israel a drought that only the prophet Elijah could break. The nation suffered for three years, until Elijah returned and challenged Israel to follow God. The prophet proved that God was Lord in a showdown with the prophets of Baal, before killing them and ending the drought.

Ahab coveted the vineyard of his subject Naboth, who refused to sell his inheritance to him. While the king sulked, Jezebel plotted to kill Naboth and get the land. Because Ahab humbled himself before God, the Lord promised to bring evil in his son's life instead of visiting it on him. Ahab was killed in a battle with Syria.

First reference 1 Kgs 16:28
Last reference Mi 6:16
Key reference 1 Kgs 16:29–30

Ahasuerus⁺ (28)

A Persian king who reigned over an empire that ran from India to Ethiopia. When his queen Vashti displeased him, Ahasuerus ordered the beautiful women of his kingdom to be gathered at the palace so he could choose a new wife. In this way he met the Jewess Esther, loved her, and made her his queen.

Not knowing that Esther was Jewish, Ahasuerus listened to his counselor, wicked Haman, who wanted to destroy the Jews. Hearing only Haman's false information, the king gave Haman permission to eradicate what he saw as a dangerous people. When Esther heard this, she came before the king and invited both men to a banquet. That night Ahasuerus discovered the faithfulness of Esther's cousin, Mordecai, who had reported a plot against the king. Ahasuerus commanded Haman to honor this Jew whom the counselor hated and had planned to kill.

On the second day of her banquet, Esther divulged Haman's plot to harm her people. Angered, the king had Haman hanged on the gallows he had built for Mordecai. Esther gave Mordecai Haman's household, and the king made Mordecai a royal advisor. Since his original law could not be changed, Ahasuerus had Mordecai write a new law that allowed the Jews to protect themselves from the attack Haman had planned.

First reference Est 1:1
Last reference Est 10:3
Key references Est 1:1; 7:5–10

Ahaz⁺ [38]

Possessor

A king of Judah who became deeply involved in paganism. God sent the kings of Syria and Israel against Judah in punishment, and Ahaz was unsuccessful in fighting off his enemies. Many people of Judah were captured and carried off. Ahaz sent to Tiglath-pileser, king of Assyria, for help, offering the temple silver and gold and the treasures of his own household to the pagan king as a gift. The Assyrian army responded by attacking Damascus but was not otherwise helpful.

When Ahaz joined the Assyrian king in Damascus, he saw and admired a pagan altar. He had it copied. When he returned to Jerusalem, he had the altars of the Lord moved and commanded Urijah the priest to use this pagan altar for worship.

Isaiah had prophesied the sign of Immanuel, "God with us," but because God did not rescue him, Ahaz became increasingly involved in paganism. He destroyed the temple vessels and closed the building to worship. Instead he built pagan temples throughout Jerusalem and established altars on high places near other cities. When he died, he was not buried with the other kings of Israel.

First reference 2 Kgs 15:38
Last reference Mi 1:1
Key references 2 Chr 28:1–5;
   Is 7:11–14

Ahaz⁺ (4)

Possessor

A descendant of Abraham through Jacob's son Benjamin, in the line of King Saul and his son Jonathan.

First reference 1 Chr 8:35
Last reference 1 Chr 9:42

Ahaziah⁺ (8)

God has seized

A king of Israel and the son of Ahab. Ahaziah reigned for two years and walked in the pagan ways of his parents. When he fell through a lattice in his chamber and was badly hurt, he sought help from the pagan god Baalzebub. God sent Elijah to the king's messenger, asking if there was no God in Israel. Twice Ahaziah sent soldiers to Elijah to demand that he come to the king. Twice Elijah called fire down on them. When a third captain came more humbly, Elijah went to the king and prophesied that he would die.

First reference 1 Kgs 22:40
Last reference 2 Chr 20:37
Key reference 1 Kgs 22:40–51

Ahaziah+ (29)

God has seized

A king of Judah, son of Joram and Athaliah. Following the advice of bad counselors, he joined with Joram, king of Israel, to fight against the Syrians. When King Joram was wounded, he went to Jezreel, where the king of Judah visited him. There Jehu killed Joram and sent his men on to Samaria, after Ahaziah. Ahaziah died of his wounds in Megiddo.

First reference 2 Kgs 8:24
Last reference 2 Chr 22:11
Key reference 2 Chr 22:2–4

Ahiezer+ (5)

Brother of help

A man of the tribe of Dan who helped Aaron number the Israelites. God made him captain of his tribe.

First reference Nm 1:12
Last reference Nm 10:25

Ahijah+ (12)

Worshipper of God

A prophet who prophesied the division of Israel into the countries of Israel and Judah. He promised Jeroboam that he would rule Israel. After the king disobeyed God, Ahijah prophesied the death of Jeroboam's son and Jeroboam's destruction.

First reference 1 Kgs 11:29
Last reference 2 Chr 10:15

Ahijah+ (4)

Worshipper of God

A descendant of Issachar. His son Baasha conspired

against King Nadab of Israel.

First reference 1 Kgs 15:27
Last reference 2 Kgs 9:9

Ahikam (20)
High

One of the men sent to consult Huldah the prophetess after King Josiah rediscovered the book of the law. Ahikam supported Jeremiah, protecting him from death, when his prophecies became unpopular. When Jeremiah was released from prison, he was given into the care of Ahikam's son Gedaliah.

First reference 2 Kgs 22:12
Last reference Jer 43:6
Key reference 2 Kgs 22:12–14

Ahilud (5)
Brother of one born

Father of Jehoshaphat. His son served as King David's recorder.

First reference 2 Sm 8:16
Last reference 1 Chr 18:15

Ahimaaz⁺ (13)
Brother of anger

Son of the priest Zadok. When Absalom forced David from his throne, Ahimaaz carried messages to David from his spy, Hushai the Archite. He also brought King David the news of his troops' victory over Absalom.

First reference 2 Sm 15:27
Last reference 1 Chr 6:53

Ahimelech+ [15]

Brother of the king

The priest of Nob who gave David the hallowed bread to feed his men, when David was fleeing from Saul. When King Saul discovered this, he had all the men in Ahimelech's priestly enclave killed. Only the priest's son Abiathar escaped.

First reference 1 Sm 21:1
Last reference Ps 52 (title)
Key references 1 Sm 21:1, 6

Ahinoam*+ [6]

Brother of pleasantness

A woman from Jezreel who became David's wife.

First reference 1 Sm 25:43
Last reference 1 Chr 3:1

Ahira [5]

Brother of wrong

A prince of the tribe of Napthali, after the Exodus.

First reference Nm 1:15
Last reference Nm 10:27

Ahithophel [20]

Brother of folly

King David's counselor who conspired with David's son Absalom to overthrow Israel's throne. Ahithophel advised Absalom to defile his father's concubines. "And the counsel of Ahithophel. . . was as if a man had enquired at the oracle of God" (2 Sm 16:23). When Absalom did not follow his counselor's advice about attacking David and it became clear that Absalom was unlikely to win, Ahithophel hanged himself.

First reference 2 Sm 15:12
Last reference 1 Chr 27:34
Key reference 2 Sm 16:23

Ahitub⁺ (5)

Brother of goodness

Son of Phineas and father of Ahiah and Ahimelech the priest of Nob.

First reference 1 Sm 14:3
Last reference 1 Sm 22:20

Ahitub⁺ (6)

Brother of goodness

A descendant of Abraham through Jacob's son Levi and a priest through the line of Aaron. Ahitub was the father of Zadok, the priest during King David's reign.

First reference 2 Sm 8:17
Last reference Ezr 7:2

Aholiab (5)

Tent of his father

An engraver and embroiderer given special ability by God to work on the tabernacle, Israel's portable worship center begun in the time of Moses. Aholiab was "a cunning workman" and taught other craftsmen.

First reference Ex 31:6
Last reference Ex 38:23

Aholibamah*⁺ (6)

Tent of the height

A wife of Esau who was "of the daughters of Canaan."

First reference Gn 36:2
Last reference Gn 36:25

Aiah+ (4)

Hawk

Father of Rizpah, who was a concubine of King Saul.

First reference 2 Sm 3:7
Last reference 2 Sm 21:11

Alphaeus+ (4)

Father of one of two apostles named James. The phrase "James the son of Alphaeus" distinguishes this James from the brother of John and the "sons of Zebedee."

First reference Mt 10:3
Last reference Acts 1:13

Amasa+ (15)

Burden

King David's nephew who became Absalom's commander during Absalom's rebellion against his father. When David regained the throne, he made Amasa commander of his army in Joab's place. When the king sent his new commander to gather the men of Judah, Joab followed Amasa, attacked him, and killed him.

First reference 2 Sm 17:25
Last reference 1 Chr 2:17
Key reference 2 Sm 19:13

Amaziah+ (35)

Strength of God

Son and successor of King Joash of Judah. Though he did right, the new king did not remove the pagan altars from the land. He killed the servants who had murdered his father in his bed but did not kill their children. After raising an army in his country, he hired one hundred thousand men from Israel. But a man of God convinced the king to rely on God, not a hired army, so Amaziah sent the Israelites home. With his own men he went to war with Edom and won; meanwhile the scorned Israelite army attacked Judah's cities, killed three thousand people, and carried away spoils. Amaziah brought back idols from Edom and began to worship them. When God sent a prophet to correct him, he would not listen, and the prophet predicted Amaziah's downfall. Amaziah confronted Jehoash, king of Israel, who tried to make peace. Judah's king refused, but when he waged war on Israel, all his men fled. Jehoash broke down Jerusalem's wall and took the precious vessels from the temple and the treasures of the king's house. Later a conspiracy grew up against Amaziah, so he fled to Lachish, where he was killed.

First reference 2 Kgs 12:21
Last reference 2 Chr 26:4
Key references 2 Chr 25:1–2, 14–16

Ammihud⁺ (6)

People of splendor

A descendant of Abraham through Joseph's son Ephraim. Ammihud was an ancestor of Joshua.

First reference Nm 1:10
Last reference 1 Chr 7:26

Amminadab⁺ (9)

A descendant of Judah. His son Nahshon became the prince of his tribe.

First reference Nm 1:7
Last reference 1 Chr 2:10

Ammishaddai (5)

People of the Almighty

A descendant of Dan. His son Ahiezer became the prince of his tribe.

First reference Nm 1:12
Last reference Nm 10:25

Amnon+ (27)

Faithful

David's firstborn son, born in Hebron to his wife Ahinoam. Amnon fell in love with his half sister Tamar. Pretending to be sick, he asked his father to send Tamar to him with food. When she came, he raped her. His love turned to hate, and he threw her out of his house. When Tamar's full brother, Absalom, heard of this, he hated Amnon and eventually had him killed.

First reference 2 Sm 3:2
Last reference I Chr 3:1
Key reference 2 Sm 13:1–2

Amon+ (16)

Skilled

An evil king of Judah who reigned for two years. He worshipped idols and "trespassed more and more" (2 Chr 33:23). Amon's servants conspired against him and killed him in his own house.

First reference 2 Kgs 21:18
Last reference Mt 1:10
Key references 2 Kgs 21:19–20;
    2 Chr 33:23

Amos+ (7)

Burdensome

A Judean prophet during the reigns of King Uzziah of Judah and King Jeroboam of Israel. He came from a rural setting in which he was a herdsman and fruit gatherer. When God called him as a prophet, he spoke to both Judah and Israel, condemning idolatry and disobedience.

First reference Am 1:1
Last reference Am 8:2

Amoz (13)

Strong

Father of the prophet Isaiah.

First reference 2 Kgs 19:2
Last reference Is 38:1

Amram⁺ (12)

High people

Father of Moses, Aaron, and Miriam.

First reference Ex 6:18
Last reference 1 Chr 24:20

Anah*⁺ (5)

Answer

Mother of Aholibamah and mother-in-law of Esau.

First reference Gn 36:2
Last reference Gn 36:25

Anah⁺ (4)

Answer

A descendant of Seir, who lived in Esau's "land of Edom." Anah discovered "mules in the wilderness" as he fed his father's donkeys.

First reference Gn 36:24
Last reference 1 Chr 1:41

Anak (9)

Strangling

Founder of a tribe in Hebron. His gigantic sons lived there when Joshua's spies searched the land.

First reference Nm 13:22
Last reference Jgs 1:20

Ananias⁺ (6)

God has favored

A Christian of Damascus whom God called to speak to Paul shortly after the future apostle's conversion. When Ananias doubted the wisdom of meeting with Paul, God told him Paul would bear the gospel to the Gentiles.

First reference Acts 9:10
Last reference Acts 22:12

Andrew (13)

Manly

Brother of Peter and one of Jesus' disciples and apostles. Andrew met Jesus and then told Peter he had found the Messiah. Jesus called both of these fishermen to leave their boat and become fishers of men. At the feeding of the five thousand, Andrew brought the boy with loaves and fish to Jesus' attention. With Philip, he brought some Greeks to meet Jesus. He was also one of the intimate group of disciples who questioned Jesus about the end times.

First reference Mt 4:18
Last reference Acts 1:13
Key references Mt 4:18–19;
   Jn 6:8–9

Annas (4)

God has favored

High priest during Jesus' ministry. Though the Romans deposed Annas in favor of his son-in-law Caiaphas, many Jews still considered him the high priest. Jesus was first brought to him after Judas's betrayal. Annas was also one of the council that sought to keep Peter from preaching.

First reference Lk 3:2
Last reference Acts 4:6

Apollos (10)

The sun

A Jewish preacher from Alexandria who had been baptized into John's baptism and knew nothing of the Holy Spirit. Aquila and Priscilla "expounded unto him the way of God more perfectly" (Acts 18:26). He preached in Greece. When a dispute arose in Corinth between church members who followed Paul and those who followed Apollos, Paul called them to recognize that they all followed Jesus.

First reference Acts 18:24
Last reference Ti 3:13
Key references Acts 18:24;
    1 Cor 3:5

Aquila (6)

Eagle

A tent-making Christian who lived in Corinth and met Paul there. Paul joined Aquila and his wife, Priscilla, in their craft. The couple became helpers in Paul's ministry and founded a house church in their home.

First reference Acts 18:2
Last reference 2 Tm 4:19

Aram⁺ (4)

The highland

A descendant of Abraham through Isaac; forebear of Jesus' earthly father, Joseph.

First reference I Chr 7:34
Last reference Lk 3:33

Araunah (9)

Strong

A Jebusite who sold his threshing floor to King David so the king could build an altar and make a sacrifice there. Same as Ornan.

First reference 2 Sm 24:16
Last reference 2 Sm 24:24

Arioch⁺ (5)

Captain of King Nebuchadnezzar's guard. When none of Nebuchadnezzar's wise men could interpret the king's dream, Arioch was to kill all the wise men. Instead he brought Daniel to the king.

First reference Dn 2:14
Last reference Dn 2:25

Aristarchus (5)

Best ruling

One of Paul's companions at Ephesus who was captured by a crowd that objected to the Christians' teaching. He accompanied Paul on various travels, including his trip to Rome.

First reference Acts 19:29
Last reference Phlm 1:24

Arphaxad (10)

A descendant of Noah through his son Shem.

First reference Gn 10:22
Last reference Lk 3:36
Key reference Gn 11:11–13

Artaxerxes⁺ (4)

Persian king who received letters objecting to the rebuilding of Jerusalem from those who opposed the Jews. Also called Longimanus.

First reference Ezr 4:7
Last reference Ezr 4:11

Artaxerxes⁺ (9)

Another name for King Darius of Persia.

First reference Ezr 7:1
Last reference Neh 13:6

Asa⁺ (59)

King of Judah, son of King Abijam. Asa reigned forty-one years and removed many idols from Judah. While the country was peaceful, he built fortified cities and established his army. When an Ethiopian army attacked, he called on the Lord and was victorious. After Azariah prophetically encouraged the king to seek the Lord, Asa led his people in making a covenant to seek God. He even removed his mother from her position as queen because she worshipped idols. But he did not remove the idols from the high places.

In the thirty-sixth year of his reign, Asa took the silver and gold from the temple and his own treasury and gave it to King Ben-hadad of Syria to convince him to end his alliance with Baasha, king of Israel, and support Judah instead. Through Hanani the prophet, God declared that Asa was not depending on Him and would end his reign in wars. The angry king imprisoned Hanani and oppressed people. Though he suffered an illness of his feet, Asa would not turn to the Lord.

First reference 1 Kgs 15:8
Last reference Mt 1:8
Key references 2 Chr 14:2–4;
   16:7–10

Asahel+ (15)

God has made

Brother of Joab, who was David's army commander. Asahel was also a commander in King David's army, overseeing twenty-four thousand men in the fourth month of each year. Following a battle at Gibeon, Asahel pursued Abner, Saul's escaping army commander, and was killed by him.

First reference 2 Sm 2:18
Last reference 1 Chr 27:7

Asaph+ (38)

Collector

A descendant of Abraham through Jacob's son Levi. Asaph was one of the key musicians serving in the Jerusalem temple. King David appointed Asaph's descendants to "prophesy with harps, with psalteries, and with cymbals" (1 Chr 25:1).

First reference 1 Chr 6:39
Last reference Ps 83 (title)

Asher (9)

Happy

A son of Jacob and Zilpah. He founded Israel's tribe of Asher.

First reference Gn 30:13
Last reference 1 Chr 7:40

Athaliah*+ (15)

God has constrained

Wife of Jehoram and mother of Ahaziah, two kings of Judah. When her son was killed by Jehu, she destroyed all possible heirs to the throne, missing only Joash, who was saved by his aunt Jehosheba. Wicked, idolatrous Athaliah ruled Judah for six years. In the seventh year of her reign, in the temple, the priest Jehoiada crowned Joash king. When Athaliah saw this, she declared it treason. Jehoiada commanded his warriors to take her outside the temple and kill her. Judah did not mourn her death.

First reference 2 Kgs 8:26
Last reference 2 Chr 24:7
Key references 2 Kgs 11:1;
  2 Chr 22:3

Augustus (4)

August

The Roman emperor who called for the census that brought Mary and Joseph to Bethlehem. He was still ruling when Paul appealed to Caesar during his imprisonment in Jerusalem. Also called Caesar Augustus.

First reference Lk 2:1
Last reference Acts 27:1

Azariah+ (9)

God has helped

King of Judah who was obedient to God but did not remove the idolatrous altars from the high places. Though Azariah ruled for fifty-two years, God made him a leper, and his son judged the people in his place. Same as Uzziah (2 Kgs 15:13).

First reference 2 Kgs 14:21
Last reference 1 Chr 3:12

Azariah⁺ (4)

God has helped

Another descendant of Abraham through Jacob's son Levi and a priest through the line of Aaron.

First reference 1 Chr 6:13
Last reference Ezr 7:1

Azariah⁺ (5)

God has helped

The Hebrew name for Abed-nego, one of Daniel's companions in exile.

First reference Dn 1:6
Last reference Dn 2:17

Azel (6)

Noble

A descendant of Abraham through Jacob's son Benjamin and through the line of King Saul and his son Jonathan.

First reference 1 Chr 8:37
Last reference 1 Chr 9:44

A: Mentioned Once

Abagtha (Est 1:10)

Abda⁺ (1 Kgs 4:6)

Abda⁺ (Neh 11:17)

Abdeel (Jer 36:26)

Abdi⁺ (Ezr 10:26)

Abdiel (1 Chr 5:15)

Abdon⁺ (1 Chr 8:23)

Abdon⁺ (2 Chr 34:20)

Abi (2 Kgs 18:2)

Abia⁺ (Lk 1:5)

Abiah*⁺ (1 Chr 2:24)

Abiah⁺ (1 Chr 7:8)

Abi-albon (2 Sm 23:31)

Abiasaph (Ex 6:24)

Abida (1 Chr 1:33)

Abidah (Gn 25:4)

Abiel⁺ (1 Chr 11:32)

Abihail⁺ (Nm 3:35)

Abihail*⁺ (1 Chr 2:29)

Abihail⁺ (1 Chr 5:14)

Abihail*⁺ (2 Chr 11:18)

Abihud (1 Chr 8:3)

Abijah⁺ (1 Kgs 14:1)

Abijah⁺ (1 Chr 24:10)

Abijah*⁺ (2 Chr 29:1)

Abijah⁺ (Neh 10:7)

Abimelech⁺ (1 Chr 18:16)

Abinadab⁺ (1 Kgs 4:11)

Abiram⁺ (1 Kgs 16:34)

Abishua⁺ (1 Chr 8:4)

Abitub (1 Chr 8:11)

Abiud (Mt 1:13)

Achaicus (1 Cor 16:17)

Achar (1 Chr 2:7)

Achaz (Mt 1:9)

Achim (Mt 1:14)

Achsa (1 Chr 2:49)

Adaiah⁺ (2 Kgs 22:1)

Adaiah⁺ (1 Chr 6:41)

Adaiah⁺ (1 Chr 8:21)

Adaiah⁺ (1 Chr 9:12)

Adaiah⁺ (2 Chr 23:1)

Adaiah⁺ (Ezr 10:29)

Adaiah⁺ (Ezr 10:39)

Adaiah⁺ (Neh 11:5)

Adaiah⁺ (Neh 11:12)

Adalia (Est 9:8)

Addar (1 Chr 8:3)

Addi (Lk 3:28)

Ader (1 Chr 8:15)

Adiel⁺ (1 Chr 4:36)

Adiel⁺ (1 Chr 9:12)

Adiel+ (1 Chr 27:25)

Adin+ (Ezr 8:6)

Adin+ (Neh 10:16)

Adina (1 Chr 11:42)

Adino (2 Sm 23:8)

Adlai (1 Chr 27:29)

Admatha (Est 1:14)

Adna+ (Ezr 10:30)

Adna+ (Neh 12:15)

Adnah+ (1 Chr 12:20)

Adnah+ (2 Chr 17:14)

Adonijah+ (2 Chr 17:8)

Adonijah+ (Neh 10:16)

Adoni-zedec (Jo 10:1)

Adoram+ (2 Sm 20:24)

Adoram+ (1 Kgs 12:18)

Agag+ (Nm 24:7)

Agee (2 Sm 23:11)

Agur (Prv 30:1)

Aharah (1 Chr 8:1)

Aharhel (1 Chr 4:8)

Ahasai (Neh 11:13)

Ahasbai (2 Sm 23:34)

Ahasuerus+ (Ezr 4:6)

Ahasuerus+ (Dn 9:1)

Ahban (1 Chr 2:29)

Aher (1 Chr 7:12)

Ahi+ (1 Chr 5:15)

Ahi+ (1 Chr 7:34)

Ahiah+ (1 Kgs 4:3)

Ahiah+ (1 Chr 8:7)

Ahian (1 Chr 7:19)

Ahiezer+ (1 Chr 12:3)

Ahihud+ (Nm 34:27)

Ahihud+ (1 Chr 8:7)

Ahijah+ (1 Chr 2:25)

Ahijah+ (1 Chr 11:36)

Ahijah+ (1 Chr 26:20)

Ahijah+ (Neh 10:26)

Ahimaaz+ (1 Sm 14:50)

Ahimaaz+ (1 Kgs 4:15)

Ahiman+ (Nm 13:22)

Ahiman+ (1 Chr 9:17)

Ahimelech+ (1 Sm 26:6)

Ahimoth (1 Chr 6:25)

Ahinadab (1 Kgs 4:14)

Ahinoam*+ (1 Sm 14:50)

Ahiram (Nm 26:38)

Ahishahar (1 Chr 7:10)

Ahishar (1 Kgs 4:6)

Ahio+ (1 Chr 8:14)

Ahlai+ (1 Chr 2:31)

Ahlai+ (1 Chr 11:41)

Ahoah (1 Chr 8:4)

Ahumai (1 Chr 4:2)

Ahuzam (1 Chr 4:6)

Ahuzzath (Gn 26:26)

Aiah+ (1 Chr 1:40)

Ajah (Gn 36:24)

Akan (Gn 36:27)

Akkub+ (1 Chr 3:24)

Akkub+ (Ezr 2:45)

Akkub+ (Neh 8:7)

Alameth (1 Chr 7:8)

Alexander+ (Mk 15:21)

Alexander+ (Acts 4:6)

Alexander+ (Acts 19:33)

Aliah (1 Chr 1:51)

Alian (1 Chr 1:40)

Allon (1 Chr 4:37)

Alphaeus+ (Mk 2:14)

Alvah (Gn 36:40)

Alvan (Gn 36:23)

Amal (1 Chr 7:35)

Amariah+ (1 Chr 6:11)

Amariah+ (2 Chr 19:11)

Amariah+ (2 Chr 31:15)

Amariah+ (Ezr 10:42)

Amariah+ (Neh 11:4)

Amariah+ (Zep 1:1)

Amasa+ (2 Chr 28:12)

Amasai+ (1 Chr 12:18)

Amasai+ (1 Chr 15:24)

Amashai (Neh 11:13)

Amasiah (2 Chr 17:16)

Amaziah+ (1 Chr 4:34)

Amaziah+ (1 Chr 6:45)

Ami (Ezr 2:57)

Ammiel+ (Nm 13:12)

Ammiel+ (1 Chr 3:5)

Ammiel+ (1 Chr 26:5)

Ammihud+ (Nm 34:20)

Ammihud+ (Nm 34:28)

Ammihud+ (2 Sm 13:37)

Ammihud+ (1 Chr 9:4)

Amminadab+ (Ex 6:23)

Amminadab+ (1 Chr 6:22)

Ammizabad (1 Chr 27:6)

Amnon+ (1 Chr 4:20)

Amon+ (Neh 7:59)

Amos+ (Lk 3:25)

Amplias (Rom 16:8)

Amram+ (1 Chr 1:41)

Amram+ (Ezr 10:34)

Amzi+ (1 Chr 6:46)

Amzi+ (Neh 11:12)

Anaiah+ (Neh 8:4)

Anaiah+ (Neh 10:22)

Anan (Neh 10:26)

Anani (1 Chr 3:24)

Ananiah (Neh 3:23)

Anathoth+ (1 Chr 7:8)

Anathoth+ (Neh 10:19)

Andronicus (Rom 16:7)

Aniam (1 Chr 7:19)

Anna* (Lk 2:36)

Antipas (Rv 2:13)

Antothijah (1 Chr 8:24)

Anub (1 Chr 4:8)

Apelles (Rom 16:10)

Aphiah (1 Sm 9:1)

Aphses (1 Chr 24:15)

Apphia* (Phlm 1:2)

Ara (1 Chr 7:38)

Arad+ (1 Chr 8:15)

Arah+ (1 Chr 7:39)

Arah+ (Neh 6:18)

Aram+ (Gn 22:21)

Archelaus (Mt 2:22)

Archippus (Col 4:17)

Ard+ (Gn 46:21)

Ard+ (Nm 26:40)

Ardon (1 Chr 2:18)

Areli (Gn 46:16)

Aretas (2 Cor 11:32)

Argob (2 Kgs 15:25)

Aridai (Est 9:9)

Aridatha (Est 9:8)

Arieh (2 Kgs 15:25)

Ariel (Ezr 8:16)

Arisai (Est 9:9)

Aristobulus (Rom 16:10)

Armoni (2 Sm 21:8)

Arnan (1 Chr 3:21)

Arod (Nm 26:17)

Artaxerxes+ (Ezr 6:14)

Artemas (Ti 3:12)

Arza (1 Kgs 16:9)

Asa+ (1 Chr 9:16)

Asahel+ (2 Chr 17:8)

Asahel+ (2 Chr 31:13)

Asahel+ (Ezr 10:15)

Asaiah+ (1 Chr 4:36)

Asaiah+ (1 Chr 6:30)

Asaiah+ (1 Chr 9:5)

Asaiah+ (2 Chr 34:20)

Asaph+ (1 Chr 9:15)

Asaph+ (1 Chr 26:1)

Asaph+ (Neh 2:8)

Asareel (1 Chr 4:16)

Asarelah (1 Chr 25:2)

Asenath* (Gn 41:45)

Aser (Lk 2:36)

Ashbea (1 Chr 4:21)

Ashchenaz (1 Chr 1:6)

Ashkenaz (Gn 10:3)

Ashpenaz (Dn 1:3)

Ashriel (1 Chr 7:14)

Ashvath (1 Chr 7:33)

Asiel (1 Chr 4:35)

Asnah (Ezr 2:50)

Asnapper (Ezr 4:10)

Aspatha (Est 9:7)

Asshur+ (Gn 10:11)

Assir⁺ (1 Chr 3:17)

Asyncritus (Rom 16:14)

Atarah* (1 Chr 2:26)

Ater⁺ (Neh 10:17)

Athaiah (Neh 11:4)

Athaliah⁺ (1 Chr 8:26)

Athaliah⁺ (Ezr 8:7)

Athlai (Ezr 10:28)

Attai⁺ (1 Chr 12:11)

Attai⁺ (2 Chr 11:20)

Azaniah (Neh 10:9)

Azarael (Neh 12:36)

Azareel⁺ (1 Chr 12:6)

Azareel⁺ (1 Chr 25:18)

Azareel⁺ (1 Chr 27:22)

Azareel⁺ (Ezr 10:41)

Azareel⁺ (Neh 11:13)

Azariah⁺ (1 Kgs 4:2)

Azariah⁺ (1 Kgs 4:5)

Azariah⁺ (1 Chr 2:8)

Azariah⁺ (1 Chr 6:9)

Azariah⁺ (1 Chr 6:36)

Azariah⁺ (2 Chr 15:1)

Azariah⁺ (2 Chr 21:2)

Azariah⁺ (2 Chr 21:2)

Azariah⁺ (2 Chr 22:6)

Azariah⁺ (2 Chr 23:1)

Azariah⁺ (2 Chr 23:1)

Azariah⁺ (2 Chr 28:12)

Azariah⁺ (2 Chr 29:12)

Azariah⁺ (2 Chr 29:12)

Azariah⁺ (Ezr 7:3)

Azariah⁺ (Neh 7:7)

Azariah⁺ (Neh 8:7)

Azariah⁺ (Neh 10:2)

Azariah⁺ (Neh 12:33)

Azariah⁺ (Jer 43:2)

Azaz (1 Chr 5:8)

Azaziah⁺ (1 Chr 15:21)

Azaziah⁺ (1 Chr 27:20)

Azaziah⁺ (2 Chr 31:13)

Azbuk (Neh 3:16)

Azgad⁺ (Ezr 8:12)

Azgad⁺ (Neh 10:15)

Aziel (1 Chr 15:20)

Aziza (Ezr 10:27)

Azmaveth⁺ (1 Chr 12:3)

Azmaveth⁺ (1 Chr 27:25)

Azriel⁺ (1 Chr 5:24)

Azriel⁺ (1 Chr 27:19)

Azriel⁺ (Jer 36:26)

Azrikam⁺ (1 Chr 3:23)

Azrikam⁺ (2 Chr 28:7)

Azubah*⁺ (1 Chr 2:18)

Azur⁺ (Jer 28:1)

Azur⁺ (Ez 11:1)

Azzan (Nm 34:26)

Azzur (Neh 10:17)

A: Mentioned Twice

Abdi⁺ (1 Chr 6:44)

Abdon⁺ (Jgs 12:13)

Abdon⁺ (1 Chr 8:30)

Abia⁺ (1 Chr 3:10)

Abiah⁺ (1 Sm 8:2)

Abiahail (Est 2:15)

Abiel⁺ (1 Sm 9:1)

Abiezer⁺ (Jo 17:2)

Abijah⁺ (Neh 12:4)

Abimael (Gn 10:28)

Abishalom (1 Kgs 15:2)

Abishur (1 Chr 2:28)

Abital (2 Sm 3:4)

Achbor⁺ (2 Kgs 22:12)

Achbor⁺ (Jer 26:22)

Achish⁺ (1 Kgs 2:39)

Adbeel (Gn 25:13)

Adin⁺ (Ezr 2:15)

Adoniram (1 Kgs 4:6)

Adrammelech (2 Kgs 19:37)

Adriel (1 Sm 18:19)

Aeneas (Acts 9:33)

Agabus (Acts 11:28)

Agar* (Gal 4:24)

Ahab⁺ (Jer 29:21)

Ahiah⁺ (1 Sm 14:3)

Ahiam (2 Sm 23:33)

Ahio⁺ (1 Chr 8:31)

Ahitub⁺ (1 Chr 6:11)

Ahitub⁺ (1 Chr 9:11)

Aholibamah⁺ (Gn 36:41)

Akkub⁺ (Ezr 2:42)

Alemeth (1 Chr 8:36)

Alexander⁺ (1 Tm 1:20)

Almodad (Gn 10:26)

Amariah⁺ (1 Chr 23:19)

Amittai (2 Kgs 14:25)

Amminadab⁺ (1 Chr 15:10)

Amok (Neh 12:7)

Amon⁺ (1 Kgs 22:26)

Amraphel (Gn 14:1)

Ananias⁺ (Acts 23:2)

Anath (Jgs 3:31)

Aner (Gn 14:13)

Appaim (1 Chr 2:30)

Arad⁺ (Nm 21:1)

Arah⁺ (Ezr 2:5)

Aran (Gn 36:28)

Arba (Jo 15:13)

Arioch⁺ (Gn 14:1)

Asahiah (2 Kgs 22:12)

Asaiah⁺ (1 Chr 15:6)

Ashur (1 Chr 2:24)

Asriel (Nm 26:31)

Asshur⁺ (Gn 10:22)

Assir⁺ (Ex 6:24)

Assir⁺ (1 Chr 6:23)

Ater⁺ (Ezr 2:16)

Ater⁺ (Ezr 2:42)

Attai⁺ (1 Chr 2:35)

Azaliah (2 Kgs 22:3)

Azariah⁺ (1 Chr 2:38)

Azariah⁺ (1 Chr 6:10)

Azariah⁺ (2 Chr 26:17)

Azariah⁺ (2 Chr 31:10)

Azariah⁺ (Neh 3:23)

Azgad⁺ (Ezr 2:12)

Azmaveth⁺ (2 Sm 23:31)

Azmaveth⁺ (1 Chr 8:36)

Azor (Mt 1:13)

Azrikam⁺ (1 Chr 8:38)

Azrikam⁺ (1 Chr 9:14)

Azubah*⁺ (1 Kgs 22:42)

A: Mentioned Three Times

Abiezer⁺ (2 Sm 23:27)

Abigail*⁺ (2 Sam 17:25)

Abinadab⁺ (1 Sm 16:8)

Achbor⁺ (Gn 36:38)

Adah⁺ (Gn 4:19)

Adoni-bezek (Jgs 1:5)

Adonikam (Ezr 2:13)

Ahio⁺ (2 Sm 6:3)

Ahisamach (Ex 31:6)

Akkub⁺ (1 Chr 9:17)

Amalek (Gn 36:12)

Amariah⁺ (1 Chr 6:7)

Amariah⁺ (Neh 10:3)

Amasai⁺ (1 Chr 6:25)

Amaziah⁺ (Am 7:10)

Aminadab (Mt 1:4)

Ammiel⁺ (2 Sm 9:4)

Anah⁺ (Gn 36:20)

Ananias⁺ (Acts 5:1)

Aram⁺ (Gn 10:22)

Asaph⁺ (2 Kgs 18:18)

Ashbel (Gn 46:21)

B

Baal-hanan⁺ (4)
Possessor of grace

A king of Edom, "before there reigned any king over the children of Israel" (Gn 36:31).

First reference Gn 36:38
Last reference I Chr 1:50

Baanah⁺ (4)
In affliction

A leader of one of the raiding bands of Saul's son Ish-bosheth. Baanah and his brother, Rechab, killed Ish-bosheth. In turn, David had the brothers killed.

First reference 2 Sm 4:2
Last reference 2 Sm 4:9

Baasha (28)
Offensiveness

The idolatrous king of Israel who fought with Asa, king of Judah. After conspiring against and killing King Nadab, he took Israel's throne. Baasha attempted to fortify Ramah, to defend Israel against Judah. But Asa bribed Ben-hadad, king of Syria, who had a covenant with both nations, to support him instead of Baasha. Asa's army tore down the unfinished fortifications at Ramah and carried the stones away. Baasha and Asa fought for the rest of their reigns. Jehu son of Hanani prophesied the destruction of Baasha's household. This occurred when Baasha's son Elah as killed by Zimri.

First reference I Kgs 15:16
Last reference Jer 41:9
Key references I Kgs 15:16,
   33; 16:1–4

Balaam (63)

Foreigner

Balak, king of Moab, sent for this Mesopotamian prophet to curse the Israelites, who were invading nearby nations and would soon come to Moab. Twice Balak called for Balaam and offered the prophet great honor if he would come, so God allowed Balaam to go to Moab. But the prophet had something perverse in mind. During his trip, his donkey first refused to follow the road then lay down upon it. Suffering a beating because of the prophet's anger, the beast spoke. Suddenly the angel of the Lord who had barred the donkey's way appeared before Balaam and reminded him that God had called for his obedience. Balaam continued on his way and would not curse Israel, no matter how the king pressed him; instead he prophesied blessings on Israel. But he gave Balak an idea: distract Israel from its faith by leading its people into idolatry (Rv 2:14–15).

First reference Nm 22:5
Last reference Rv 2:14
Key references Nm 22:18;
   23:12; Rv 2:14–15

Balak (43)

Waster

The king of Moab who saw the Israelites heading toward his country and sent for the Mesopotamian prophet Balaam to curse the intruders. At first, Balaam would not come to Moab. When he did come, Balak was angered by his unwillingness to curse Israel. Though Balak brought the prophet to numerous idolatrous high places and made many offerings, he could not sway the prophet's mind because God had told Balaam that Israel was blessed. But in the end Balaam did suggest that the king might influence Israel by leading the people into idolatry—and the idea was successful (Nm 25:1–2).

First reference Nm 22:2
Last reference Mi 6:5
Key reference Nm 22:5–6

Bani⁺ (4)
Built

A priest who helped Ezra explain the law to exiles returned to Jerusalem; father of a rebuilder of the city walls.

First reference Neh 3:17
Last reference Neh 9:5

Barabbas (11)
Son of Abba

A man variously described by the Gospel writers as a murderer, a robber, and one accused of sedition. Barabbas was in prison when Jesus came to trial, and Pilate offered the Jewish people a choice concerning which of the two men he should release for the Passover. At the instigation of the chief priests, the people chose Barabbas. He was released, and

Jesus died on the cross instead.

First reference Mt 27:16
Last reference Jn 18:40
Key references Mt 27:17, 21–22

Barak (14)

Lightning

The judge Deborah's battle captain, who refused to enter battle without her support. With Deborah, he went to Kadesh and joined battle against the Canaanite king Jabin's captain Sisera. Barak successfully routed the troops, but Sisera was killed by a woman—Jael, wife of Heber the Kenite.

First reference Jgs 4:6
Last reference Heb 11:32
Key references Jgs 4:8, 15–16

Barnabas (29)

Son of prophecy

A Cypriot Christian who sold some land and gave the profits to the church. After Saul's conversion, Barnabas introduced this previous persecutor of the church to the apostles and spoke up for him. When the Jerusalem church heard that Gentiles of Antioch had been converted, they sent Barnabas to them, and he became one of the "prophets and teachers" at that church. Saul and Barnabas were sent on a missionary journey; in Lycaonia, the people wrongly proclaimed them gods. Together the two taught against the Judaizers, who wanted Gentiles to be circumcised. But these missionaries disagreed over the addition of John Mark to their ministry and separated. Barnabas and Mark went to Cyprus. Same as Joses (Acts 4:36).

First reference Acts 4:36
Last reference Col 4:10
Key references Acts 9:26–27; 11:22–24

Bartholomew (4)
Son of Tolmai

One of Jesus' disciples. Probably the same as Nathanael.

First reference Mt 10:3
Last reference Acts 1:13

Baruch+ (23)
Blessed

A scribe who wrote down all the words the prophet Jeremiah received from God. Baruch went to the temple and read these prophecies to the people. When he read them to the princes of the land, they warned him and Jeremiah to hide while they told Jehoiakim, king of Judah. After the king destroyed the first copy of the prophecies, Baruch rewrote it at Jeremiah's dictation. The proud men who opposed Jeremiah falsely accused Baruch of setting Jeremiah against Judah and trying to deliver the nation into the hands of the Chaldeans.

First reference Jer 32:12
Last reference Jer 45:2
Key reference Jer 36:4

Barzillai+ (11)
Iron-hearted

An elderly man who brought food and supplies to King David and his soldiers as they fled from the army of David's son Absalom. When David returned to Jerusalem, Barzallai conducted him over the Jordan River. David invited him to Jerusalem, but Barzillai sent Chimham, who was probably his son, in his place.

First reference 2 Sm 17:27
Last reference Neh 7:63

Bashemath*+ (5)

Ishmael's daughter and a wife of Esau. Mother of Reuel, Nahath, Zerah, Shammah, and Mizzah. Possibly the same as Bashemath (Gn 26:34).

First reference Gn 36:3
Last reference Gn 36:17

Bath-sheba* (11)
Daughter of an oath

The beautiful wife of the warrior Uriah the Hittite. When King David saw her bathing on her rooftop, he desired her and committed adultery with her, and she became pregnant. To solve his problem, he arranged for Uriah to die in battle and then married Bath-sheba. But God was displeased and the child died. After David repented, God gave them a son, Solomon, who became heir to David's throne. When David's son Adonijah tried to take the throne just before the king's death, Bath-sheba intervened, asking David to remember his promise. Later she intervened with Solomon when Adonijah sought to marry Abishag, David's concubine.

First reference 2 Sm 11:3
Last reference Ps 51 (title)
Key references 2 Sm 11:3–4;
1 Kgs 1:11

Becher⁺ (4)

Young camel

A descendant of Abraham through Jacob's son Benjamin.

First reference Gn 46:21
Last reference 1 Chr 7:8

Bela⁺ (4)

A gulp

A king of Edom, "before there reigned any king over the children of Israel" (Gn 36:31).

First reference Gn 36:32
Last reference 1 Chr 1:44

Bela⁺ (6)

A gulp

A descendant of Abraham through Jacob's son Benjamin. Bela was Benjamin's firstborn son.

First reference Nm 26:38
Last reference 1 Chr 8:3

Belshazzar (8)

A Babylonian king who saw handwriting on the wall and sought to have it interpreted. When his own soothsayers could not do so, the prophet Daniel read it to him. That night, Belshazzar was killed and Darius the Mede took his throne.

First reference Dn 5:1
Last reference Dn 8:1

Belteshazzar (10)

A Babylonian name given to the exiled Israelite Daniel upon entering King Nebuchadnezzar's service.

First reference Dn 1:7
Last reference Dn 10:1

Benaiah⁺ (24)
God has built

One of David's three mighty men and a commander in King David's army who oversaw the Cherethites and Pelethites. Because King Solomon's brother Adonijah and his battle leader Joab threatened to take his throne, Solomon commanded Benaiah to kill them. The king rewarded Benaiah by giving him Joab's command.

First reference 2 Sm 8:18
Last reference 1 Chr 27:6
Key references 1 Kgs 2:22–25, 29–34; 1 Chr 11:24

Benaiah⁺ (24)
God has built

A commander in King David's army who oversaw twenty-four thousand men in the eleventh month of each year.

First reference 2 Sm 8:18
Last reference 1 Chr 27:6
Key references 1 Kgs 2:22–25, 29-34; 1 Chr 11:24

Benaiah⁺ (5)
God has built

A Levite musician who performed in celebration when King David brought the ark of the covenant to Jerusalem.

First reference 1 Chr 15:18
Last reference 1 Chr 16:6

Ben-hadad⁺ [4]

Son of Hadad

King of Syria who supported Asa, king of Judah, against Israel.

First reference 1 Kgs 15:18
Last reference 2 Chr 16:4

Ben-hadad⁺ [18]

Son of Hadad

Another king of Syria who fought against King Ahab of Israel. When his army lost, Ben-hadad fled. Again Syria fought Israel and lost, and Ben-hadad fled once more. He asked for mercy, and Ahab made a covenant with him. Elisha came to Damascus at a time when Ben-hadad was ill, and the king asked the prophet if he would live. Though Elisha told his messenger he would recover, he also prophesied his death. Ben-hadad was murdered by Hazael, who took over his throne.

First reference 1 Kgs 20:1
Last reference 2 Kgs 8:9

Ben-hadad⁺ [4]

Son of Hadad

Another Syrian king, son of Hazael. Amos prophesied the burning of his palaces.

First reference 2 Kgs 13:3
Last reference Am 1:4

Benjamin⁺ [17]

Son of the right hand

Jacob's youngest son and the only full brother of Joseph. Their mother,

Rachel, died when Benjamin was born. He became his father Jacob's favorite after Joseph was sold into slavery by his brothers. During a famine, Jacob sent his other sons to Egypt to get food but fearfully kept Benjamin home. Joseph, then prime minister of Egypt, imprisoned Simeon and insisted that his half brothers bring Benjamin to him. When they returned, Joseph gave his brothers more food but ordered that a silver cup be hidden in Benjamin's sack. When their half brothers came to Benjamin's defense, Joseph knew they had experienced a change of heart.

First reference Gn 35:18
Last reference I Chr 8:1

Beor⁺ [8]

A lamp

Father of the false prophet Balaam. Same as Bosor.

First reference Nm 22:5
Last reference Mi 6:5

Beriah⁺ [6]

In trouble

A descendant of Abraham through Jacob's son Asher.

First reference Gn 46:17
Last reference I Chr 7:31

Bethuel [9]

Destroyed of God

Son of Abraham's brother Nahor. Seeing God's hand in Jacob's request, Bethuel gave his daughter Rebekah in marriage to Isaac. He sent Rebekah off with a generous dowry.

First reference Gn 22:22
Last reference Gn 28:5

Bezaleel[+] (8)
In the shadow of God

A craftsman given special ability by God to work on the tabernacle, Israel's portable worship center begun in the time of Moses. Bezaleel was skilled in "cunning works" in gold, silver, brass, precious stones, and wood, along with teaching other craftsmen.

First reference Ex 31:2
Last reference 2 Chr 1:5

Bichri (8)
Youthful

Father of an Israelite who rebelled against King David.

First reference 2 Sm 20:1
Last reference 2 Sm 20:22

Bildad (5)

One of three friends of Job who mourned his losses for a week then accused him of wrongdoing. God ultimately chastised the three for their criticism of Job, commanding them to sacrifice burnt offerings while Job prayed for them.

First reference Jb 2:11
Last reference Jb 42:9

Bilhah (10)
Timid

Rachel's handmaid, whom she gave to Jacob to bear children for her. As Jacob's concubine, Bilhah had two sons, Dan and Naphtali. Jacob's son Reuben also slept with her.

First reference Gn 29:29
Last reference 1 Chr 7:13

Boaz [22]

A relative of Naomi who acted as kinsman-redeemer for her and her daughter-in-law Ruth when they returned to Israel after their husbands' deaths. Ruth worked in Boaz's field, and he looked after her, having heard of her faithfulness to Naomi. At Naomi's urging, Ruth offered herself in marriage to Boaz. He accepted the responsibility of kinsman-redeemer. He bought back Naomi's husband's inherited land and promised that his first child would perpetuate Ruth's first husband's name. The couple married and had a son, Obed, who became the grandfather of King David. Same as Booz.

First reference Ru 2:1
Last reference 1 Chr 2:12
Key references Ru 2:8–16;
4:9–11

Bukki[+] [4]
Wasteful

A descendant of Abraham through Jacob's son Levi and a priest through the line of Aaron.

First reference 1 Chr 6:5
Last reference Ezr 7:4

B: Mentioned Once

Baal+ (1 Chr 5:5)

Baal-hanan+ (1 Chr 27:28)

Baalis (Jer 40:14)

Baana+ (1 Kgs 4:12)

Baana+ (Neh 3:4)

Baanah+ (1 Kgs 4:16)

Baara* (1 Chr 8:8)

Baaseiah (1 Chr 6:40)

Bakbakkar (1 Chr 9:15)

Balac (Rv 2:14)

Bani+ (2 Sm 23:36)

Bani+ (1 Chr 6:46)

Bani+ (1 Chr 9:4)

Bani+ (Ezr 10:34)

Bani+ (Ezr 10:38)

Bani+ (Neh 10:14)

Bani+ (Neh 11:22)

Barachias (Mt 23:35)

Bariah (1 Chr 3:22)

Bar-jesus (Acts 13:6)

Barjona (Mt 16:17)

Barsabas+ (Acts 1:23)

Barsabas+ (Acts 15:22)

Bartimaeus (Mk 10:46)

Baruch+ (Neh 11:5)

Barzillai+ (2 Sm 21:8)

Bashemath*+ (Gn 26:34)

Basmath* (1 Kgs 4:15)

Bath-shua* (1 Chr 3:5)

Bavai (Neh 3:18)

Bazlith (Neh 7:54)

Bazluth (Ezr 2:52)

Bealiah (1 Chr 12:5)

Bebai+ (Neh 10:15)

Becher+ (Nm 26:35)

Bechorath (1 Sm 9:1)

Bedan+ (1 Sm 12:11)

Bedan+ (1 Chr 7:17)

Bedeiah (Ezr 10:35)

Beeliada (1 Chr 14:7)

Beera (1 Chr 7:37)

Beerah (1 Chr 5:6)

Beeri+ (Gn 26:34)

Beeri+ (Hos 1:1)

Bela+ (1 Chr 5:8)

Belah (Gn 46:21)

Ben (1 Chr 15:18)

Benaiah+ (1 Chr 4:36)

Benaiah+ (1 Chr 27:34)

Benaiah+ (2 Chr 20:14)

Benaiah+ (2 Chr 31:13)

Benaiah+ (Ezr 10:25)

Benaiah+ (Ezr 10:30)

Benaiah+ (Ezr 10:35)

Benaiah+ (Ezr 10:43)

Benammi (Gn 19:38)

Ben-hail (2 Chr 17:7)

Ben-hanan (1 Chr 4:20)

Beninu (Neh 10:13)

Benjamin+ (1 Chr 7:10)

Benjamin+ (Ezr 10:32)

Benjamin+ (Neh 3:23)

Benjamin+ (Neh 12:34)

Ben-oni (Gn 35:18)

Ben-zoheth (1 Chr 4:20)

Bera (Gn 14:2)

Berachah (1 Chr 12:3)

Berachiah (1 Chr 6:39)

Beraiah (1 Chr 8:21)

Berechiah+ (1 Chr 3:20)

Berechiah+ (1 Chr 9:16)

Berechiah+ (1 Chr 15:17)

Berechiah+ (1 Chr 15:23)

Berechiah+ (2 Chr 28:12)

Bered (1 Chr 7:20)

Beri (1 Chr 7:36)

Beriah+ (1 Chr 7:23)

Berodach-baladan
   (2 Kgs 20:12)

Besodeiah (Neh 3:6)

Beth-rapha (1 Chr 4:12)

Beth-zur (1 Chr 2:45)

Bezai+ (Neh 10:18)

Bezaleel+ (Ezr 10:30)

Bezer (1 Chr 7:37)

Bidkar (2 Kgs 9:25)

Bigtha (Est 1:10)

Bigthan (Est 2:21)

Bigthana (Est 6:2)

Bigvai+ (Ezr 8:14)

Bigvai+ (Neh 10:16)

Bilgah+ (1 Chr 24:14)

Bilgai (Neh 10:8)

Bilhan+ (1 Chr 7:10)

Bimhal (1 Chr 7:33)

Binnui+ (Ezr 8:33)

Binnui+ (Ezr 10:30)

Binnui+ (Ezr 10:38)

Binnui+ (Neh 7:15)

Binnui+ (Neh 12:8)

Birsha (Gn 14:2)

Birzavith (1 Chr 7:31)

Bishlam (Ezr 4:7)

Bithiah* (1 Chr 4:18)

Biztha (Est 1:10)

Blastus (Acts 12:20)

Boanerges (Mk 3:17)

Bosor (2 Pt 2:15)

Bukki+ (Nm 34:22)
Bunah (1 Chr 2:25)
Bunni+ (Neh 9:4)
Bunni+ (Neh 10:15)

Bunni+ (Neh 11:15)
Buz+ (Gn 22:21)
Buz+ (1 Chr 5:14)
Buzi (Ez 1:3)

B: Mentioned Twice

Baal+ (1 Chr 8:30)
Baanah+ (2 Sm 22:39)
Bakbuk (Ezr 2:51)
Baladan (2 Kgs 20:12)
Bani+ (Ezr 2:10)
Bani+ (Neh 9:4)
Barachel (Jb 32:2)
Barkos (Ezr 2:53)
Baruch+ (Neh 3:20)
Bebai+ (Ezr 2:11)
Bedad (Gn 36:35)
Benaiah+ (Ez 11:1)
Beno (1 Chr 24:26)
Beor+ (Gn 36:32)

Berechiah+ (Zec 1:1)
Beriah+ (1 Chr 8:13)
Beriah+ (1 Chr 23:10)
Besai (Ezr 2:49)
Bezai+ (Ezr 2:17)
Bigvai+ (Ezr 2:2)
Bigvai+ (Ezr 2:14)
Bilgah+ (Neh 12:5)
Bilhan+ (Gn 36:27)
Bilshan (Ezr 2:2)
Binea (1 Chr 8:37)
Binnui+ (Neh 3:24)
Bocheru (1 Chr 8:38)
Bukkiah (1 Chr 25:4)

B: Mentioned Three Times

Baanah+ (Ezr 2:2)
Bakbukiah (Neh 11:17)
Bebai+ (Ezr 8:11)
Benaiah+ (2 Sm 23:30)

Berechiah+ (Neh 3:4)
Bernice* (Acts 25:13)
Bethlehem (1 Chr 2:51)
Booz (Mt 1:5)

C

Caiaphas (9)

The dell

The Jewish high priest who judged Jesus at His trial. Caiaphas, who feared Roman authority, felt it was expedient to kill one man to protect his people and so accepted false testimony against Jesus. Since he could not kill anyone, he sent Jesus to Pilate for a death sentence. Following the resurrection of Jesus, Caiaphas tried to stop Peter from preaching.

First reference Mt 26:3
Last reference Acts 4:6

Cain (19)

Lance

Adam and Eve's first son who became jealous of his brother, Abel, when God refused Cain's unrighteous offering but accepted Abel's offering. Cain killed Abel and did not admit it when God asked where his brother was. For his sin, God made him "a fugitive and a vagabond" (Gn 4:12). Cain moved to the land of Nod, had children, and built the city of Enoch.

First reference Gn 4:1
Last reference Jude 1:11
Key references Gn 4:9; Heb 11:4

Cainan (7)

Fixed

Grandson of Seth and great-grandson of Adam and Eve. He lived for 910 years.

First reference Gn 5:9
Last reference Lk 3:37

Caleb⁺ (28)

Forcible

Jephunneh's son, sent by Moses to spy out Canaan before the Israelites entered the Promised Land. When ten other spies warned that they could not win the land, Caleb believed Israel could do it. God blessed Caleb and Joshua, the only spies who believed the land could be taken. Of the twelve, only these two entered the Promised Land. For his faithfulness, Caleb received Hebron as an inheritance. Caleb promised his daughter Achsah to the man who could conquer Kirjath-sepher. After his brother Othniel took it, Caleb kept his promise and the couple married.

First reference Nm 13:6
Last reference 1 Chr 6:56

Key references Nm 13:30; 32:11–12; Jo 14:13

Canaan (9)

Humiliated

Son of Ham and grandson of Noah. Noah cursed Canaan because his father, Ham, did not cover Noah when he became drunk and fell asleep, naked, in his tent. Canaan became the ancestor of the Phoenicians and other peoples living between the Phoenician city of Sidon and Gaza.

First reference Gn 9:18
Last reference 1 Chr 1:13

Carmi⁺ (4)

Gardener

A descendant of Abraham through Jacob's son Reuben.

First reference Gn 46:9
Last reference 1 Chr 5:3

Carmi⁺ (4)

Gardener

A descendant of Abraham through Jacob's son Judah.

First reference Jo 7:1
Last reference 1 Chr 4:1

Cephas (5)

The rock

A name Jesus gave the apostle Peter. It is used most often in the book of 1 Corinthians. Same as Peter.

First reference Jn 1:42
Last reference Gal 2:9

Chedorlaomer (5)

The king of Elam in the days of Abram. Chedorlaomer was part of a victorious battle alliance that kidnapped Abram's nephew Lot.

First reference Gn 14:1
Last reference Gn 14:17

Chenaanah⁺ (4)

Humiliated

A false prophet who told King Ahab to fight against Ramoth-gilead.

First reference 1 Kgs 22:11
Last reference 2 Chr 18:23

Chimham (4)

Pining

Possibly a son of Barzillai, who offered him to King David to serve in his place. David probably gave Chimham a land grant near Bethlehem (Jer 41:17).

First reference 2 Sm 19:37
Last reference Jer 41:17

Chushan-rishathaim (4)

Cushan of double wickedness

A Mesopotamian king into whose hands God gave the disobedient Israelites. When they repented, He raised up Othniel, Caleb's younger brother, to deliver the nation. Same as Cushan.

First reference Jgs 3:8
Last reference Jgs 3:10

Cornelius (10)

A God-fearing centurion of the Italian band. In a vision, an angel told him to call for Peter. After Peter traveled to see Cornelius and preached to him and his companions, the Holy Spirit fell on them. They were the first Gentiles Peter baptized.

First reference Acts 10:1
Last reference Acts 10:31

Cush⁺ (6)

A grandson of Noah through his son Ham.

First reference Gn 10:6
Last reference 1 Chr 1:10

Cushi⁺ (8)

A Cushite

The messenger who brought David the news that his son Absalom was dead.

First reference 2 Sm 18:21
Last reference 2 Sm 18:32

Cyrus (23)

The king of Persia who commanded that the temple in Jerusalem be rebuilt. He ordered all his people to give donations to help the Jews, and he returned the temple vessels that Nebuchadnezzar of Babylon had taken. When opposers objected to the work, the Jews reminded them of Cyrus's command, and the work went forward again. The prophet Daniel also lived and prospered during the early part of Cyrus's reign.

First reference 2 Chr 36:22
Last reference Dn 10:1
Key references 2 Chr 36:23;
 Ezr 5:13–15

C: Mentioned Once

Calcol (1 Chr 2:6)

Caleb+ (1 Chr 2:50)

Candace* (Acts 8:27)

Carcas (Est 1:10)

Careah (2 Kgs 25:23)

Carpus (2 Tm 4:13)

Carshena (Est 1:14)

Chalcol (1 Kgs 4:31)

Chelal (Ezr 10:30)

Chelluh (Ezr 10:35)

Chelub+ (1 Chr 4:11)

Chelub+ (1 Chr 27:26)

Chelubai (1 Chr 2:9)

Chenaanah+ (1 Chr 7:10)

Chenani (Neh 9:4)

Chenaniah+ (1 Chr 26:29)

Chesed (Gn 22:22)

Chileab (2 Sm 3:3)

Chislon (Nm 34:21)

Chloe* (1 Cor 1:11)

Chuza (Lk 8:3)

Cis (Acts 13:21)

Claudia* (2 Tm 4:21)

Claudius+ (Acts 23:26)

Clement (Phil 4:3)

Cleopas (Lk 24:18)

Cleophas (Jn 19:25)

Conaniah (2 Chr 35:9)

Core (Jude 1:11)

Cosam (Lk 3:28)

Coz (1 Chr 4:8)

Crescens (2 Tm 4:10)

Cush+ (Ps 7)

Cushan (Hb 3:7)

Cushi+ (Jer 36:14)

Cushi+ (Zep 1:1)

Cyrenius (Lk 2:2)

C: Mentioned Twice

Chenaniah⁺ (1 Chr 15:22)

Cheran (Gn 36:26)

Cherub (Ezr 2:59)

Chilion (Ru 1:2)

Col-hozeh (Neh 3:15)

Cononiah (2 Chr 31:12)

Cozbi* (Nm 25:15)

Crispus (Acts 18:8)

C: Mentioned Three Times

Caleb⁺ (1 Chr 2:18)

Claudius⁺ (Acts 11:28)

Coniah (Jer 22:24)

D

Dan (10)

Judge

Son of Jacob and Bilhah, Rachel's maid. Before his death, Jacob prophesied that Dan would judge his people and be as a "serpent by the way, an adder in the path" (Gn 49:17).

First reference Gn 30:6
Last reference I Chr 2:2

Daniel+ (80)

An Old Testament major prophet. As a child Daniel was taken into exile in Babylon. Because he refused to defile himself with meat and wine from the king's table, God blessed him with knowledge and wisdom. Daniel described and interpreted a dream about an image of various metals and clay for King Nebuchadnezzar, and the king made him ruler over the province of Babylon. Daniel revealed the meaning of a second dream to Nebuchadnezzar, predicting his downfall until he worshipped the Lord. During King Belshazzar's reign, Daniel interpreted the meaning of the mysterious handwriting on the wall. For this Daniel was made third ruler in the kingdom, but Belshazzar died that night. After Darius the Mede took over the kingdom of Babylonia and planned to make Daniel head of the whole kingdom, other leaders plotted against Daniel. Knowing he would not worship anyone but the Lord, they convinced the king to punish any person who worshipped anyone but the king for thirty days. For disobeying this law, Daniel was thrown into the lions' den. But God closed the beasts' mouths. When his favored man came out safely, Darius honored the Lord. Daniel prospered in the reigns of Darius and Cyrus the Persian. Same as Belteshazzar.

First reference Ez 14:14
Last reference Mk 13:14
Key references Dn 1:8, 17; 2:31–45; 6:22–23

Darius⁺ [16]

Darius Hystaspes, king of Persia, followed in the footsteps of King Cyrus and supported the Jews in their efforts to rebuild Jerusalem. When those who opposed the rebuilding wrote to Darius, he looked into the question and then ordered the opposition to allow the building to continue.

First reference Ezr 4:5
Last reference Zec 7:1

Darius⁺ [8]

Darius the Mede, king of Persia during part of the prophet Daniel's life. Darius wanted to promote Daniel, but Daniel's enemies plotted against him. When Daniel refused to worship the king, Daniel was thrown into the lions' den despite Darius's efforts to save him. God protected his servant, and Darius glorified God.

First reference Dn 5:31
Last reference Dn 11:1

Dathan (10)

With Korah and Abiram, Dathan conspired against Moses, declaring that all the people of Israel were holy. Dathan stayed in his tent when Moses called the conspirators before God, so Moses came to him. The ground broke open at Dathan's feet and swallowed him, his family, and his possessions.

First reference Nm 16:1
Last reference Ps 106:17

David (1,139)

Loving

Popular king of Israel. As a young shepherd and musician, David was anointed king by the prophet Samuel in the place of disobedient King Saul. David vanquished the Philistine giant Goliath, and Saul brought young David to his court, where the king's son Jonathan befriended him. Because the new hero became popular with the people, Saul became jealous and first sent David to war then sought to kill him. With Jonathan's help, David fled. David escaped to Nob, where he received help from the priests, who were then killed by Saul. So began a period of war between the two men. Though David twice had opportunities to kill Saul, he would not touch the Lord's anointed. Fearing Saul, David eventually fled into Philistine territory but would not fight against his own people. He concealed from Achish, king of Gath, the fact that his troops never raided Israel. When Achish prepared for battle against

Israel, the king's troops refused to have David's men in their ranks, so David never fought against Saul for the Philistines. Following the battle with the Philistines and the deaths of Saul and his sons, David was anointed king of Judah. Saul's remaining son, Ish-bosheth, was made king of Israel, but following Ish-bosheth's murder, these northern tribes made David their king. David defeated the Philistines and brought the ark of the covenant to Jerusalem. But God would not let him build a temple. The king continued to defeat his foreign enemies, until he fell into sin with Bathsheba and killed her husband, Uriah. Though David repented, this began a period of family troubles. David's son Amnon raped his half sister Tamar, and in retaliation her brother Absalom killed Amnon then attempted to take the throne. Though David's troops overcame Absalom's army, David grieved at the death of his rebellious son. Before David's death, when his son Adonijah tried to usurp the throne, David quickly had Solomon anointed king. David wrote many of the psalms and sang a song of praise about the victories God brought him (2 Sm 22). Despite his failings, scripture refers to David as a man after God's own heart (Acts 13:22).

First reference Ru 4:17
Last reference Rv 22:16
Key references 1 Sm 16:13;
   18:6–9; 24:6–7; 2 Sm 12:13, 22

Deborah*+ (9)
Bee

Israel's only female judge and prophetess, she held court under a palm tree. Deborah called Barak to lead warriors into battle against the Canaanite army commander, Sisera. But Barak would fight only if Deborah went with him. For this, she prophesied that God would hand Sisera over to a woman. Deborah supported Barak as he gathered his troops on Mount Tabor, and she advised him to go into battle. With him she sang a song of victory that praised the Lord.

First reference Jgs 4:4
Last reference Jgs 5:15

Delilah* (6)
Languishing

A woman with whom the Israelite judge Samson fell in love. Bribed by the Philistines to discover the source of her lover's strength, Delilah nagged Samson until he told her that if his head was shaved, he would become weak. When this was done, Samson became weak and the Philistines overpowered him.

First reference Jgs 16:4
Last reference Jgs 16:18

Deuel (4)
Known of God

Father of Eliasaph, who was a prince of the tribe of Gad.

First reference Nm 1:14
Last reference Nm 10:20

Dinah* (8)

Justice

Daughter of Jacob and Leah, who was sexually assaulted by the prince Shechem. Her brothers retaliated, killing the men of his city.

First reference Gn 30:21
Last reference Gn 46:15

Dishan (5)

Antelope

A descendant of Seir, who lived in Esau's "land of Edom."

First reference Gn 36:21
Last reference 1 Chr 1:42

Dishon+ (4)

Antelope

A descendant of Seir, who lived in Esau's "land of Edom."

First reference Gn 36:21
Last reference 1 Chr 1:38

Doeg (6)

Anxious

King Saul's chief herds-man, who told the king that David had visited Nob. Doeg slaughtered the priests of Nob at Saul's command.

First reference 1 Sm 21:7
Last reference Ps 52 (title)

D: Mentioned Once

Dalaiah (1 Chr 3:24)

Dalphon (Est 9:7)

Damaris* (Acts 17:34)

Daniel+ (1 Chr 3:1)

Dara (1 Chr 2:6)

Darda (1 Kgs 4:31)

Darius+ (Neh 12:22)

Debir (Jo 10:3)

Deborah*+ (Gn 35:8)

Dekar (1 Kgs 4:9)

Delaiah+ (1 Chr 24:18)

Delaiah+ (Neh 6:10)

Demetrius+ (3 Jn 1:12)

Diblaim (Hos 1:3)

Dibri (Lv 24:11)

Dionysius (Acts 17:34)

Diotrephes (3 Jn 1:9)

Dodai (1 Chr 27:4)

Dodavah (2 Chr 20:37)

Dodo+ (Jgs 10:1)

Drusilla* (Acts 24:24)

D: Mentioned Twice

Daniel+ (Ezr 8:2)

Darkon (Ezr 2:56)

Dedan+ (Gn 10:7)

Delaiah+ (Ezr 2:60)

Delaiah+ (Jer 36:12)

Demetrius+ (Acts 19:24)

Diklah (Gn 10:27)

Dodo+ (2 Sm 23:9)

Dodo+ (2 Sm 23:24)

Dorcas* (Acts 9:36)

Dumah (Gn 25:14)

D: Mentioned Three Times

Dedan+ (Gn 25:3)

Demas (Col 4:14)

Didymus (Jn 11:16)

Dishon+ (Gn 36:25)

E

Ebed+ (5)
Servant

Father of Gaal. His son incited the men of Shechem against King Abimelech.

First reference Jgs 9:26
Last reference Jgs 9:35

Ebed-melech (6)
Servant of a king

An Ethiopian eunuch who rescued Jeremiah from a dungeon by reporting his situation to King Zedekiah. Jeremiah prophesied that God would deliver the faithful eunuch.

First reference Jer 38:7
Last reference Jer 39:16

Eber+ (9)
Other side

Great-grandson of Shem and descendant of Noah.

First reference Gn 10:21
Last reference 1 Chr 1:25

Eglon (5)
Calf-like

A king of Moab who attacked Israel. Eglon subjugated the Israelites for eighteen years until he was killed by the Israelite judge Ehud.

First reference Jgs 3:12
Last reference Jgs 3:17

Ehud+ (8)
United

The second judge of Israel who subdued the oppressing

Moabites. A left-handed man, Ehud killed Eglon, the obese king of Moab, with a hidden dagger while pretending to be on a peace mission.

First reference Jgs 3:15
Last reference Jgs 4:1

Elah⁺ (4)

King of Israel, a contemporary of King Asa of Judah. Elah was killed by Zimri, who usurped his throne.

First reference 1 Kgs 16:6
Last reference 1 Kgs 16:14

Elah⁺ (4)

Father of Hoshea. His son killed King Pekah of Israel and usurped his throne.

First reference 2 Kgs 15:30
Last reference 2 Kgs 18:9

Eleazar⁺ (63)

God is helper

Aaron's third son. His older brothers Nadab and Abihu were killed by God for illicit worship practices, so Eleazar became the chief over the Levites. He oversaw the temple worship, including the use of the temple vessels, meat offerings, and anointing oil, and was in charge of the tabernacle. When Aaron died, Eleazar became high priest. With Moses, God commanded him to count the Israelites. After Israel came to the Promised Land, Eleazar and Joshua divided the territory among Israel's tribes. He died and was buried on a hill belonging to his son Phinehas.

First reference Ex 6:23
Last reference Ezr 7:5
Key references Nm 4:16; 26:1–2; Dt 10:6

Eli (33)

Lofty

The high priest in Shiloh, where the ark of the covenant rested for a time. He rebuked Hannah for being drunk (though she wasn't) as she prayed for God to give her a child. When her son Samuel was born, Hannnah brought him to Eli and dedicated him to God. Eli acted as Samuel's foster father and trained him in the priesthood. But Eli's own sons, Hophni and Phinehas, did not know the Lord and sinned greatly. Because Eli honored them above God, the priest had done little to restrain them. Yet God promised to raise up a faithful priest in their place. Samuel began to hear the Word of God, and Eli encouraged him to listen. Though his own sons were spiritual failures, Eli did much better with his foster son. Samuel went on to be a powerful prophet of the Lord. The Lord had told Eli that his sons would die on the same day, and they did—in a battle with the Philistines, who stole the ark. When Eli heard the news of his sons' deaths, he fell backward in his chair and broke his neck.

First reference 1 Sm 1:3
Last reference 1 Kgs 2:27
Key references 1 Sm 1:13–14; 2:29; 3:8–9

Eliab+ (5)

God of his father

A prince of Zebulun who assisted Moses in taking the census of his tribe.

First reference Nm 1:9
Last reference Nm 10:16

Eliab+ (5)

God of his father

Father of Dathan and Abiram. His sons rebelled against Moses.

First reference Nm 16:1
Last reference Dt 11:6

Eliab+ (5)

God of his father

First son of Jesse and an older brother of King David. The prophet Samuel, sent by God to anoint the successor to King Saul, thought the tall and good-looking Eliab would be the Lord's choice—but God said, "The Lord seeth not as man seeth; for man looketh on the outward appearance, but the Lord looketh on the heart" (1 Sm 16:7). A warrior in Saul's army, Eliab criticized his youngest brother when David questioned Israelite soldiers about their fear of Goliath.

First reference 1 Sm 16:6
Last reference 2 Chr 11:18

Eliakim+ (9)

God of raising

King Hezekiah of Judah's palace administrator. Eliakim confronted the king of Assyria's messengers who tried to convince Hezekiah and his people to submit to Assyria.

First reference 2 Kgs 18:18
Last reference Is 37:2

Elias (30)

God of Jehovah

Greek form of the name *Elijah,* used in six New Testament books.

First reference Mt 11:14
Last reference Jas 5:17

Eliasaph⁺ (5)

God is gatherer

A prince of Gad who helped Moses take a census of his tribe.

First reference Nm 1:14
Last reference Nm 10:20

Eliashib⁺ (5)

God will restore

A Levite worship leader, son of Jehoiakim and grandson of Jeshua, who returned from Babylon.

First reference Ezr 10:6
Last reference Neh 12:23

Eliashib⁺ (7)

God will restore

High priest during the rebuilding of Jerusalem's walls. He defiled the temple by assigning Tobiah the Ammonite a room there.

First reference Neh 3:1
Last reference Neh 13:28

Eliezer⁺ (14)

God of help

A son of Moses by his wife, Zipporah.

First reference Ex 18:4
Last reference 1 Chr 26:25

Elihu+ (7)

God of him

A young man who became a mediator in the discussion between Job and his comforters. Unlike the comforters, God did not accuse Elihu of any wrong.

First reference Jb 32:2
Last reference Jb 36:1

Elijah+ (68)

God of Jehovah

One of the Old Testament's major prophets, Elijah came from Tishbe, in Gilead. His prophecy that no rain would fall in Israel except at his command angered wicked King Ahab, and Elijah had to flee across the Jordan River and on to Zarephath. God hid him for three years and sent him to Mount Carmel. At Carmel he had a showdown with the priests of Baal that proved the Lord was God. Baal could not ignite the offering made by the pagans, but God sent fire from heaven that lit a water-soaked offering made by Elijah. The people of Israel worshipped God, and rain fell. Angry that Elijah had all the priests of Baal killed, Queen Jezebel threatened his life, and the discouraged prophet fled to Horeb. God gave Elijah the prophet Elisha as a disciple. Elijah returned to Ahab to prophesy the ruling couple's end, and Ahab repented. Following Ahab's death, Elijah prophesied the death of King Ahaziah, who consulted the god of Ekron when he was ill. Knowing God would take Elijah to heaven, his disciple Elisha asked to receive a double portion of his spirit. Elijah said that if Elisha saw his ascension into heaven, he would have it. Suddenly a chariot with horses of fire appeared before the two men, and Elijah went up into heaven in a whirlwind. Same as Elias.

First reference I Kgs 17:1
Last reference Mal 4:5
Key references I Kgs 17:1–6;
    18:21–40; 2 Kgs 2:11

Elimelech (6)
God of the king

Naomi's husband. He died in Moab, where the family had moved from Bethlehem to escape a famine.

First reference Ru 1:2
Last reference Ru 4:9

Eliphaz⁺ (9)
God of gold

A son of Esau by his wife Adah and a nephew of Jacob.

First reference Gn 36:4
Last reference I Chr 1:36

Eliphaz⁺ (6)
God of gold

One of three friends of Job who mourned his losses for a week then accused him of wrongdoing. God ultimately chastised the three for their criticism of Job, commanding them to sacrifice burnt offerings while Job prayed for them.

First reference Jb 2:11
Last reference Jb 42:9

Elisabeth* (9)

God of the oath

Wife of Zacharias and mother of John the Baptist. For many years Elisabeth had been barren, but her husband received a vision promising she would conceive. When Elisabeth heard, she rejoiced at God's favor. Her cousin Mary visited Elisabeth for three months after learning that she would bear the Messiah.

First reference Lk 1:5
Last reference Lk 1:57

Elisha (58)

God of supplication

The prophet Elijah's successor and disciple, Elisha saw Elijah carried up to heaven in a whirlwind of fire and received a double portion of his spirit. Taking over the role of prophet, Elisha performed many miracles for individuals—he healed a polluted water source for the people of Jericho, provided oil for a widow, and caused a "great woman" of Shunem to have a child then brought him back to life after he died. He fed one hundred people from twenty loaves of bread, prefiguring Christ's feeding of the five thousand and the three thousand. At Elisha's command, Naaman, captain of the Syrian king, bathed in the Jordan and was healed of leprosy. At Elisha's request, God blinded a host of Syrian warriors. Elisha led them to Samaria then persuaded the king of Israel to send them home. This ended the incursion of Syria's raiding bands on

Israel. The prophet prophesied the recovery and then the death of King Ben-hadad of Syria and told King Jeroboam of Israel that he would strike Syria three times but not fully defeat that nation. After Elisha died, some men put a body into his tomb for safekeeping. The man's body touched the prophet's bones and was revived. Same as Eliseus.

First reference 1 Kgs 19:16
Last reference 2 Kgs 13:21
Key references 2 Kgs 2:9;
    4:8–37; 5:8–19

Elishama (6)
God of hearing

A descendant of Abraham through Joseph's son Ephraim. Elishama was an ancestor of Joshua.

First reference Nm 1:10
Last reference 1 Chr 7:26

Elishama⁺ (4)

A son of King David, born in Jerusalem. Same as Elishua.

First reference 2 Sm 5:16
Last reference 1 Chr 14:7

Elizur (5)
God of the rock

A prince of Reuben who helped Moses take a census of his tribe and who led the tribe out of Sinai.

First reference Nm 1:5
Last reference Nm 10:18

Elkanah⁺ (10)

Father of the prophet Samuel. Elkanah's wife Hannah was barren and prayed to have a child. When God gave her Samuel, Elkanah agreed with her that their son should become a priest under the high priest Eli.

First reference 1 Sm 1:1
Last reference 1 Chr 6:34

Elnathan⁺ [4]

God is the giver

Grandfather of King Jehoiachin of Judah.

First reference 2 Kgs 24:8
Last reference Jer 36:25

Enan [5]

Having eyes

Forefather of a prince of Naphtali who helped Moses take a census of his tribe.

First reference Nm 1:15
Last reference Nm 10:27

Enoch⁺ [9]

Initiated

A descendant of Seth, son of Adam. "Enoch walked with God: and he was not; for God took him" (Gn 5:24). He was immediately translated into eternity. Same as Henoch (1 Chr 1:3).

First reference Gn 5:18
Last reference Jude 1:14

Enos [7]

Mortal

Son of Seth, Adam's son, and forebear of Jesus' earthly father, Joseph. Same as Enosh.

First reference Gn 4:26
Last reference Lk 3:38

Ephraim (11)
Double fruit

Joseph and his wife Asenath's second son. Ephraim and his brother, Manasseh, were adopted and blessed by Jacob. But Ephraim received the greater blessing, for Jacob insisted he would be the greater brother. Eventually the brothers superseded Jacob's oldest sons, Reuben and Simeon.

First reference Gn 41:52
Last reference 1 Chr 7:22
Key references Gn 48:5,
    17–19

Ephron (12)
Fawn-like

The Hittite from whom Abraham bought the cave of Machpelah, where he buried Sarah. Though Ephron wanted to give Abraham the land, Abraham insisted on buying it.

First reference Gn 23:8
Last reference Gn 50:13
Key reference Gn 23:10–11

Er⁺ (9)
Watchful

Judah's firstborn son, who was wicked. "The Lord. . . slew him" (Gn 38:10). Both he and his brother Onan died in Canaan.

First reference Gn 38:3
Last reference 1 Chr 2:3

Esaias (21)
God has saved

Greek form of the name *Isaiah,* used in the New Testament.

First reference Mt 3:3
Last reference Rom 15:12
Key reference Lk 4:14–21

Esau (82)

Rough

The oldest son of Isaac and Rebekah and the twin brother of Jacob. Esau was a good hunter and the favorite of his father, but he sold his birthright to Jacob for some lentil stew. Then he disturbed his parents by marrying two Hittite women. His mother, Rebekah, and his brother, Jacob, plotted to trick Isaac into giving Jacob the elder son's blessing, and they succeeded, creating bad feelings between the brothers. Because Esau received a lesser blessing, he plotted to kill Jacob, who had to flee. Years later, before Jacob returned to his homeland, he sent word to his brother. Fearing Esau's anger, he sent a peace offering of cattle before him. But Esau's rage had cooled, and he greeted him joyfully, refusing the gift Jacob offered. When the brothers' cattle became too many for them to live on the same land, Esau moved to Mount Seir. His descendants became the Edomites, called after Esau's nickname, which came from the red stew for which he sold his birthright; *Edom* means "red." Same as Edom.

First reference Gn 25:25
Last reference Heb 12:16
Key references Gn 25:30–33; 27:41; 36:6–8

Esther* (56)

The Jewish wife of Persian king Ahasuerus. Angered by his first wife, Vashti, the king sought a new bride from among the most beautiful women of his kingdom. As a result of this search, he found Esther, fell in love with her, married her, and made her his queen. Ahasuerus's favorite counselor, Haman, lied to the king and plotted to kill the Jewish people. Esther's cousin Mordecai, who had raised her, convinced the new queen to confront her husband. When she expressed her doubts, he told her: "For if thou altogether holdest thy peace at this time, then shall there enlargement and deliverance arise to the Jews from another place; but thou and thy father's house shall be destroyed: and who knoweth whether thou art come to the kingdom for such a time as this?" (Est 4:14). The queen boldly went to the king, though it could have meant her death to appear before him unrequested. She asked that he and Haman come to a banquet. On the second day of the banquet, Esther told the king of Haman's plan to kill her people. Angered, Ahasuerus had Haman killed, and Esther and her people were saved. Same as Hadassah.

First reference Est 2:7
Last reference Est 9:32
Key reference Est 4:14–16

Eve* (4)
Life-giver

Adam's wife, "the mother of all living." Tempted by the serpent, Eve ate the forbidden fruit of the tree of the knowledge of good and evil and offered it to her husband, who also ate. Suddenly fearful of God because of their sin, they hid from Him. God placed a curse on Adam and Eve. For her part, Eve would suffer greatly during childbirth, desire her husband, and be ruled over by him. God removed the couple from the Garden of Eden. Eve and Adam first had two children named in the Bible—Cain and Abel. After Cain murdered Abel, God gave them another child, Seth.

First reference Gn 3:20
Last reference 1 Tm 2:13

Ezer⁺ (4)

Treasure, help

A descendant of Seir, who lived in Esau's "land of Edom."

First reference Gn 36:21
Last reference 1 Chr 1:42

Ezra⁺ (24)

Aid

An Israelite scribe and teacher of the law who returned from the Babylonian Exile along with some priests, Levites, temple servants, and other Israelites. Ezra had received the backing of King Artaxerxes of Persia and returned with money and the temple vessels. Ezra also had the right to appoint magistrates and judges in Israel. When they reached Jerusalem, the officials told Ezra that many men of Israel had intermarried with the people around them and followed their ways. Ezra prayed for the people, read them the law, and called them to confess their sin. All Israel repented and put away their foreign spouses.

First reference Ezr 7:1
Last reference Neh 12:36
Key reference Ezr 7:6

E: Mentioned Once

Ebal⁺ (1 Chr 1:22)

Ebed⁺ (Ezr 8:6)

Eber⁺ (1 Chr 8:12)

Eber⁺ (Neh 12:20)

Eden⁺ (2 Chr 29:12)

Eden⁺ (2 Chr 31:15)

Ehi (Gn 46:21)

Eker (1 Chr 2:27)

Eladah (1 Chr 7:20)

Elah⁺ (1 Kgs 4:18)

Elah⁺ (1 Chr 4:15)

Elah⁺ (1 Chr 9:8)

Elam⁺ (1 Chr 8:24)

Elam⁺ (1 Chr 26:3)

Elam⁺ (Ezr 8:7)

Elam⁺ (Neh 10:14)

Elam⁺ (Neh 12:42)

Elasah⁺ (Ezr 10:22)

Elasah⁺ (Jer 29:3)

Elead (1 Chr 7:21)

Eleazar⁺ (1 Sm 7:1)

Eleazar⁺ (Ezr 8:33)

Eleazar⁺ (Ezr 10:25)

Eleazar⁺ (Neh 12:42)

Eliab⁺ (1 Chr 6:27)

Eliab⁺ (1 Chr 12:8)

Eliada⁺ (2 Chr 17:17)

Eliadah (1 Kgs 11:23)

Eliakim⁺ (Neh 12:41)

Eliam⁺ (2 Sm 11:3)

Eliam⁺ (2 Sm 23:34)

Eliasaph⁺ (Nm 3:24)

Eliashib⁺ (1 Chr 3:24)

Eliashib⁺ (1 Chr 24:12)

Eliashib⁺ (Ezr 10:24)

Eliashib⁺ (Ezr 10:27)

Eliashib⁺ (Ezr 10:36)

Elidad (Nm 34:21)

Eliel⁺ (1 Chr 5:24)

Eliel⁺ (1 Chr 6:34)

Eliel⁺ (1 Chr 8:20)

Eliel⁺ (1 Chr 8:22)

Eliel⁺ (1 Chr 11:46)

Eliel⁺ (1 Chr 11:47)

Eliel⁺ (1 Chr 12:11)

Eliel⁺ (1 Chr 15:9)

Eliel⁺ (1 Chr 15:11)

Eliel⁺ (2 Chr 31:13)

Elienai (1 Chr 8:20)

Eliezer⁺ (Gn 15:2)

Eliezer⁺ (1 Chr 15:24)

Eliezer⁺ (1 Chr 27:16)

Eliezer+ (2 Chr 20:37)

Eliezer+ (Ezr 8:16)

Eliezer+ (Ezr 10:18)

Eliezer+ (Ezr 10:23)

Eliezer+ (Ezr 10:31)

Eliezer+ (Lk 3:29)

Elihoenai (Ezr 8:4)

Elihoreph (1 Kgs 4:3)

Elihu+ (1 Sm 1:1)

Elihu+ (1 Chr 12:20)

Elihu+ (1 Chr 26:7)

Elihu+ (1 Chr 27:18)

Elijah+ (Ezr 10:21)

Elika (Sm 23:25)

Elioenai+ (1 Chr 4:36)

Elioenai+ (1 Chr 7:8)

Elioenai+ (1 Chr 26:3)

Elioenai+ (Ezr 10:22)

Elioenai+ (Ezr 10:27)

Elioenai+ (Neh 12:41)

Eliphal (1 Chr 11:35)

Eliphelet+ (2 Sm 23:34)

Eliphelet+ (1 Chr 3:6)

Eliphelet+ (1 Chr 3:8)

Eliphelet+ (1 Chr 8:39)

Eliphelet+ (Ezr 8:13)

Eliphelet+ (Ezr 10:33)

Eliseus (Lk 4:27)

Elishama+ (2 Kgs 25:25)

Elishama+ (1 Chr 2:41)

Elishama+ (2 Chr 17:8)

Elishama+ (Jer 41:1)

Elishaphat (2 Chr 23:1)

Elisheba* (Ex 6:23)

Elizaphan+ (Nm 34:25)

Elkanah+ (1 Chr 9:16)

Elkanah+ (1 Chr 12:6)

Elkanah+ (1 Chr 15:23)

Elkanah+ (2 Chr 28:7)

Elmodam (Lk 3:28)

Elnaam (1 Chr 11:46)

Elnathan+ (Ezr 8:16)

Elnathan+ (Ezr 8:16)

Elnathan+ (Ezr 8:16)

Elpalet (1 Chr 14:5)

Eluzai (1 Chr 12:5)

Elymas (Acts 13:8)

Elzabad+ (1 Chr 12:12)

Elzabad+ (1 Chr 26:7)

Emmanuel (Mt 1:23)

Emmor (Acts 7:16)

Enosh (1 Chr 1:1)

Epaenetus (Rom 16:5)

Ephah*+ (1 Chr 2:46)

Ephah+ (1 Chr 2:47)

Ephai (Jer 40:8)

Epher+ (1 Chr 4:17)

Epher+ (1 Chr 5:24)

Ephlal (1 Chr 2:37)

Ephod (Nm 34:23)

Ephrath* (1 Chr 2:19)

Er+ (1 Chr 4:21)

Er+ (Lk 3:28)

Eran (Nm 26:36)

Erastus+ (Rom 16:23)

Eshek (1 Chr 8:39)

Esli (Lk 3:25)

Etam (1 Chr 4:3)

Ethan+ (1 Chr 6:42)

Ethbaal (1 Kgs 16:31)

Ethnan (1 Chr 4:7)

Ethni (1 Chr 6:41)

Eubulus (2 Tm 4:21)

Eunice* (2 Tm 1:5)

Euodias* (Phil 4:2)

Eutychus (Acts 20:9)

Ezar (1 Chr 1:38)

Ezbai (1 Chr 11:37)

Ezbon+ (Gn 46:16)

Ezbon+ (1 Chr 7:7)

Ezer+ (1 Chr 4:4)

Ezer+ (1 Chr 7:21)

Ezer+ (1 Chr 12:9)

Ezer+ (Neh 3:19)

Ezer+ (Neh 12:42)

Ezra+ (1 Chr 4:17)

Ezra+ (Neh 12:1)

Ezri (1 Chr 27:26)

E: Mentioned Twice

Ebal⁺ (Gn 36:23)

Eder (1 Chr 23:23)

Eglah (2 Sm 3:5)

Ehud⁺ (1 Chr 7:10)

Elah⁺ (Gn 36:41)

Elam⁺ (Gn 10:22)

Elam⁺ (Ezr 2:7)

Elam⁺ (Ezr 2:31)

Elam⁺ (Ezr 10:2)

Eldaah (Gn 25:4)

Eldad (Nm 11:26)

Eleasah⁺ (1 Chr 2:39)

Eleasah⁺ (1 Chr 8:37)

Eleazar⁺ (2 Sm 23:9)

Eleazar⁺ (Mt 1:15)

Elhanan⁺ (2 Sm 21:19)

Elhanan⁺ (2 Sm 23:24)

Eliah (1 Chr 8:27)

Eliahba (2 Sm 23:32)

Eliakim⁺ (2 Kgs 23:34)

Eliathah (1 Chr 25:4)

Elioenai⁺ (1 Chr 3:23)

Eliphalet (2 Sm 5:16)

Elipheleh (1 Chr 15:18)

Elishua (2 Sm 5:15)

Eliud (Mt 1:14)

Elizaphan⁺ (Nm 3:30)

Elkanah⁺ (Ex 6:24)

Elkanah⁺ (1 Chr 6:25)

Elkanah⁺ (1 Chr 6:26)

Elon⁺ (Gn 26:34)

Elon⁺ (Gn 46:14)

Elon⁺ (Jgs 12:11)

Elzaphan (Ex 6:22)

Epaphroditus (Phil 2:25)

Epher⁺ (Gn 25:4)

Ephratah* (1 Chr 2:50)

Erastus⁺ (Acts 19:22)

Eri (Gn 46:16)

Esh-baal (1 Chr 8:33)

Eshban (Gn 36:26)

Eshcol (Gn 14:13)

Eshtemoa (1 Chr 4:17)

Eshton (1 Chr 4:11)

Ethan⁺ (1 Kgs 4:31)

Ethan⁺ (1 Chr 2:6)

Evi (Nm 31:8)

Evil-merodach (2 Kgs 25:27)

Ezekias (Mt 1:9)

Ezekiel (Ez 1:3)

E: Mentioned Three Times

Ebiasaph (1 Chr 6:23)

Edom (Gn 25:30)

Eleazar+ (1 Chr 23:21)

Eliab+ (1 Chr 15:18)

Eliada+ (2 Sm 5:16)

Eliakim+ (Mt 1:13)

Elishah (Gn 10:4)

Elishama+ (Jer 36:12)

Elpaal (1 Chr 8:11)

Epaphras (Col 1:7)

Ephah+ (Gn 25:4)

Esar-haddon (2 Kgs 19:37)

Esrom (Mt 1:3)

Ethan+ (1 Chr 6:44)

F

Felix (9)

Happy

Governor of Judea before whom Paul appeared after the Roman guard rescued him from his appearance at the Jewish council. Felix, hoping for a bribe and wanting to please the Jews, delayed making a decision in Paul's case. When his successor, Porcius Festus, came, they heard his case together and sent Paul to Caesar in Rome.

First reference Acts 23:24
Last reference Acts 25:14
Key reference Acts 24:24–26

Festus (13)

Festal

The governor of Judea who replaced Felix. He heard Paul's case and determined to send Paul to Rome, since the apostle had appealed to Caesar. When Festus brought the case before King Agrippa, Agrippa agreed. Also called Porcius Festus.

First reference Acts 24:27
Last reference Acts 26:32
Key reference Acts 25:24–25

F: Mentioned Once

Fortunatus (1 Cor 16:17)

G

Gaal (9)
Loathing

A would-be ruler who got the men of Shechem drunk and convinced them to rise up against their king, Abimelech. Zebul, the ruler of the city, warned the king of their planned ambush. Abimelech stealthily returned to his city, fought, and won. Gaal and his relatives were banished from Shechem.

First reference Jgs 9:26
Last reference Jgs 9:41

Gad⁺ (6)
Attack

A son of Jacob and Leah's handmaid Zilpah. At Gad's birth Leah said, "A troop cometh," so she gave him a name meaning "attack." Jacob prophesied that a troop would overcome Gad but that he would at last overcome.

First reference Gn 30:11
Last reference 1 Chr 5:11

Gad⁺ (13)
Attack

A prophet who warned David, when he ran from Saul, to leave Moab and return to Judea. When King David sinned by taking a census of the people, Gad came to him with God's choices for punishment and a way to end it.

First reference 1 Sm 22:5
Last reference 2 Chr 29:25
Key references 1 Sm 22:5;
   1 Chr 21:9–14

Gallio [3]

Deputy (proconsul) of Achaia who refused to hear the case when the Jews accused Paul of breaking the law.

First reference Acts 18:12
Last reference Acts 18:17

Gamaliel+ [5]

Reward of God

Leader of the tribe of Manasseh under Moses during the Exodus.

First reference Nm 1:10
Last reference Nm 10:23

Gedaliah+ [27]

God has become great

The ruler appointed by Nebuchadnezzar over the remnant of Jews left behind in Judah at the time of the Babylonian Exile. When the prophet Jeremiah was freed from prison, he chose to stay with Gedaliah and the people of Judah instead of heading for Babylon. Gedaliah persuaded the captains of Judah not to worry about serving the Chaldeans. Though one of his captains warned about a plot against him, Gedaliah refused to believe it. Ishmael, the son of Nethaniah, another captain, killed Gedaliah and all his men with him at Mizpah.

First reference 2 Kgs 25:22
Last reference Jer 43:6
Key references Jer 40:6–9, 16; 41:2

Gehazi (12)

Valley of a visionary

The prophet Elisha's servant, who pointed out to Elisha that the Shunnamite woman had no son. Elisha promised her one in a year. Gehazi later laid Elisha's staff on her son in an attempt to bring him back to life. After Elisha healed the Syrian captain Naaman of leprosy and refused gifts, Gehazi followed him to elicit money and clothing from him. For this, Gehazi was made leprous.

First reference 2 Kgs 4:12
Last reference 2 Kgs 8:5
Key references 2 Kgs 4:14;
    5:25–27

Gemariah⁺ (4)

God has perfected

A scribe and prince of Judah in whose room Baruch read the prophecies of Jeremiah. Son of Shaphan.

First reference Jer 36:10
Last reference Jer 36:25

Gera⁺ (4)

Grain

Father of Shimei. Shimei cursed David but later recognized him as king.

First reference 2 Sm 16:5
Last reference 1 Kgs 2:8

Gershom⁺ (5)

Refugee

Moses and Zipporah's firstborn son.

First reference Ex 2:22
Last reference 1 Chr 26:24

Gershom+ (7)

Refugee

Firstborn son of Levi. Same as Gershon.

First reference 1 Chr 6:16
Last reference 1 Chr 15:7

Gershon (18)

Refugee

Firstborn son of Levi. From his line came the Libnites and Shimites. His clan carried the curtains of the tabernacle, its cords, and the equipment. Same as Gershom (1 Chr 6:16).

First reference Gn 46:11
Last reference 1 Chr 23:6
Key reference Gn 46:11

Gideon (39)

Warrior

The fifth judge of Israel, whom God raised up to lead his nation against the Midianites. The angel of the Lord appeared to Gideon when he was hiding his threshing from the enemy, told him God was with him, and called him a "mighty man of valour." Gideon's many doubts did not keep him from obeying God. He made an offering to the Lord then tore down the local altar to the pagan god Baal and cut down its grove, for which the men of his town wanted to kill him. The Spirit of God came upon Gideon, and he sent to the tribes of Manasseh, Asher, Zebulun, and Naphtali, who came to him. Doubtful that God would save Israel, several times Gideon sought proof by placing a fleece on the floor and asking God to make either the fleece or the floor wet; every time God answered his request. When Israel gathered to fight Midian, God reduced Gideon's forces, cutting out the fearful and identifying the rest by the way they drank water. Gideon attacked Midian with only three hundred men. Holding trumpets and pitchers filled with lamps, the men drew near the Midianite camp. They blew the trumpets and broke the pitchers, and their enemy fled. Gideon and his troops followed, capturing two princes and two kings and killing them. Same as Gedeon, Jerubbaal, and Jerubbesheth.

First reference Jgs 6:11
Last reference Jgs 8:35
Key references Jgs 6:11;
    7:6–7, 20–22

Gideoni (5)
Warlike

Father of Abidan, a captain of the Benjaminites who helped Moses take a census and lead his people toward the Promised Land.

First reference Nm 1:11
Last reference Nm 10:24

Gilead+ (11)
Heap of testimony

A descendant of Abraham through Joseph's son Manasseh.

First reference Nm 26:29
Last reference 1 Chr 7:17

Gog+ (10)

A prince of Magog, a place perhaps in Scythia but certainly from the "north parts" (Ez 39:2), against whom Ezekiel prophesied. God spoke of Gog's destruction and graves in Israel. In the book of Revelation, "Gog and Magog" refers to the Lord's last enemies.

First reference Ez 38:2
Last reference Rv 20:8

Goliath (6)
Exile

A nine-foot-nine-inch-tall Philistine champion who was well armored and carried a spear that had a shaft like a weaver's beam. He challenged any Israelite to a fight; the losing nation would become the winner's servants. David fought Goliath with a slingshot, killed him, and then cut off his head.

First reference I Sm 17:4
Last reference I Chr 20:5

Gomer+ (4)
Completion

Firstborn son of Japheth, Noah's son.

First reference Gn 10:2
Last reference I Chr 1:6

G: Mentioned Once

Gabbai (Neh 11:8)

Gaddi (Nm 13:11)

Gaddiel (Nm 13:10)

Gaham (Gn 22:24)

Gaius+ (Acts 19:29)

Gaius+ (Acts 20:4)

Gaius+ (3 Jn 1:1)

Galal+ (1 Chr 9:15)

Gamul (1 Chr 24:17)

Gashmu (Neh 6:6)

Gazez+ (1 Chr 2:46)

Gazez+ (1 Chr 2:46)

Geber+ (1 Kgs 4:13)

Geber+ (1 Kgs 4:19)

Gedaliah+ (Ezr 10:18)

Gedaliah+ (Jer 38:1)

Gedaliah+ (Zep 1:1)

Gedeon (Heb 11:32)

Gemalli (Nm 13:12)

Gemariah+ (Jer 29:3)

Genubath (1 Kgs 11:20)

Gera+ (Gn 46:21)

Gera+ (Jgs 3:15)

Gershom+ (Jgs 18:30)

Gershom+ (Ezr 8:2)

Gesham (1 Chr 2:47)

Geuel (Nm 13:15)

Gibbar (Ezr 2:20)

Gibea (1 Chr 2:49)

Gilalai (Neh 12:36)

Gilead+ (1 Chr 5:14)

Ginnetho (Neh 12:4)

Gispa (Neh 11:21)

Gog+ (1 Chr 5:4)

Gomer+ (Hos 1:3)

Guni+ (1 Chr 5:15)

G: Mentioned Twice

Gadi (2 Kgs 15:14)

Gahar (Ezr 2:47)

Gaius+ (Rom 16:23)

Galal+ (1 Chr 9:16)

Gamaliel+ (Acts 5:34)

Gareb (2 Sm 23:38)

Gazzam (Ezr 2:48)

Gedaliah+ (1 Chr 25:3)

Gedor+ (1 Chr 4:4)

Gedor+ (1 Chr 8:31)

Gether (Gn 10:23)

Giddalti (1 Chr 25:4)

Giddel+ (Ezr 2:47)

Giddel+ (Ezr 2:56)

Gilead+ (Jgs 11:1)

Ginath (Kgs 16:21)

Ginnethon (Neh 10:6)

G: Mentioned Three Times

Gatam (Gn 36:11)

Gera+ (1 Chr 8:3)

Geshem (Neh 2:19)

Guni+ (Gn 46:24)

H

Hadad+ [4]

A king of Edom, "before there reigned any king over the children of Israel" (Gn 36:31).

First reference Gn 36:35
Last reference I Chr 1:47

Hadad+ [7]

Israel's Edomite adversary who arose after Solomon turned from the Lord. Hadad formed a marauding band that attacked Israel for the rest of Solomon's reign.

First reference I Kgs 11:14
Last reference I Kgs 11:25

Hadadezer [9]

Hadad is his help

Syrian king of Zobah whose troops David defeated along with the Syrians of Damascus who supported Hadadezer. Same as Hadarezer.

First reference 2 Sm 8:3
Last reference I Kgs 11:23

Hadarezer [12]

Hadad is his help

Syrian king of Zobar whom David defeated along with the Syrians of Damascus who supported him. Later, Hadarezer hired out his men to fight King David for the Ammonites. After they lost, Hadarezer made peace with Israel. Same as Hadadezer.

First reference 2 Sm 10:16
Last reference I Chr 19:19

Hagar* (12)

Sarai's Egyptian maid who became a surrogate wife to Abram so he and Sarai could have a child. When Hagar conceived, she despised Sarai and fled from her. The angel of the Lord told Hagar to return and submit to Sarai. After Sarai's own child, Isaac, was born, she threw Hagar and her son, Ishmael, out of the camp. God provided Hagar with water in the wilderness and promised to make Ishmael into a great nation.

First reference Gn 16:1
Last reference Gn 25:12
Key references Gn 16:1–2, 15;
   21:10

Haggai (11)

Festive

A prophet of Judah who wrote the book that bears his name. With the prophet Zechariah, he encouraged the disheartened Jews to continue in their efforts to rebuild the temple. During the era of Haggai's prophecies and the temple building project, the Jews prospered. God promised this second temple would be greater than the original temple that Solomon had built.

First reference Ezr 5:1
Last reference Hg 2:20
Key references Ezr 6:14; Hg
   2:9–10

Haggith* (5)

Festive

One of several wives of King David and mother of David's son Adonijah.

First reference 2 Sm 3:4
Last reference I Chr 3:2

Ham (12)

Hot

The youngest of Noah's three sons. After the flood, when Noah became drunk and lay naked in his tent, Ham looked on and reported it to his brothers. For this, Noah cursed Ham's youngest son and blessed the brothers who covered him without looking. Ham fathered four sons, from whom came many of Israel's worst enemies.

First reference Gn 5:32
Last reference I Chr 1:8
Key references Gn 9:22–25; 10:6

Haman (53)

King Ahasuerus's wicked counselor, who plotted to eradicate the Jews from the Persian kingdom. When Mordecai, the cousin of Ahasuerus's wife, Queen Esther, refused to bow before the king, Haman decided to destroy all the Jews. The counselor extracted permission from the king to create a law to that end. But Mordecai heard of his plan and reported it to the queen. When Haman came to the court one day, the king asked what should be done to honor a man in whom the king delighted. Thinking the king meant himself, Haman suggested that the man be dressed in the king's clothes, placed on a horse, and his good deeds proclaimed as he was led throughout the streets. To the counselor's horror, the king commanded Haman to do this for his enemy, Mordecai. Queen Esther invited Haman and the king to a banquet. The proud counselor was honored until the second day of the feast, when the queen revealed the truth of his plans to the king. Ahasuerus, angry at the deceit of his counselor, had him hanged on the gallows that Haman had erected to destroy Mordecai.

First reference Est 3:1
Last reference Est 9:24
Key references Est 3:5–11

Hammedatha (5)

Father of Haman, the villain of the story of Esther.

First reference Est 3:1
Last reference Est 9:24

Hamor (3)
Ass

A prince of Shechem whose son raped Dinah, Jacob's daughter. Hamor arranged a marriage, but Dinah's brothers, angered at the situation, killed all the men in his city.

First reference Gn 33:19
Last reference Jgs 9:28
Key references Gn 34:2, 8–10, 24–26

Hanameel (4)

God has favored

The prophet Jeremiah's cousin, from whom Jeremiah bought land as a sign from God.

First reference Jer 32:7
Last reference Jer 32:12

Hanani⁺ (4)

Father of King Jehu of Israel.

First reference 1 Kgs 16:1
Last reference 2 Chr 20:34

Hananiah⁺ (4)

God has favored

A son of King David's musician Heman, who was "under the hands of [his] father for song in the house of the Lord" (1 Chr 25:6).

First reference 1 Chr 25:4
Last reference 1 Chr 25:23

Hananiah⁺ (8)

God has favored

A false prophet who told King Zedekiah of Judah that the king of Babylon's yoke had been broken. He claimed that within two years, the temple vessels and King Jehoiakim's exiled son Jeconiah would be returned. Jeremiah was not convinced. God gave him a prophecy that denied Hananiah's and promised to take the false prophet's life within a year. Hananiah died in the seventh month.

First reference Jer 28:1
Last reference Jer 28:17

Hananiah+ (5)

God has favored

The Hebrew name of Daniel's friend better known as Shadrach.

First reference Dn 1:6
Last reference Dn 2:17

Hannah* (13)

Favored

Hannah could not bear a child, but her husband, Elkanah, loved her, though his second wife abused her. Distraught, Hannah went to the temple to pray and promised God that if He gave her a child, she would give the boy to Him for his whole life. As she fervently prayed in the temple, Eli the priest mistook her praying for drunkenness; then he discovered how wrong he had been. In time, Hannah conceived and bore Samuel. When he was weaned, the couple brought the boy to Eli to foster. Samuel became a powerful prophet of Israel who crowned Saul and David king.

First reference 1 Sm 1:2
Last reference 1 Sm 2:21
Key references 1 Sm 1:11;
    15–16

Hanoch+ (4)

A descendant of Abraham through Jacob's son Reuben.

First reference Gn 46:9
Last reference 1 Chr 5:3

Hanun+ (9)

Favored

An Ammonite king to whom David sent comforters after his father died. The princes of Ammon convinced Hanun these men were spies. So the new king shaved half their beards off, cut off half their clothing, and sent them home. Then Hanun hired Syrian warriors and unsuccessfully attacked Israel.

First reference 2 Sm 10:1
Last reference I Chr 19:6

Haran⁺ (6)

Rest, mountaineer, parched

Brother of Abram. Haran died while they were still in Ur of the Chaldees. His son, Lot, traveled to Canaan with Abram and Sarai.

First reference Gn 11:26
Last reference Gn 11:31

Harim⁺ (6)

Snub-nosed

One of twenty-four priests in David's time who was chosen by lot to serve in the tabernacle. Harim was also forefather of a man who repaired Jerusalem's walls under Nehemiah.

First reference I Chr 24:8
Last reference Neh 12:15

Hatach (4)

One of King Ahasuerus's eunuchs, who attended Queen Esther. He acted as a messenger between her and Mordecai when Mordecai discovered Haman's plot.

First reference Est 4:5
Last reference Est 4:10

Hazael (23)

God has seen

A king of Syria anointed to his position by Elijah. Before becoming king, while Hazael served the Syrian king Ben-hadad, he was sent to Elisha to ask if the king would recover from an illness. Elisha replied that he would recover but told Hazael he would die. Hazael suffocated Ben-hadad and took his throne. Throughout his reign Hazael fought Israel and Judah. King Jehoash of Judah bribed him not to attack Jerusalem. Because Jehoash did not obey God, he continually fought Hazael and his son, Ben-hadad. Hazael oppressed Israel through King Jehoahaz's reign.

First reference 1 Kgs 19:15
Last reference Am 1:4

Key references 1 Kgs 19:15; 2 Kgs 8:8–10; 12:18; 13:22

Heber⁺ (5)

Community, across

A descendant of Abraham through Jacob's son Asher.

First reference Gn 46:17
Last reference Lk 3:35

Heber⁺ (4)

Called Heber the Kenite, he was the husband of Jael, the woman who killed the Canaanite commander Sisera.

First reference Jgs 4:11
Last reference Jgs 5:24

Hebron (7)

Association

A descendant of Abraham through Jacob's son Levi.

First reference Ex 6:18
Last reference 1 Chr 24:23

Helez⁺ (4)

Strength

A commander in King David's army overseeing twenty-four thousand men in the seventh month of each year.

First reference 2 Sm 23:26
Last reference 1 Chr 27:10

Helon (5)

Strong

Father of a prince of Zebulun who helped Moses take a census of his tribe.

First reference Nm 1:9
Last reference Nm 10:16

Heman⁺ (14)

A descendant of Abraham through Jacob's son Levi. Heman was one of the key musicians serving in the Jerusalem temple. King David appointed Heman's descendants to "prophesy with harps, with psalteries, and with cymbals" (1 Chr 25:1).

First reference 1 Chr 6:33
Last reference Ps 88 (title)

Henadad (4)

Favor of Hadad

Father of a man who repaired Jerusalem's walls and led a revival under Nehemiah.

First reference Ezr 3:9
Last reference Neh 10:9

Hepher[+] (5)

Shame

A descendant of Abraham through Jacob's son Joseph.

First reference Nm 26:32
Last reference Jo 17:3

Herod[+] (11)

Heroic

Known as Herod the Great, this evil king of Judea killed several of his own sons and completed many building projects, including improvements on the temple. He was much hated by those he ruled. When the wise men from the East appeared, looking for the king of the Jews, Herod feared for his throne and killed all the male toddlers and infants in Bethlehem. But Joseph and his family had escaped into Egypt. Upon Herod's death, Joseph, Mary, and Jesus returned from Egypt but, fearing to live in the land ruled by his son, moved to Nazareth.

First reference Mt 2:1
Last reference Acts 23:35

Herod[+] (22)

Heroic

Herod Antipas, son of Herod the Great, ruled as tetrarch of Galilee and Perea. John the Baptist opposed Antipas's marriage to Herodias, Antipas's brother's wife, saying that their union was unlawful. When the ruler's stepdaughter danced publicly and pleased him, Herod offered her whatever she wanted. He sorrowfully fulfilled her request—John the Baptist's head on a plate. Hearing of Jesus' miracles, Herod believed John had returned from the dead. When Pilate learned that Jesus was from Galilee, he passed him on to Herod to judge. Herod mocked Him and dressed Him in fine clothing. The two rulers became friends that day.

First reference Mt 14:1
Last reference Acts 12:21

Herod⁺ (5)

Heroic

Grandson of Herod the Great who ruled over the tetrarchy of Philip and Lysanias, Herod Agrippa I had the apostle James killed and arrested. Seeing that this pleased the Jewish leaders, he also imprisoned Peter. Herod Agrippa died suddenly and horribly

when the people of Tyre and Sidon declared him a god and he did not correct them.

First reference Acts 12:1
Last reference Acts 13:1

Herodias* (6)

Heroic

Granddaughter of Herod the Great whose second marriage was opposed by John the Baptist. When Herodias's daughter asked what she should request from Herod Antipas, she pushed her to ask for John the Baptist's head on a plate.

First reference Mt 14:3
Last reference Lk 3:19

Heth (14)

Terror

A descendant of Noah through his son Ham. Abraham bought a burial site for his wife, Sarah, from the descendants of Heth.

First reference Gn 10:15
Last reference 1 Chr 1:13

Hezekiah⁺ (125)

Strengthened of God

King of Judah, son of Ahaz, who did right in God's eyes. Hezekiah removed pagan worship from the kingdom and kept God's commandments. Under his command, the Levites cleansed the temple and worship was restored. When the Assyrian king Sennacherib attacked his nation, Hezekiah gave him a large tribute. Sennacherib sent officials to confer with Hezekiah's aides and try to convince his people to side with Sennacherib against their king and God. As Assyria threatened, Isaiah brought the king a comforting prophecy. Sennacherib sent a message to Hezekiah that belittled God and threatened Judah. Hezekiah brought the letter before God and asked Him to save Judah. Again, Isaiah prophesied the Assyrians' fall. Hezekiah became ill to the point of death, and Isaiah told him he would not recover. After weeping and praying, the king received a message from the prophet that God had extended his life by fifteen years and would deliver and defend Jerusalem from its enemies. Isaiah confirmed this with the sign of a shadow moving back ten steps.

After Hezekiah showed the emissaries of the king of Babylon all that was in his house, Isaiah told him everything in his house would be carried away to that land. His sons would also be taken away and made eunuchs to the Babylonian king. Same as Ezekias.

First reference 2 Kgs 16:20
Last reference Mi 1:1
Key references 2 Kgs 18:1–7;
    19:4–7; 20:9–11

Hezron⁺ (12)
Courtyard

A descendant of Abraham through Jacob's son Judah.

First reference Gn 46:12
Last reference 1 Chr 4:1

Hilkiah⁺ (8)
Portion of God

A priest and father of Eliakim. His son met King Sennacherib's messengers for King Hezekiah of Judah.

First reference 2 Kgs 18:18
Last reference Is 36:22

Hilkiah⁺ (19)
Portion of God

High priest during the reign of King Josiah of Judah. He oversaw the counting of the money collected for the work of restoring the temple, discovered the book of the law, and consulted the prophetess Huldah about that discovery.

First reference 2 Kgs 22:4
Last reference Jer 29:3
Key reference 2 Kgs 22:8

Hiram+ [18]

Milk

A king of Tyre who provided cedar trees and workmen for building in Israel. "Hiram was ever a lover of David" (1 Kgs 5:1) and offered David cedar trees and workmen to build a home. As he prepared to build the temple, Solomon ordered cedar and cypress from Hiram. The two men made a treaty, and Solomon gave Hiram twenty cities in Galilee. When Solomon built a fleet of ships, Hiram provided experienced seamen to aid Solomon's sailors. Hiram's own fleet brought back almug wood, which was used to make supports for the temple.

First reference 2 Sm 5:11
Last reference 1 Chr 14:1
Key references 1 Kgs 5:1, 8

Hiram+ [4]

Milk

A skilled craftsman who was especially gifted in working brass, Hiram came from Tyre to help build Solomon's house and make utensils for the temple.

First reference 1 Kgs 7:13
Last reference 1 Kgs 7:45

Hodijah+ [4]

Celebrated

A Levite who helped Ezra to explain the law to exiles returned to Jerusalem. Hodijah was among a group of Levites who led a revival among the Israelites in the time of Nehemiah.

First reference Neh 8:7
Last reference Neh 10:13

Hoglah* (4)

Partridge

One of five daughters of Zelophehad, an Israelite who died during the wilderness wanderings. The women asked Moses if they could inherit their father's property in the Promised Land (a right normally reserved for sons), and God ruled that they should.

First reference Nm 26:33
Last reference Jo 17:3

Hophni (5)

Pugilist

Son of the high priest Eli, who had honored Hophni and his brother Phinehas more than the Lord. The brothers did not know the Lord, misused their priestly office, and disobeyed the law. A man of God prophesied that they would die on the same day. When the Philistines attacked and took the ark of the covenant, both Hophni and Phinehas were killed.

First reference 1 Sm 1:3
Last reference 1 Sm 4:17

Hosah (4)

Hopeful

A Levite who was chosen by lot to guard the west side of the house of the Lord.

First reference 1 Chr 16:38
Last reference 1 Chr 26:16

Hoshea⁺ (8)

Deliverer

The Israelite who conspired against King Pekah, killed him, and took his throne. Hoshea became a vassal to King Shalmaneser of Assyria but rebelliously sent messengers to the king of Egypt. Shalmaneser imprisoned Hoshea, captured Samaria, and carried the Israelites off to Assyria.

First reference 2 Kgs 15:30
Last reference 2 Kgs 18:10

Hur+ (6)
White

Father of a craftsman who devised metal and stone designs for the tabernacle.

First reference Ex 31:2
Last reference 2 Chr 1:5

Huram+ (8)

Variation of the name Hiram. Same as Hiram (2 Sm 5:11).

First reference 2 Chr 2:3
Last reference 2 Chr 9:21

Hushai (14)
Hasty

King David's friend Hushai the Archite remained in Jerusalem when Absalom ousted the king from the city. At David's request, Hushai became Absalom's advisor, with the intent of protecting David. When Ahithophel wanted to attack his father quickly, Hushai advised against it; then he sent a warning to David to escape.

First reference 2 Sm 15:32
Last reference 1 Chr 27:33
Key references 2 Sm 15:32–34; 16:18

Husham (4)
Hastily

A king of Edom, "before there reigned any king over the children of Israel" (Gn 36:31).

First reference Gn 36:34
Last reference 1 Chr 1:46

H: Mentioned Once

Haahashtari (1 Chr 4:6)

Habaziniah (Jer 35:3)

Hachmoni (1 Chr 27:32)

Hadad⁺ (1 Chr 1:30)

Hadar⁺ (Gn 25:15)

Hadar⁺ (Gn 36:39)

Hadassah* (Est 2:7)

Hadlai (2 Chr 28:12)

Hadoram⁺ (1 Chr 18:10)

Hadoram⁺ (2 Chr 10:18)

Hagab (Ezr 2:46)

Hagaba (Neh 7:48)

Hagabah (Ezr 2:45)

Haggeri (1 Chr 11:38)

Haggiah (1 Chr 6:30)

Hakkatan (Ezr 8:12)

Hakkoz (1 Chr 24:10)

Hallohesh (Neh 10:24)

Halohesh (Neh 3:12)

Hammoleketh* (1 Chr 7:18)

Hanan⁺ (1 Chr 8:23)

Hanan⁺ (1 Chr 11:43)

Hanan⁺ (Neh 8:7)

Hanan⁺ (Neh 10:22)

Hanan⁺ (Neh 10:26)

Hanan⁺ (Jer 35:4)

Hamuel (1 Chr 4:26)

Hanani⁺ (2 Chr 16:7)

Hanani⁺ (Ezr 10:20)

Hanani⁺ (Neh 12:36)

Hananiah⁺ (1 Chr 8:24)

Hananiah⁺ (2 Chr 26:11)

Hananiah⁺ (Ezr 10:28)

Hananiah⁺ (Neh 3:8)

Hananiah⁺ (Neh 3:30)

Hananiah⁺ (Neh 7:2)

Hananiah⁺ (Neh 10:23)

Hananiah⁺ (Neh 12:41)

Hananiah⁺ (Jer 36:12)

Hananiah⁺ (Jer 37:13)

Haniel (1 Chr 7:39)

Hanniel (Nm 34:23)

Hanoch⁺ (Gn 25:4)

Hanun⁺ (Neh 3:13)

Hanun⁺ (Neh 3:30)

Haran⁺ (1 Chr 2:46)

Haran⁺ (1 Chr 23:9)

Harbona (Est 1:10)

Harbonah (Est 7:9)

Hareph (1 Chr 2:51)

Harhaiah (Neh 3:8)

Harhas (2 Kgs 22:14)

Harim+ (Ezr 10:31)

Harim+ (Neh 10:5)

Harim+ (Neh 10:27)

Hariph+ (Neh 7:24)

Hariph+ (Neh 10:19)

Harnepher (1 Chr 7:36)

Haroeh (1 Chr 2:52)

Harum (1 Chr 4:8)

Harumaph (Neh 3:10)

Haruz (2 Kgs 21:19)

Hasadiah (1 Chr 3:20)

Hasenuah (1 Chr 9:7)

Hashabiah+ (1 Chr 6:45)

Hashabiah+ (1 Chr 9:14)

Hashabiah+ (1 Chr 26:30)

Hashabiah+ (1 Chr 27:17)

Hashabiah+ (2 Chr 35:9)

Hashabiah+ (Ezr 8:19)

Hashabiah+ (Ezr 8:24)

Hashabiah+ (Neh 3:17)

Hashabiah+ (Neh 10:11)

Hashabiah+ (Neh 11:15)

Hashabiah+ (Neh 11:22)

Hashabiah+ (Neh 12:21)

Hashabiah+ (Neh 12:24)

Hashabnah (Neh 10:25)

Hashabniah+ (Neh 3:10)

Hashabniah+ (Neh 9:5)

Hashbadana (Neh 8:4)

Hashem (1 Chr 11:34)

Hashub+ (Neh 3:11)

Hashub+ (Neh 3:23)

Hashub+ (Neh 10:23)

Hashub+ (Neh 11:15)

Hashubah (1 Chr 3:20)

Hashum+ (Neh 8:4)

Hashum+ (Neh 10:18)

Hashupha (Neh 7:46)

Hasrah (2 Chr 34:22)

Hassenaah (Neh 3:3)

Hasshub (1 Chr 9:14)

Hasupha (Ezr 2:43)

Hathath (1 Chr 4:13)

Hattil (Ezr 2:57)

Hattush+ (1 Chr 3:22)

Hattush+ (Ezr 8:2)

Hattush+ (Neh 3:10)

Hattush+ (Neh 10:4)

Hattush+ (Neh 12:12)

Hazaiah (Neh 11:5)

Hazelelponi* (1 Chr 4:3)

Haziel (1 Chr 23:9)

Hazo (Gn 22:22)

Heber+ (1 Chr 4:18)

Heber+ (1 Chr 5:13)

Heber+ (1 Chr 8:17)

Heber+ (1 Chr 8:22)

Hege (Est 2:3)

Heldai+ (1 Chr 27:15)

Heldai+ (Zec 6:10)

Heleb (2 Sm 23:29)

Heled (1 Chr 11:30)

Helem+ (1 Chr 7:35)

Helem+ (Zec 6:14)

Helez+ (1 Chr 2:39)

Hephzibah* (2 Kgs 21:2)

Heli (Lk 3:23)

Helkai (Neh 12:15)

Hemam (Gn 36:22)

Hemath (1 Chr 2:55)

Hemdan (Gn 36:26)

Hen (Zec 6:14)

Henoch+ (1 Chr 1:3)

Henoch+ (1 Chr 1:33)

Hepher+ (1 Chr 4:6)

Hepher+ (1 Chr 11:36)

Hephzibah (2 Kgs 21:1)

Heresh (1 Chr 9:15)

Hermas (Rom 16:14)

Hermes (Rom 16:14)

Hermogenes (2 Tm 1:15)

Herodion (Rom 16:11)

Hesed (1 Kgs 4:10)

Hezeki (1 Chr 8:17)

Hezekiah+ (1 Chr 3:23)

Hezion (1 Kgs 15:18)

Hezir+ (1 Chr 24:15)

Hezir+ (Neh 10:20)

Hezrai (2 Sm 23:35)

Hezro (1 Chr 11:37)

Hiddai (2 Sm 23:30)

Hiel (1 Kgs 16:34)

Hilkiah+ (1 Chr 6:45)

Hilkiah+ (1 Chr 26:11)

Hilkiah+ (Jer 1:1)

Hillel (Jgs 12:13)

Hirah (Gn 38:1)

Hizkiah (Zep 1:1)

Hizkijah (Neh 10:17)

Hod (1 Chr 7:37)

Hodaiah (1 Chr 3:24)

Hodaviah+ (1 Chr 5:24)

Hodaviah+ (1 Chr 9:7)

Hodaviah+ (Ezr 2:40)

Hodesh* (1 Chr 8:9)

Hodevah (Neh 7:43)

Hodiah* (1 Chr 4:19)

Hodijah+ (Neh 10:18)

Hoham (Jo 10:3)

Homam (1 Chr 1:39)

Horam (Jo 10:33)

Hori+ (Nm 13:5)

Hoshaiah+ (Neh 12:32)

Hoshaiah+ (Jer 42:1)

Hoshama (1 Chr 3:18)

Hoshea+ (Dt 32:44)

Hoshea+ (1 Chr 27:20)

Hoshea+ (Neh 10:23)

Hotham (1 Chr 7:32)

Hothan (1 Chr 11:44)

Hupham (Nm 26:39)

Huppah (1 Chr 24:13)

Hur+ (1 Kgs 4:8)

Hur+ (1 Chr 4:1)

Hur+ (Neh 3:9)

Hurai (1 Chr 11:32)

Huram+ (1 Chr 8:5)

Huri (1 Chr 5:14)

Hushah (1 Chr 4:4)

Hushim+ (Gn 46:23)

Hushim+ (1 Chr 7:12)

Huz (Gn 22:21)

H: Mentioned Twice

Habaiah (Ezr 2:6)

Habakkuk (Hb 1:1)

Hachaliah (Neh 1:1)

Hadad+ (1 Chr 1:50)

Hadoram+ (Gn 10:27)

Haggi (Gn 46:16)

Hakupha (Ezr 2:51)

Hammelech (Jer 36:26)

Hanan+ (1 Chr 8:38)

Hanan+ (Ezr 2:46)

Hanan+ (Neh 10:10)

Hanani+ (1 Chr 25:4)

Hanani+ (Neh 1:2)

Hananiah+ (1 Chr 3:19)

Harhur (Ezr 2:51)

Harim+ (Ezr 2:32)

Harsha (Ezr 2:52)

Hashabiah+ (1 Chr 25:3)

Hatipha (Ezr 2:54)

Hatita (Ezr 2:42)

Havilah+ (Gn 10:7)

Havilah+ (Gn 10:29)

Hazarmaveth (Gn 10:26)

Helah* (1 Chr 4:5)

Helek (Nm 26:30)

Herod+ (Acts 25:13)

Hezekiah+ (Ezr 2:16)

Hobab (Nm 10:29)

Hothir (1 Chr 25:4)

Hul (Gn 10:23)

Huldah* (2 Kgs 22:14)

Hur+ (Nm 31:8)

Hur+ (1 Chr 2:50)

Hushim*+ (1 Chr 8:8)

Hymenaeus (1 Tm 1:20)

H: Mentioned Three Times

Hamul (Gn 46:12)

Hamutal* (2 Kgs 23:31)

Hashum+ (Ezr 2:19)

Hebron (1 Chr 2:42)

Hegai (Est 2:8)

Heman+ (1 Kgs 4:31)

Hezron+ (Gn 46:9)

Hilkiah+ (Neh 8:4)

Hori+ (Gn 36:22)

Hosea (Hos 1:1)

Huppim (Gn 46:21)

Hur+ (Ex 17:10)

Huram+ (2 Chr 4:11)

I

Iddo⁺ (4)

Father of the prophet Zechariah.

First reference Ezr 5:1
Last reference Zec 1:7

Immer⁺ (5)

Talkative

Forefather of a Levite who returned to Jerusalem following the Babylonian captivity.

First reference 1 Chr 9:12
Last reference Neh 11:13

Isaac (132)

Laughter

The son of Abraham and Sarah whom God promised to the long-barren couple as part of His covenant promise. After Sarah gave Abraham her servant Hagar to bear him a son, Ishmael, Sarah bore Isaac. God tested Abraham by asking him to sacrifice Isaac at Moriah. When Isaac commented on the lack of a lamb to sacrifice, Abraham replied that God would provide it. At the site of sacrifice, Abraham built an altar and placed his son atop it. But the angel of the Lord stopped the sacrifice, and God provided a ram instead. Abraham sent a servant to his brother Nahor's household to find a wife for Isaac. The man returned with Nahor's daughter Rebekah; Isaac married her and loved her. Rebekah had trouble conceiving, so Isaac prayed for a child. She bore two sons, Esau and Jacob. Esau was Isaac's favorite, but Jacob fooled his elderly, blind father into giving him the blessing of the firstborn child. Isaac had to give Esau a lesser blessing, which caused Esau to hate his brother and required Jacob to leave for a time. Isaac lived to be 180 years old, and his sons buried him.

First reference Gn 17:19
Last reference Jas 2:21
Key references Gn 22:7–9;
    24:3–4; 25:19–34

Isaiah (32)

God has saved

A prophet of Jerusalem who served during the last year of the reign of King Uzziah and through the reigns of Jotham, Ahaz, and Hezekiah. This aristocratic prophet was married to a prophetess and had at least two children. Isaiah warned Ahaz of an attack by Syria. He supported Ahaz and Hezekiah as the Assyrians became aggressive and sought to expand their empire. But the prophet warned against making treaties with foreign nations. When Sennacherib, king of Assyria, attacked Judah and encouraged the people of Judah not to fight against him, Isaiah counseled Hezekiah to pray and prophesied that a spirit would enter the Assyrian king and he would return to his own land. Later he promised that God would not let Assyria enter Jerusalem. It happened as Isaiah had foretold. Hezekiah became sick, and Isaiah prophesied that he would die. Yet when the king prayed, God promised him fifteen more years of life. Isaiah proved it to the king by causing a shadow to go backward on the steps of Ahaz. But after Hezekiah showed his wealth to messengers from the king of Babylon, Isaiah foretold that everything in his house, including his sons, would be captured by Babylon. Same as Esaias.

First reference 2 Kgs 19:2
Last reference Is 39:8
Key references 2 Kgs 19:20–24; 20; Is 1:1

Iscariot (11)

Inhabitant of Kerioth

Surname of Judas, the disciple who betrayed Jesus. Same as Judas (Mt 10:4).

First reference Mt 10:4
Last reference Jn 14:22
Key references Mk 14:10; Jn 13:2, 26

Ish-bosheth (12)

Man of shame

King Saul's son who was made king over Israel by Abner, the captain of Saul's army. Ish-bosheth offended Abner by claiming that the captain had slept with Saul's concubine. So Abner turned to David, who sent word to Ish-bosheth and demanded that he return David's wife Michal. Ish-bosheth took her from her second husband and sent her to David. Baanah and Rechab killed Ish-bosheth. The murderers took his head to David, who had them killed and buried the dead king's head in Abner's tomb.

First reference 2 Sm 2:8
Last reference 2 Sm 4:12
Key references 2 Sm 3:7; 4:5–8

Ishmael+ (19)

God will hear

Son of Hagar the Egyptian and Abram. Ishmael was born after Abram's barren wife, Sarai (later called Sarah), encouraged her husband to have a child with her maid. God rejected Ishmael, who was not the son of His covenant promise. But He promised to bless Ishmael and make him fruitful so he would found a great nation. Because Ishmael mocked Isaac, Sarah's son, Sarah insisted that Hagar and Ishmael be cast out of the camp. But God watched over them, and they made a home in the wilderness of Paran.

First reference Gn 16:11
Last reference I Chr 1:31
Key references Gn 17:18, 20;
  21:9–12

Ishmael+ (23)

An army captain of Judah under Gedaliah, the governor of Judah who was appointed by King Nebuchadnezzar of Babylon. Under the influence of the Ammonite king Baalis, Ishmael killed the governor and his men and fled with the people of Judah toward Egypt. When the captain Johanan came to him, the people followed Johanan, and Ishmael escaped to the Ammorites.

First reference 2 Kgs 25:23
Last reference Jer 41:18
Key references Jer 40:13–16;
  41:2–3, 15

Israel (55)

He will rule as God

The name given to Jacob by God when he wrestled

with Him at Peniel. After renaming him, God again appeared to Israel, confirmed His covenant promises, and blessed him. Of his twelve sons, Israel loved Joseph more than the others, gave him a coat of many colors to show his preferred status, and put him in a position of authority. For this, Israel's other sons hated Joseph. They sold him into slavery and convinced their father that Joseph was dead. When famine came to the land, Israel sent all his sons except Benjamin to Egypt for food. Joseph had risen to second-in-command of the kingdom there, but his brothers did not recognize him. Joseph demanded that they leave Simeon with him as a hostage and bring Benjamin to Egypt. Israel reluctantly agreed to send Benjamin. When his sons returned again, telling him Egypt's second-in-command was Joseph, Israel could hardly believe it. At God's command Israel traveled to Egypt with all his family and flocks. Joseph met them in Goshen and was reunited with his father. With Pharaoh's approval, Joseph gave his family land in Goshen to settle on. Israel blessed Joseph's sons, Ephraim and Manasseh, taking them as his own sons. But he gave the younger, Ephraim, the greater blessing, saying he would be the greater one. Then he blessed all his sons and asked that he be buried in the field at Machpelah with his forefathers. When Israel died, Joseph had him embalmed and buried him as he requested. Same as Jacob (Gn 25:26).

First reference Gn 32:28
Last reference Ezr 8:18
Key references Gn 35:10–12;
    42:1–2; 48:1–5

Issachar+ (7)

He will bring a reward

Leah and Jacob's fifth son and Jacob's ninth son. His mother saw him as God's payment to her because she gave her servant, Zilpah, to Jacob. Issachar had four sons.

First reference Gn 30:18
Last reference 1 Chr 7:1

Ithamar (21)

Coast of the palm tree

A son of Aaron and his wife, Elisheba. With his father and brothers, Ithamar served as a priest. Moses became angry at Ithamar and his brother Eleazar because they would not eat the sin offering in the tabernacle. Ithamar oversaw the Gershonites and the duties of the sons of Merari in the tabernacle.

First reference Ex 6:23
Last reference Ezr 8:2
Key references Nm 3:4;
    4:28, 33

Ittai+ (7)
Near

A Gittite who remained faithful to King David when Absalom tried to overthrow him. David set Ittai over a third of the people who followed him out of Jerusalem.

First reference 2 Sm 15:19
Last reference 2 Sm 18:12

Izhar (8)

Anointing

A descendant of Abraham through Jacob's son Levi.

First reference Ex 6:18
Last reference 1 Chr 23:18

I: Mentioned Once

Ibneiah (1 Chr 9:8)

Ibnijah (1 Chr 9:8)

Ibri (1 Chr 24:27)

Idbash (1 Chr 4:3)

Iddo+ (1 Kgs 4:14)

Iddo+ (1 Chr 6:21)

Iddo+ (1 Chr 27:21)

Iddo+ (Ezr 8:17)

Igal+ (Nm 13:7)

Igal+ (2 Sm 23:36)

Igdaliah (Jer 35:4)

Igeal (1 Chr 3:22)

Ilai (1 Chr 11:29)

Immer+ (1 Chr 24:14)

Immer+ (Neh 3:29)

Immer+ (Jer 20:1)

Imna (1 Chr 7:35)

Imnah+ (1 Chr 7:30)

Imnah+ (2 Chr 31:14)

Imrah (1 Chr 7:36)

Imri+ (1 Chr 9:4)

Imri+ (Neh 3:2)

Iphedeiah (1 Chr 8:25)

Ir (1 Chr 7:12)

Ira+ (2 Sm 20:26)

Irad (Gn 4:18)

Iri (1 Chr 7:7)

Irnahash (1 Chr 4:12)

Iru (1 Chr 4:15)

Iscah (Gn 11:29)

Ishbah (1 Chr 4:17)

Ishbi-benob (2 Sm 21:16)

Ishi+ (1 Chr 2:31)

Ishi+ (1 Chr 4:20)

Ishi+ (1 Chr 4:42)

Ishi+ (1 Chr 5:24)

Ishiah (1 Chr 7:3)

Ishijah (Ezr 10:31)

Ishma (1 Chr 4:3)

Ishmael+ (2 Chr 19:11)

Ishmael+ (2 Chr 23:1)

Ishmael+ (Ezr 10:22)

Ishmaiah (1 Chr 27:19)

Ishmerai (1 Chr 8:18)

Ishod (1 Chr 7:18)

Ishpan (1 Chr 8:22)

Ishuah (Gn 46:17)

Ishuai (1 Chr 7:30)

Ishui (1 Sm 14:49)

Ismachiah (2 Chr 31:13)

Ismaiah (1 Chr 12:4)

Ispah (1 Chr 8:16)

Issachar+ (1 Chr 26:5)

Isshiah+ (1 Chr 24:21)

Isshiah+ (1 Chr 24:25)

Isuah (1 Chr 7:30)

Isui (Gn 46:17)

Ithai (1 Chr 11:31)

Ithiel+ (Neh 11:7)

Ithiel+ (Prv 30:1)

Ithmah (1 Chr 11:46)

Ithra (2 Sm 17:25)

Ithran+ (1 Chr 7:37)

Ittai+ (2 Sm 23:29)

Izehar (Nm 3:19)

Izrahiah (1 Chr 7:3)

Izri (1 Chr 25:11)

I: Mentioned Twice

Ibzan (Jgs 12:8)

I-chabod (1 Sm 4:21)

Iddo⁺ (Neh 12:4)

Imla (2 Chr 18:7)

Imlah (1 Kgs 22:8)

Immanuel (Is 7:14)

Immer⁺ (Ezr 2:59)

Ira⁺ (2 Sm 23:28)

Iram (Gn 36:43)

Irijah (Jer 37:13)

Ishbak (Gn 25:2)

Ishmael⁺ (1 Chr 8:38)

Ithran⁺ (Gn 36:26)

Ithream (2 Sm 3:5)

I: Mentioned Three Times

Ibhar (2 Sm 5:15)

Iddo⁺ (2 Chr 9:29)

Ikkesh (2 Sm 23:36)

Ira⁺ (2 Sm 23:26)

J

Jaalam (4)

Occult

A son of Esau, whose father's blessing as older brother was taken by the scheming Jacob.

First reference Gn 36:5
Last reference I Chr 1:35

Jabin+ (7)

The king of Canaan who had Sisera as the captain of his army. Since there was peace between Jabin and Heber the Kenite, Sisera fled to Heber's tents, where Heber's wife, Jael, killed him. God used this event to subdue Jabin.

First reference Jgs 4:2
Last reference Ps 83:9

Jacob+ (278)

Supplanter

Isaac and Rebekah's son who was born clinging to the heel of his twin brother, Esau. When they were adults and the exhausted hunter, Esau, came home and asked Jacob for his lentil stew, Jacob offered to sell it to him for his birthright. Esau accepted. When Isaac was old and blind, he asked Esau to hunt game for him and promised his blessing. Rebekah overheard and warned Jacob. Together they plotted to gain the blessing of the eldest son for Jacob. Jacob covered himself with goatskins so he would seem as hairy as his brother, fed his father goat stew, and received the firstborn's greater blessing. Esau had to make do with a lesser one. To evade Esau's anger, Jacob fled to his uncle Laban's household. During his trip there, God promised to bring Jacob many descendants and bless the earth through them. Tricked by Laban, Jacob married both his daughters, Leah and Jacob's beloved Rachel. From them and their handmaids, Bilhah and Zilpah, Jacob had twelve sons, who became the founders of Israel's twelve tribes. After deceiving his father-in-law, Jacob fled toward home. He met God, wrestled with Him, was renamed Israel, and began to understand God's deliverance. When he again met Esau, Jacob discovered that his fears were groundless. Esau was no longer angry. Same as Israel.

First reference Gn 25:26
Last reference Heb 11:21
Key references Gn 27:27–29, 39–40; 32:28–30

Jael* (6)
Ibex

The wife of Heber the Kenite, Jael killed the Canaanite commander Sisera when he fled to her tent following his defeat by the Israelites. She invited him in and took a tent peg and drove it through his temple. This death fulfilled the Israelite judge Deborah's prophecy.

First reference Jgs 4:17
Last reference Jgs 5:24

Jair+ (4)
Enlightener

A descendant of Manasseh who captured twenty-three

cities of Bashan and named them Havvoth-jair.

First reference Nm 32:41
Last reference 1 Chr 2:22

James⁺ (21)

Zebedee's son and John's brother. With John, this fisherman was called by Jesus to become a fisher of men as one of His disciples. James was part of the intimate group of disciples who witnessed the healing of Simon's mother-in-law, the raising of Jairus's daughter, and the transfiguration of Jesus. With his brother, he boldly sought to call down fire on an unbelieving village and asked to sit at Jesus' right or left hand in glory. He was among the disciples who asked when the temple would fall, and he spent the night in Gethsemane with Jesus. Following Jesus' death, James remained with the disciples in the upper room in prayer. He was executed by Herod Agrippa I.

First reference Mt 4:21
Last reference Acts 12:2
Key references Mk 1:17–20;
    5:37; 9:2–3; Acts 12:1–2

James⁺ (4)

Son of Alphaeus and disciple of Jesus. Scripture only mentions him in lists of the disciples. He was one of those in the upper room, praying, following Jesus' death.

First reference Mt 10:3
Last reference Acts 1:13

James⁺ (17)

Jesus' brother, called James the less (younger). When the people of the synagogue were astonished at Jesus' teachings, they asked if this was not the brother of James. James became a leader in the Jerusalem church. After returning from Arabia, Paul visited him. When he saw that Paul had received God's grace, James and some other disciples accepted him for ministry. Freed from prison, Peter requested that James be informed, and James spoke for the disciples during the Jerusalem Council, which had convened to address the subject of Gentile circumcision. Paul again consulted James on this subject when he returned to Jerusalem. This James is believed by many to be the writer of the book of James in the New Testament.

First reference Mt 13:55
Last reference Jude 1:1
Key references Mk 6:3; 15:40;
    1 Cor 15:7; Gal 2:9

Jamin⁺ (4)

Right hand

A descendant of Abraham through Jacob's son Simeon.

First reference Gn 46:10
Last reference 1 Chr 4:24

Japheth (11)

Expansion

Noah's third son, who joined his family in the ark. After leaving the ark, when Noah became drunk and lay unclothed in his tent, Japheth and his brother Shem covered their father without looking at him.

For this, Noah asked that God would bless him. Japheth had seven sons and became forefather of the coastland peoples.

First reference Gn 5:32
Last reference 1 Chr 1:5

Jared (6)
A descent

A descendant of Adam through Adam's son Seth. Jared was the second-longest-lived indiviual in the Bible at 962 years. Same as Jered.

First reference Gn 5:15
Last reference Lk 3:37

Jason (4)
About to cure

A Christian from Thessalonica whose house was attacked by jealous Jews who dragged him and other Christians before the city officials. The Jews claimed the Christians had said there was another King, Jesus. After taking money from the Christians as security, the Roman officials released them.

First reference Acts 17:5
Last reference Acts 17:9

Javan (4)
Effervescing

A grandson of Noah through his son Japheth. Javan had four sons.

First reference Gn 10:2
Last reference 1 Chr 1:7

Jeconiah (7)
God will establish

King of Judah and son of King Jehoiakim. King

Nebuchandnezzar carried Jeconiah and his nobles to Babylon. Hananiah prophesied that he would return to Jerusalem, but, through Jeremiah, God revealed that he would not. Same as Coniah, Jechonias, and Jehoiachin.

First reference 1 Chr 3:16
Last reference Jer 29:2

Jedaiah⁺ [4]

One of twenty-four priests in David's time who was chosen by lot to serve in the tabernacle.

First reference 1 Chr 9:10
Last reference Neh 7:39

Jedaiah⁺ [5]

A priest who returned from exile with Zerubbabel and lived in Jerusalem. The prophet Zechariah prophesied that there would be a memorial to him in the temple.

First reference Neh 11:10
Last reference Zec 6:14

Jeduthun [17]

Laudatory

A descendant of Abraham through Jacob's son Levi. Jeduthun was one of the key musicians serving in the Jerusalem temple. King David appointed Jeduthun's descendants to "prophesy with harps, with psalteries, and with cymbals" (1 Chr 25:1).

First reference 1 Chr 9:16
Last reference Ps 77 (title)

Jehoahaz⁺ [16]

Jehovah seized

King of Israel and son of King Jehu, Jehoahaz did

what was evil in God's sight. He fought with and lost battles to Hazael, king of Syria. When he sought the Lord concerning the oppression Hazael's nation inflicted upon Israel, God provided a savior.

First reference 2 Kgs 10:35
Last reference 2 Chr 25:25
Key reference 2 Kgs 13:4–5

Jehoahaz⁺ (5)

King of Judah, son of King Josiah. This evil king reigned only three months before Pharaoh-necho of Egypt captured Jehoahaz and sent him to Egypt, where he died. Same as Shallum (2 Kgs 15:10).

First reference 2 Kgs 23:30
Last reference 2 Chr 36:4

Jehoash⁺ (8)

Jehovah fired

Another name for Joash (2 Kgs 11:2).

First reference 2 Kgs 11:21
Last reference 2 Kgs 14:13

Jehoash⁺ (8)

Jehovah fired

An evil king of Israel, son of King Jehoahaz. Jehoash regained from Hazael, king of Syria, the cities Hazael had won from Israel in battle. Jehoash fought King Amaziah of Judah, broke down Jerusalem's wall, and took gold and silver from the temple and the king. With hostages, he returned to Samaria. Same as Joash (2 Kgs 13:9).

First reference 2 Kgs 13:10
Last reference 2 Kgs 14:17

Jehoiachin (10)

Jehovah will establish

King of Judah and son of King Jehoiakim, this evil king reigned only three months before King Nebuchadnezzar of Babylon carried him and the best of his people to Babylon. In the thirty-seventh year of Jehoiachin's captivity, King Evil-merodach brought him out of prison and gave him preferential treatment. Same as Coniah, Jeconiah, and Jeconias.

First reference 2 Kgs 24:6
Last reference Jer 52:31

Jehoiada⁺ (20)

Jehovah known

Father of Benaiah, a commander in King David's army, who also served Solomon.

First reference 2 Sm 8:18
Last reference I Chr 27:5

Jehoiada⁺ (28)

Jehovah known

The high priest who made a covenant with Judah's army's leaders to protect young King Joash. For six years Jehoiada protected Joash from his grandmother Athaliah, who had usurped Judah's throne. In the seventh year, the priest anointed and crowned Joash. When Athaliah objected, he had her killed then made a covenant between Joash and his people. At the king's command, Jehoiada took up a collection for refurbishing the temple, which Athaliah had caused to be damaged. Because Jehoiada had done much good for the people, he was buried with the kings of Judah.

First reference 2 Kgs 11:4
Last reference 2 Chr 24:25
Key references 2 Chr 23:1;
  24:6–7, 15–16

Jehoiakim (37)

Jehovah will raise

Originally named Eliakim, he was a son of King Josiah of Judah. After the Egyptian pharaoh Necho killed Josiah and later deposed his son Jehoahaz, the pharaoh made Eliakim king of Judah and changed his name to Jehoiakim. Following Necho's defeat by King Nebuchadnezzar, Jehoiakim served the Babylonian king. But three years later, Jehoiakim rebelled. When Jeremiah's prophetic, warning words were read to this wicked king, piece by piece he burned the scroll they were written on—so God declared that Babylon would destroy Judah. Nebuchadnezzar attacked and defeated Jerusalem, bound Jehoiakim in chains, and carried him to Babylon, along with most of the people of Judah. Following Jehoiakim's capture, a prophet told how he murdered another prophet who spoke out against him then had his body dumped in a common burial ground. Same as Eliakim (2 Kgs 23:34).

First reference 2 Kgs 23:34
Last reference Dn 1:2
Key references 2 Kgs 23:34;
  24:1; Jer 26:20–23;
  36:22–24

Jehoram⁺ (15)

Jehovah raised

Firstborn son of King Jehoshaphat of Judah. After Jehoram became king, he killed all his brothers. He married the daughter of King Ahab of Israel and led his nation into idolatry. Philistines and Arabians invaded Judah and captured Jehoram's family. As God had warned, Jehoram died, unmourned, of an incurable bowel disease. He was not buried in the kings' tombs. Same as Joram (2 Kgs 8:21).

First reference 1 Kgs 22:50
Last reference 2 Chr 22:11
Key references 2 Chr 21:4–6, 11, 20

Jehoram⁺ (7)

King of Israel, son of Ahab and brother of Ahaziah, from whom he inherited the throne. Though he did not worship Baal, neither did Jehoram stop his nation from worshipping Jeroboam's golden calves. With Jehoshaphat, king of Judah, he went to war against Moab. Discouraged, they consulted the prophet Elijah, who told them how to win their battle. Jehoram was killed by Jehu (1 Kgs 19:16), who took his throne. Same as Joram (2 Kgs 8:16).

First reference 2 Kgs 1:17
Last reference 2 Chr 22:7

Jehoshaphat⁺ (4)

Jehovah judged

An official in King David's court who was his recorder.

First reference 2 Sm 8:16
Last reference 1 Chr 18:15

Jehoshaphat⁺ (75)

Jehovah judged

King of Judah who inherited the throne from his father, Asa. Though he had blessings and "riches and honour in abundance" (2 Chr 17:5; 18:1), he repeatedly allied himself with the unfaithful land of Israel. Though he followed God, Jehoshaphat became inconsistent in his obedience and did not completely end idolatry in Judah. Despite the warning of the prophet Micaiah, he joined King Ahab of Israel in a disastrous attack on Ramoth-gilead. Later, as a great army came against his own nation, Jehoshaphat sought the Lord. When King Jehoram of Israel asked Jehoshaphat to join him in attacking Moab, Judah's king suggested they consult a prophet. Elijah gave them the winning battle plan.

First reference 1 Kgs 15:24
Last reference 2 Chr 22:9
Key references 1 Kgs 22:4–5, 43; 2 Kgs 3:11–20; 2 Chr 18:1, 31; 20:5–12

Jehu⁺ (5)

Jehovah (is) He

A prophet who prophesied the destruction of Baasha, king of Israel, and Baasha's heirs. He also confronted King Jehoshaphat of Judah with his inconsistent faith.

First reference 1 Kgs 16:1
Last reference 2 Chr 20:34

Jehu+ (50)
Jehovah (is) He

A king of Israel. God commanded Elijah to anoint Jehu king to destroy King Ahab and his dynasty. Stunned, Jehu received Elijah's servant and the anointing. Jehu killed kings Joram of Israel and Ahaziah of Judah. Then he killed Jezebel by commanding servants to throw her from a window, made the Samaritans slaughter Ahab's sons, and killed forty-two of King Ahaziah's relatives. After calling the priests of Baal and the idol's worshippers together, Jehu had his men put them all to the sword. But Jehu did not walk carefully in God's ways and lost part of Israel to Syria.

First reference 1 Kgs 19:16
Last reference Hos 1:4
Key references 2 Kgs 9:6–10, 23–24, 27, 33; 10:18–27

Jehudi (4)
Descendant of Jehudah

Nethaniah's son who carried a message from King Josiah's court to Jeremiah's scribe, commanding him to read Judah's princes the word God sent through the prophet.

First reference Jer 36:14
Last reference Jer 36:23

Jeiel+ (4)

A Levite worship leader who played a harp as the ark of the covenant was brought into Jersualem.

First reference 1 Chr 15:18
Last reference 1 Chr 16:5

Jephthah (29)

He will open

The eighth judge of Israel, Jephthah the Gileadite was Gilead's son by a prostitute. His half brothers drove him out, and he went to the land of Tob. When the Ammonites fought Israel, he became Gilead's leader. He unsuccessfully tried to make peace with these enemies. Then Jephthah promised God that he would give Him whatever greeted him when he came home, should he be victorious. After winning the battle, his daughter, his only child, came to greet him on his return. After giving his daughter a two-month reprieve, Jephthah kept his vow. For passing over Ephraim's land, he battled the Ephraimites. Jephthah judged Israel for six years. Same as Jephthae.

First reference Jgs 11:1
Last reference 1 Sm 12:11
Key references Jgs 11:5–10, 29–30

Jephunneh⁺ (15)

He will be prepared

Father of Caleb, one of two spies (along with Joshua) who argued in favor of entering the Promised Land.

First reference Nm 13:6
Last reference 1 Chr 6:56

Jerahmeel⁺ (6)

God will be compassionate

A descendant of Abraham through Jacob's son Pharez.

First reference 1 Chr 2:9
Last reference 1 Chr 2:42

Jeremiah+ (135)

God will rise

A prophet of Judah during the reigns of kings Josiah, Jehoahaz, Jehoiakim, Jehoiachin, and Zedekiah. Following Assyria's destruction of Israel, Babylon threatened Judah. The turmoil of his age was clearly reflected in the gloomy prophecies of Jeremiah. He condemned Judah for idolatry and called the nation to repentance. God warned of Judah's destruction and mourned over it, yet Jerusalem refused to repent, and Jeremiah warned of the people's judgment. When Pashur (Jer 20:1), chief officer of the temple, heard Jeremiah's prophecies, he put him in the stocks. Released, the prophet spoke against this false prophet, predicting the fall of Judah to Babylon. Pashur was only one of many men who became angry with the prophet, because Jeremiah contended with kings and false prophets as he spoke God's Word. Before the fall of Jerusalem, Jeremiah was imprisoned and accused of deserting to the enemy. For a while he was cast into a muddy cistern. When Jerusalem fell, Nebuchadnezzar treated him well. Jeremiah warned the remnant of people who remained in Judah not to go to Egypt. But the commanders of Judah took the people, including Jeremiah, there anyway. Jeremiah may have died in Egypt. Same as Jeremias and Jeremy.

First reference 2 Chr 35:25
Last reference Dn 9:2
Key references Jer 1:1, 5;
    20:1–6; 21:3–6; 35:8–17;
    37:12–15; 38:6

Jeremiah+ (4)

A priest who renewed the covenant under Nehemiah.

First reference Neh 10:2
Last reference Neh 12:34

Jeroboam+ (90)

The people will contend

A servant of King Solomon who had authority over the forced labor for the tribes of Ephraim and Manasseh. The prophet Ahijah the Shilonite prophesied that Jeroboam would be king over ten tribes of Israel when Solomon died. Solomon heard this and sought to kill Jeroboam, who fled to Egypt. Israel rebelled against Solomon's son, King Rehoboam, and made Jeroboam king. Fearing that his people would return to Rehoboam if they worshipped in Jerusalem, Jeroboam I established idolatrous worship in Israel. Because Jeroboam did not obey God, the prophet Abijah warned the king's wife that God would cut off all the men of Jeroboam's household and burn his house. Jeroboam's son became ill and died. When Jeroboam went to war with King Abijah of Judah, God routed Jeroboam. Israel never regained its power during Jeroboam's lifetime.

First reference 1 Kgs 11:26
Last reference 2 Chr 13:20
Key references 1 Kgs 12:20,
    28; 2 Chr 13:14–16, 20

Jeroboam⁺ (14)

The people will contend

King of Israel, son of King Joash, Jeroboam II continued the idolatrous worship established by Jeroboam I (1 Kgs 11:26). God used Jeroboam II to regain Israel's lost territory, and he even took the Syrian capital, Damascus. The prophet Amos predicted Jeroboam's death by the sword.

First reference 2 Kgs 13:13
Last reference Am 7:11
Key references 2 Kgs 14:25–27; Am 7:11

Jerubbaal (14)

Baal will contend

A name given to Gideon by his father after he destroyed the altars to Baal.

First reference Jgs 6:32
Last reference 1 Sm 12:11
Key reference Jgs 6:32

Jeshua⁺ (4)

He will save

A priest in the time of King Hezekiah who helped to distribute the people's freewill offerings to his fellow priests.

First reference 1 Chr 24:11
Last reference 2 Chr 31:15

Jeshua⁺ (12)

He will save

High priest who returned from exile with Zerubbabel and built the temple altar with him. With the priests and Levites, Jeshua took part in a praise service when the temple foundation was laid. When Judah's adversaries wanted to help build the temple, Jeshua and other leaders refused to allow it.

First reference Ezr 2:2
Last reference Neh 12:26
Key reference Ezr 3:2

Jeshua⁺ (5)

He will save

A Levite who helped Ezra to explain the law to exiles returned to Jerusalem. Jeshua was among a group of Levites who led a revival among the Israelites in the time of Nehemiah.

First reference Neh 8:7
Last reference Neh 12:24

Jesse (47)

Extant

Father of David. Jesse had seven of his sons pass before the prophet Samuel, but none was the king Samuel was seeking. Only when the youngest, David, was brought before Samuel did the prophet anoint him king of Israel. Jesse allowed his youngest son to become King Saul's harpist and then his armor bearer. After David returned home, his father sent him to bring food to his brothers, who were with Saul's army, and there David fought Goliath. The prophet Isaiah foresaw the coming of the Messiah with the words "There shall come forth a rod out the stem of Jesse, and a Branch shall grow out of his roots" (Is 11:1). Jesus' earthly lineage stems from Jesse, through David.

First reference Ru 4:17
Last reference Rom 15:12
Key references 1 Sm 16:8–11; Is 11:1

Jesus+ (981)

Jehovah saved

God's Son and humanity's Savior, Jesus existed from the beginning. Through the Holy Spirit, He became incarnated within the womb of Mary and was born in a humble Bethlehem stable. He grew up in Nazareth, learning the carpentry trade of His earthly father, Joseph. At twelve he amazed the religious leaders of Jerusalem with his understanding of spiritual things. Jesus began His ministry when he was about thirty. Baptized by his cousin John, Jesus went into the wilderness, where He was tempted by Satan but did not fail. After announcing His new ministry in the synagogue, He called twelve disciples to leave their work and follow Him. With them, He traveled through Israel, teaching and calling people to repentance and new relationship with God. During His ministry, Jesus preached about the kingdom of God and corrected the false beliefs of the Pharisees and Sadducees. Jesus taught the spiritual ruler Nicodemus that he needed to be born again. In the Sermon on the Mount, He gave the multitudes a short course in what it meant to truly love God and serve Him. With signs and miracles, He proved His own divine status and drew curious crowds to whom He preached. Jesus healed many people of illnesses and broke through their spiritual darkness. But when He raised Lazarus from the dead, the chief priests and Pharisees began to plot to kill Him because they feared they would lose control of the Jewish people and the Roman authorities would remove them from power. As His enemies sought to kill Him, Jesus entered Jerusalem on a donkey. The people spread garments before him and greeted Him as the Messiah, calling out, "Hosanna." A week later, after Judas betrayed Him, the crowd agreed with the chief priests and cried, "Crucify Him!" Following an illegal trial, Jesus, who had done no wrong, died for humanity's sin on the cross. After His resurrection, three days later, He showed Himself to Mary Magdalene and then the disciples and others. He appeared to the faithful for forty days then commissioned the apostles to spread the Good News, afterward ascending to heaven. The book of Revelation pictures Jesus as the Lamb who is Lord of lords and King of kings. He will return to judge the world. Finally He will establish a New Jerusalem, where He will live with those who trust in Him.

First reference Mt 1:1
Last reference Rv 22:21
Key references Mt 5–7;
    Mk 11:7–9; Lk 4:18; 24:28–32;
    Jn 1:1, 14; 3:3–21; 20:10–22;
    Rv 17:14; 19:11–16; 21:1–3

Jether+ (4)

Father of Amasa, one of David's army commanders.

First reference 1 Kgs 2:5
Last reference 1 Chr 2:17

Jethro (10)

His excellence

Moses' father-in-law, for whom Moses kept flocks until God called him to Egypt. For a time, Moses' wife, Zipporah, along with her two sons, lived with Jethro. The four of them joined up at Mt. Sinai. There Jethro advised Moses to appoint others who could help him rule over the people. Same as Hobab.

First reference Ex 3:1
Last reference Ex 18:12

Jeush+ (4)

Hasty

A son of Esau.

First reference Gn 36:5
Last reference 1 Chr 1:35

Jezebel* (22)

Chaste

A Sidonian princess who married King Ahab of Israel, Jezebel killed or persecuted Israel's prophets, including Elijah, who fled from her wrath after he killed the priests of her god Baal. When Ahab coveted Naboth's vineyard, Jezebel arranged for charges of blasphemy to be brought against Naboth. After Naboth was stoned, she commanded Ahab to take the vineyard. God ordered Jehu to strike Jezebel down. After assassinating her son, King Joram, Jehu went to Jezreel. There he commanded Jezebel's slaves to throw her from a window. When he ordered her burial, only her skull, her feet, and the palms of her hands were left, fulfilling Elijah's prophecy that dogs would eat her.

First reference 1 Kgs 16:31
Last reference Rv 2:20
Key references 1 Kgs 18:13;
    19:1–3; 21:8–16;
    2 Kgs 9:7–10

Joab+ (133)

Jehovah fathered

Though he displeased David when he killed Saul's army commander, Abner, for many years Joab was commander of David's army. He fought the Ammonites for David and obeyed David's command to put Uriah the Hittite on the front lines so he would be killed. Joab sought to bring David and his estranged son Absalom together by sending a wise woman to the king with a story similar to David's own. David immediately guessed that Joab was behind her story and allowed the exiled Absalom to come home. Two years later, Joab intervened again to bring Absalom into his father's favor. David set Amasa as commander over Joab, but he sent Joab and a third of the army into battle against Absalom, who was trying to dethrone his father. Though David asked Joab to deal gently with his son, when the commander heard that Absalom was caught in a tree, Joab killed him. Joab killed Amasa, too, and again commanded the whole army. He obeyed David— but not God—when he took a census of Israel. At the end of David's life, Joab supported David's son Adonijah as king instead of Solomon. On his deathbed, David warned Solomon not to let Joab die peacefully. Solomon had Joab killed in the tabernacle, where he had fled.

First reference 1 Sm 26:6
Last reference Ps 60 (title)
Key references 2 Sm 3:26–30; 11:14–17; 14:2–3; 18:14; 1 Kgs 2:33–34

Joah⁺ (6)

Jehovah brothered

An officer of King Hezekiah of Judah. With Eliakim and Shebna, he confronted the king of Assyria's messengers, who tried to convince Hezekiah and his people to submit to Assyria.

First reference 2 Kgs 18:18
Last reference Is 36:22

Joash⁺ (9)

Father of Gideon, Joash stood up for his son when their neighbors wanted to kill Gideon for destroying the altar of Baal.

First reference Jgs 6:11
Last reference Jgs 8:32

Joash⁺ (18)

King of Judah, son of King Ahaziah. Joash was hidden from his wicked grandmother Athaliah and protected by the priest Jehoiada, who instructed him. Though he followed the Lord, Joash did not remove idolatry from the nation. He ordered that money be collected to refurbish the temple. But when Hazael, king of Syria, was about to attack, Joash took the gold from the temple and his own house and sent it as tribute to Hazael. Joash was killed by his servants, who formed a conspiracy against him. Same as Jehoash (2 Kgs 11:21).

First reference 2 Kgs 11:2
Last reference 2 Chr 25:25
Key references 2 Chr 22:11; 24:2, 25

Joash⁺ (16)

Another name for Jehoash (2 Kgs 13:10), a king of Israel.

First reference 2 Kgs 13:9
Last reference Am 1:1

Job⁺ (59)
Hated, persecuted

A righteous man from the land of Uz whom God tested to prove to Satan that Job was not faithful to Him because he had many physical blessings. For a time, God gave Job into Satan's power. First Job lost his cattle and servants. Then a messenger came with news that all his children had been killed. Yet Job continued to worship God. Satan then covered Job with sores, and his wife told him, "Curse God, and die" (Jb 2:9). Yet he still remained faithful. Three comfortless comforters, his friends, came to share his misery. For a week they were silent. But when Job began to speak, they answered with accusations that he had done something wrong. Eliphaz, Bildad, and Zophar took turns attempting to convince him that he needed to repent. Job made his case against them. Aware that no one is completely righteous before God, though Job remained at a loss to understand what he had done wrong, he voiced many moving expressions of faith. A young man, Elihu, confronted them with God's justice and power, until God intervened and made Job aware of his own lack of understanding. Job repented. God rebuked his three friends and restored all of Job's original blessings.

First reference Jb 1:1
Last reference Jas 5:11
Key references Jb 1:21; 9:1–3; 13:12, 15; 19:25–27; 38:1–3; 40:4–5; 42:1–17

Jobab⁺ (4)

A king of Edom, "before there reigned any king over the children of Israel" (Gn 36:31).

First reference Gn 36:33
Last reference 1 Chr 1:45

Johanan⁺ (15)

Jehovah favored

A rebellious Jewish leader. Johanan supported the new Chaldean governor, Gedaliah, after the fall of Jerusalem. Following the governor's murder, he disobeyed God and took the remaining Israelites to Egypt.

First reference 2 Kgs 25:23
Last reference Jer 43:5
Key reference Jer 43:2

John⁺ (90)

Called "the Baptist," John was Jesus' cousin. He was born to the elderly couple Zacharias and Elisabeth after an angel told the doubtful Zacharias of the expected birth then temporarily struck him dumb for unbelief. Before Jesus began His ministry, John preached a message of repentance in the desert and, in the Jordan River, baptized those who confessed their sins. He also confronted the Pharisees and Sadducees with their lack of repentance. John foretold that another worthier than he would baptize with the Holy Spirit. He hesitantly baptized Jesus and saw the Spirit of God descend on Him. Because John had objected to Herod the tetrarch's marriage to Herod's brother's wife, Herodias, the ruler threw John into prison. Yet Herod was afraid to kill John, because the people believed he was a prophet. From prison, John sent word to ask Jesus if He was the expected Messiah. Jesus replied by telling the messengers to report on the healings they had seen and the preaching they had heard. When Herod's stepdaughter danced before his birthday guests, Herod offered to give her whatever she wanted. Her mother, Herodias, pressed her to ask for John the Baptist's head. Herod reluctantly gave her what she asked for. John's disciples took his body and buried it.

First reference Mt 3:1
Last reference Acts 19:4
Key references Mt 3:7–10;
 11:2–4; 14:1–12;
 Mk 1:6–8; Lk 1:5–20

John⁺ (35)

A son of Zebedee and brother of James, John became Jesus' disciple when the Master called the brothers to leave their fishing boat and follow Him. Describing himself in his Gospel as the disciple whom Jesus loved, John indicated their intimate relationship. As Jesus' closest disciples, he, James, and Peter experienced events such as the healings of Peter's mother-in-law and Jairus's daughter and the transfiguration of Jesus. Jesus called Zebedee's sons the Sons of Thunder, perhaps for their quick-tempered personalities. When a town refused to house the Master and his men, the brothers wanted to call down fire on them. These two overly confident men asked Jesus if they could sit at his left and right hands in glory. John and James fell asleep in the Garden of Gethsemane as Jesus prayed before His arrest. John may also have been the "another disciple" who was known to the high priest and brought Peter into the courtyard during Jesus' trial (Jn 18:15). At the crucifixion, Jesus placed his mother, Mary, in John's care. After Jesus' death and resurrection, John was often with Peter. Together they investigated the empty tomb and went fishing while they awaited their new ministry. John was with Peter when he healed the beggar at the temple gate. John wrote the Gospel and letters that bear his name and the book of Revelation.

First reference Mt 4:21
Last reference Rv 22:8
Key references Mt 4:21–22;
    17:1–3; Mk 10:35–37;
    Jn 13:23; 19:26; 20:1–2

John+ (5)

Also called Mark, he joined his cousin Barnabas and the apostle Paul on Paul's first missionary journey but left them at Perga. This caused Paul to lose confidence in John Mark for a time.

First reference Acts 12:12
Last reference Acts 15:37

Joiada (4)

Jehovah knows

A high priest and descendant of the high priest Jeshua (Ezr 2:2).

First reference Neh 12:10
Last reference Neh 13:28

Joiakim (4)

Jehovah will raise

A high priest and descendant of the high priest Jeshua (Ezr 2:2). Joiakim returned to Jerusalem with Zerubbabel.

First reference Neh 12:10
Last reference Neh 12:26

Jokshan (4)

Insidious

A son of Abraham by his second wife, Keturah.

First reference Gn 25:2
Last reference 1 Chr 1:32

Joktan (6)

He will be made little

A descendant of Noah through his son Shem. Joktan had thirteen sons.

First reference Gn 10:25
Last reference I Chr 1:23

Jonadab (5)

Jehovah largessed

A friend and cousin of David's son Amnon, "a very subtil man" (2 Sm 13:3), who advised him to pretend to be ill so his half sister Tamar would come to him. He reported Amnon's death to King David, telling him that Absalom had killed his brother.

First reference 2 Sm 13:3
Last reference 2 Sm 13:35

Jonadab (7)

Jehovah largessed

The Rechabite who commanded his descendants not to drink any wine.

First reference Jer 35:6
Last reference Jer 35:19

Jonah (19)

A dove

An Old Testament minor prophet whom God commanded to preach in Nineveh, home of Israel's Assyrian enemies. Fearing God would give mercy to his enemies, Jonah fled on a ship headed for Tarshish. When a tempest struck the ship, the fearful sailors threw the disobedient prophet overboard. Jonah was swallowed by a fish. When he praised God, the fish vomited him onto land. Jonah went to Nineveh, and the people repented. The angry prophet, wanting to die, fled the city. God pointed out that Jonah had more compassion for a plant that died than for the people of the city. Same as Jona and Jonas (Mt 12:39).

First reference 2 Kgs 14:25
Last reference Jon 4:9
Key references Jon 1:10–15;
   4:10–11

Jonas⁺ (9)

Greek form of the name *Jonah*, used in the New Testament.

First reference Mt 12:39
Last reference Lk 11:32

Jonathan⁺ (96)

Jehovah given

Eldest son of King Saul. He and his armor bearer attacked the Philistines at Michmash and brought them into confusion so Saul and his men could attack them. Jonathan and David became great friends, and Jonathan made a covenant with him. When Saul jealously tried to kill David, Jonathan warned his friend. He spoke well of David to his father and earned him a reprieve, but again Saul's anger raged against David, who fled. David later consulted Jonathan, who spoke to his father then warned David away for good. When Saul again fought the Philistines, Jonathan was killed in battle.

First reference 1 Sm 13:2
Last reference Jer 38:26
Key references 1 Sm 14:6–15;
   18:1–4; 20:1–23; 31:2

Jonathan⁺ (6)

Son of Abiathar, the high priest during King David's reign. He acted as messenger to David for the counselor Hushai. When David made Solomon king, Jonathan brought the news to David's son Adonijah.

First reference 2 Sm 15:27
Last reference 1 Kgs 1:43

Joram⁺ (7)

Jehovah raised

King of Judah and son of King Jehoshaphat. Edom revolted during his reign. When Joram fought them, his troops fled. Same as Jehoram (1 Kgs 22:50).

First reference 2 Kgs 8:21
Last reference Mt 1:8

Joram⁺ (19)

Jehovah raised

Son of King Ahab and king of Israel. When he went to war with King Ahaziah of Judah against the Syrians, Joram was wounded. While he was recovering in Jezreel, he was killed by Jehu, who took his throne. Same as Jehoram (2 Kgs 1:17).

First reference 2 Kgs 8:16
Last reference 2 Chr 22:7
Key references 2 Kgs 8:28–29;
    9:21–24

Josedech (6)

Jehovah righted

Father of the high priest Joshua, who took part in rebuilding the temple.

First reference Hg 1:1
Last reference Zec 6:11

Joseph⁺ (217)

Let him add

Son of Jacob and Rachel. Joseph was Jacob's favorite son, which made his other sons jealous. Joseph angered his brothers when he told them of his dream that he would rule over them. While watching their flocks, the brothers plotted to kill Joseph. They threw him into an empty pit then sold him to some passing traders. Killing a goat, they dipped Joseph's robe in it and told Jacob he had been killed by a wild animal. Carried to Egypt, Joseph became a slave to the captain of Pharaoh's guard. After the captain's wife accused him of trying to seduce her, Joseph landed in prison, where he interpreted the dreams of two of Pharaoh's servants. Given an opportunity to interpret Pharaoh's dream, he became second-in-command in Egypt. During the famine he had predicted, Joseph's ten half brothers came to buy food from him and did not recognize him. Joseph tested them to be certain they would not treat his full brother, Benjamin, as they had treated him. After his

brothers passed the test, Joseph revealed himself. The family was reunited in Egypt, where they settled in Goshen.

First reference Gn 30:24
Last reference Heb 11:22
Key references Gn 37:3–8, 24–28; 41:14–40; 42:6–28; 44:16–34; 45:3–10

Joseph[+] (15)

Let him add

Husband of Mary and earthly father of Jesus. The carpenter Joseph was betrothed to Mary when she conceived Jesus. He planned to divorce her quietly, but an angel told him not to fear marrying her, for she would bear the Messiah. With Mary, he traveled to Bethlehem, where the child was born. He was with Mary when

Jesus was dedicated at the temple and when they visited the temple when Jesus was twelve years old.

First reference Mt 1:16
Last reference Jn 6:42
Key references Mt 1:18–25;
  Lk 2:4–7

Joseph⁺ (6)

Let him add

A wealthy man of Arimathea and member of the Sanhedrin who became Jesus' disciple. After Jesus' death, Joseph went to Pilate and asked for His body, which Joseph laid in his own tomb.

First reference Mt 27:57
Last reference Jn 19:38

Joshua⁺ (202)

Jehovah saved

Moses' right-hand man, Joshua son of Nun led Israel to victory against the Amalekites. He spied out Canaan before the Israelites entered it and came back with a positive report. Because of his faith, he was one of only two men of his generation who entered the Promised Land. God chose Joshua to succeed Moses as Israel's leader. After Moses' death, Joshua led the Israelites into the Promised Land. After they crossed the Jordan River, Joshua led his warriors to attack Jericho using trumpets, the ark of the covenant, and their own voices. The walls fell flat from God's power. Through their own disobedience, the Israelites lost at Ai; then they won when they obeyed God. Joshua renewed their covenant with God and wrote a copy of Moses' law then continued to conquer the new land. As they fought the king of Jerusalem and his allies, Joshua needed a longer day and asked God to make the sun stand still. It remained in place until Israel won. When Joshua was old and the land had not all been conquered, God promised to win the land for His people, so Joshua allotted all the lands to the tribes of Israel and charged the people to obey God. Same as Hoshea (Dt 32:44) and Jesus (Heb 4:8).

First reference Ex 17:9
Last reference 1 Kgs 16:34
Key references Nm 14:6–7, 30; 27:18–23; Jo 6:2–21; 10:12–13; 13:1, 6; 24:15

Joshua+ (11)

Jehovah saved

The high priest who served under Governor Zerubbabel. Through their leadership, Israel rebuilt the temple. The prophet Zechariah saw a vision of Joshua. Satan accused him as he stood in filthy garments, but an angel reclothed him in clean clothes symbolizing righteousness.

First reference Hg 1:1
Last reference Zec 6:11
Key references Hg 1:14; Zec 3:1–10

Josiah+ (52)

Founded of God

Son of King Amon of Judah, Josiah became king when he was eight years old and followed the Lord closely through his life.

Josiah collected money and repaired the temple. When the book of the law was discovered by Hilkiah the priest, Josiah had it read to him and consulted the prophetess Huldah. Then Josiah read the book to the elders of his nation, made a covenant to follow the Lord, and caused his people to follow his example. He put down idolatry in the land and celebrated the Passover. Josiah died in battle against Necho, king of Egypt, who fought him at Carchemish.

First reference 1 Kgs 13:2
Last reference Zep 1:1
Key references 2 Kgs 22:1–2, 10–13; 23:1–3, 5, 21, 29; 2 Chr 34:1–3, 31–33; 35:20–24

Jotham⁺ (4)

Jehovah is perfect

The youngest son of Jerubbaal (also known as Gideon). Jotham hid from his brother Abimelech, who tried to kill all his brothers.

First reference Jgs 9:5
Last reference Jgs 9:57

Jotham⁺ (19)

Jehovah is perfect

Son of Azariah, king of Judah, Jotham governed for his father, who had become a leper. After he inherited the throne, he built the upper gate of the temple and obeyed God, but he did not destroy idolatry in the land. He defeated the Ammonites and received tribute from them.

First reference 2 Kgs 15:5
Last reference Mi 1:1
Key references 2 Kgs 15:32–35; 2 Chr 27:1–5

Jozadak (5)

Jehovah righted

Father of Jeshua, the high priest who returned to Israel with Zerubbabel.

First reference Ezr 3:2
Last reference Neh 12:26

Judah⁺ (43)

Celebrated

Fourth son of Jacob and Leah. Judah convinced his brothers not to kill Joseph but to sell him to some Midianite traders instead. Because Judah would not give his widowed daughter-in-law his third son as a husband, she sat by the roadside and pretended she was a harlot. Judah went to her and she had twins. In Egypt, Judah spoke up for Benjamin when he was accused of stealing Joseph's cup and offered himself in Benjamin's place. His father's final blessing described Judah as one whom his brothers would praise.

First reference Gn 29:35
Last reference Jer 38:22
Key references Gn 37:26–27; 44:18–34; 49:8–9

Judas⁺ (2)

Celebrated

The disciple who betrayed Jesus, usually identified as Judas Iscariot. He was given his position by Jesus and was put in charge of the money, but he was not honest with it (Jn 12:6). Judas went to the chief priests and promised to betray Jesus for thirty pieces of silver. At the Last Supper, Jesus predicted Judas's betrayal and even handed him a morsel of food to indicate his identity as the betrayer. Sorrowful at his own betrayal, following Jesus' death, Judas returned the money to the priests and hanged himself. Same as Iscariot.

First reference Mt 10:4
Last reference Acts 1:25
Key references Mt 27:3–5;
    Mk 14:10; Jn 13:2, 26

J: Mentioned Once

Jaakan (Dt 10:6)

Jaakobah (1 Chr 4:36)

Jaala (Neh 7:58)

Jaalah (Ezr 2:56)

Jaanai (1 Chr 5:12)

Jaare-oregim (2 Sm 21:19)

Jaasau (Ezr 10:37)

Jaasiel (1 Chr 27:21)

Jaazaniah+ (2 Kgs 25:23)

Jaazaniah+ (Jer 35:3)

Jaazaniah+ (Ez 8:11)

Jaazaniah+ (Ez 11:1)

Jaaziel (1 Chr 15:18)

Jabal (Gn 4:20)

Jabin+ (Jo 11:1)

Jachan (1 Chr 5:13)

Jachin+ (1 Chr 24:17)

Jadau (Ezr 10:43)

Jaddua+ (Neh 10:21)

Jadon (Neh 3:7)

Jahath+ (1 Chr 4:2)

Jahath+ (1 Chr 24:22)

Jahath+ (2 Chr 34:12)

Jahaziah (Ezr 10:15)

Jahaziel+ (1 Chr 12:4)

Jahaziel+ (1 Chr 16:6)

Jahaziel+ (2 Chr 20:14)

Jahaziel+ (Ezr 8:5)

Jahdai (1 Chr 2:47)

Jahdiel (1 Chr 5:24)

Jahdo (1 Chr 5:14)

Jahmai (1 Chr 7:2)

Jahzeel (Gn 46:24)

Jahzerah (1 Chr 9:12)

Jahziel (1 Chr 7:13)

Jair+ (1 Chr 20:5)

Jair+ (Est 2:5)

Jakan (1 Chr 1:42)

Jakeh (Prv 30:1)

Jakim+ (1 Chr 8:19)

Jakim+ (1 Chr 24:12)

Jalon (1 Chr 4:17)

Jambres (2 Tm 3:8)

Jamin+ (1 Chr 2:27)

Jamin+ (Neh 8:7)

Jamlech (1 Chr 4:34)

Janna (Lk 3:24)

Jannes (2 Tm 3:8)

Japhia+ (Jo 10:3)

Jarah (1 Chr 9:42)

Jaresiah (1 Chr 8:27)

Jarib+ (1 Chr 4:24)

Jarib⁺ (Ezr 8:16)

Jarib⁺ (Ezr 10:18)

Jaroah (1 Chr 5:14)

Jashen (2 Sm 23:32)

Jashobeam⁺ (1 Chr 12:6)

Jashub⁺ (Ezr 10:29)

Jashubi-lehem (1 Chr 4:22)

Jasiel (1 Chr 11:47)

Jason (Rom 16:21)

Jathniel (1 Chr 26:2)

Jaziz (1 Chr 27:31)

Jeaterai (1 Chr 6:21)

Jeberechiah (Is 8:2)

Jecamiah (1 Chr 3:18)

Jecholiah* (2 Kgs 15:2)

Jecoliah* (2 Chr 26:3)

Jedaiah⁺ (1 Chr 4:37)

Jedaiah⁺ (Neh 3:10)

Jediael⁺ (1 Chr 11:45)

Jediael⁺ (1 Chr 12:20)

Jediael⁺ (1 Chr 26:2)

Jedidah* (2 Kgs 22:1)

Jedidiah (2 Sm 12:25)

Jeezer (Nm 26:30)

Jehaleleel (1 Chr 4:16)

Jehalelel (2 Chr 29:12)

Jehdeiah⁺ (1 Chr 24:20)

Jehdeiah⁺ (1 Chr 27:30)

Jehezekel (1 Chr 24:16)

Jehiah (1 Chr 15:24)

Jehiel⁺ (1 Chr 9:35)

Jehiel⁺ (1 Chr 11:44)

Jehiel⁺ (1 Chr 27:32)

Jehiel⁺ (2 Chr 21:2)

Jehiel⁺ (2 Chr 29:14)

Jehiel⁺ (2 Chr 31:13)

Jehiel⁺ (2 Chr 35:8)

Jehiel⁺ (Ezr 8:9)

Jehiel⁺ (Ezr 10:2)

Jehiel⁺ (Ezr 10:21)

Jehiel⁺ (Ezr 10:26)

Jehizkiah (2 Chr 28:12)

Jehoadah (1 Chr 8:36)

Jehohanan⁺ (1 Chr 26:3)

Jehohanan⁺ (2 Chr 17:15)

Jehohanan⁺ (2 Chr 23:1)

Jehohanan⁺ (Ezr 10:28)

Jehohanan⁺ (Neh 12:13)

Jehohanan⁺ (Neh 12:42)

Jehoiada⁺ (1 Chr 12:27)

Jehoiada⁺ (1 Chr 27:34)

Jehoiada⁺ (Neh 3:6)

Jehoiada⁺ (Jer 29:26)

Jehoiarib⁺ (1 Chr 9:10)

Jehoiarib⁺ (1 Chr 24:7)

Jehonathan⁺ (1 Chr 27:25)

Jehonathan+ (2 Chr 17:8)

Jehonathan+ (Neh 12:18)

Jehoram+ (2 Chr 17:8)

Jehoshabeath* (2 Chr 22:11)

Jehoshaphat+ (1 Kgs 4:17)

Jehoshaphat+ (1 Chr 15:24)

Jehosheba* (2 Kgs 11:2)

Jehoshua (Nm 13:16)

Jehoshuah (1 Chr 7:27)

Jehozabad+ (1 Chr 26:4)

Jehozabad+ (2 Chr 17:18)

Jehu+ (1 Chr 2:38)

Jehu+ (1 Chr 4:35)

Jehu+ (1 Chr 12:3)

Jehubbah (1 Chr 7:34)

Jehucal (Jer 37:3)

Jehudijah (1 Chr 4:18)

Jehush (1 Chr 8:39)

Jeiel+ (1 Chr 5:7)

Jeiel+ (2 Chr 20:14)

Jeiel+ (2 Chr 26:11)

Jeiel+ (2 Chr 29:13)

Jeiel+ (2 Chr 35:9)

Jeiel+ (Ezr 8:13)

Jeiel+ (Ezr 10:43)

Jekamiah (1 Chr 2:41)

Jekuthiel (1 Chr 4:18)

Jemima* (Jb 42:14)

Jephthae (Heb 11:32)

Jephunneh+ (1 Chr 7:38)

Jerahmeel+ (1 Chr 24:29)

Jerahmeel+ (Jer 36:26)

Jered+ (1 Chr 1:2)

Jered+ (1 Chr 4:18)

Jeremai (Ezr 10:33)

Jeremiah+ (1 Chr 5:24)

Jeremiah+ (1 Chr 12:4)

Jeremiah+ (1 Chr 12:10)

Jeremiah+ (1 Chr 12:13)

Jeremias (Mt 16:14)

Jeremoth+ (1 Chr 8:14)

Jeremoth+ (1 Chr 23:23)

Jeremoth+ (1 Chr 25:22)

Jeremoth+ (Ezr 10:26)

Jeremoth+ (Ezr 10:27)

Jeribai (1 Chr 11:46)

Jeriel (1 Chr 7:2)

Jerijah (1 Chr 26:31)

Jerimoth+ (1 Chr 7:7)

Jerimoth+ (1 Chr 7:8)

Jerimoth+ (1 Chr 12:5)

Jerimoth+ (1 Chr 24:30)

Jerimoth+ (1 Chr 25:4)

Jerimoth+ (1 Chr 27:19)

Jerimoth+ (2 Chr 11:18)

Jerimoth+ (2 Chr 31:13)

Jerioth* (1 Chr 2:18)

Jeroham+ (1 Chr 8:27)

Jeroham+ (1 Chr 9:8)

Jeroham+ (1 Chr 12:7)

Jeroham+ (1 Chr 27:22)

Jeroham+ (2 Chr 23:1)

Jerubbesheth (2 Sm 11:21)

Jerusha* (2 Kgs 15:33)

Jerushah* (2 Chr 27:1)

Jesaiah+ (1 Chr 3:21)

Jesaiah+ (Neh 11:7)

Jeshaiah+ (1 Chr 26:25)

Jeshaiah+ (Ezr 8:7)

Jeshaiah+ (Ezr 8:19)

Jesharelah (1 Chr 25:14)

Jeshebeab (1 Chr 24:13)

Jesher (1 Chr 2:18)

Jeshishai (1 Chr 5:14)

Jeshohaiah (1 Chr 4:36)

Jeshua+ (Ezr 8:33)

Jeshua+ (Neh 3:19)

Jeshua+ (Neh 8:17)

Jeshua+ (Neh 10:9)

Jesiah+ (1 Chr 12:6)

Jesiah+ (1 Chr 23:20)

Jesimiel (1 Chr 4:36)

Jesui (Nm 26:44)

Jesus+ (Heb 4:8)

Jesus+ (Col 4:11)

Jether+ (Jgs 8:20)

Jether+ (1 Chr 2:32)

Jether+ (1 Chr 4:17)

Jether+ (1 Chr 7:38)

Jeuel (1 Chr 9:6)

Jeush+ (1 Chr 7:10)

Jeush+ (2 Chr 11:19)

Jeuz (1 Chr 8:10)

Jeziah (Ezr 10:25)

Jeziel (1 Chr 12:3)

Jezliah (1 Chr 8:18)

Jezoar (1 Chr 4:7)

Jezrahiah (Neh 12:42)

Jezreel+ (1 Chr 4:3)

Jibsam (1 Chr 7:2)

Jidlaph (Gn 22:22)

Jimna (Nm 26:44)

Jimnah (Gn 46:17)

Joab+ (1 Chr 2:54)

Joab+ (1 Chr 4:14)

Joab+ (Ezr 8:9)

Joah+ (1 Chr 26:4)

Joah+ (2 Chr 34:8)

Joahaz (2 Chr 34:8)

Joanna+ (Lk 3:27)

Joash+ (1 Chr 4:22)

Joash+ (1 Chr 7:8)

Joash+ (1 Chr 12:3)

Joash+ (1 Chr 27:28)

Joatham (Mt 1:9)

Job+ (Gn 46:13)

Jobab+ (Jo 11:1)

Jobab+ (1 Chr 8:9)

Jobab+ (1 Chr 8:18)

Joed (Neh 11:7)

Joel+ (1 Chr 4:35)

Joel+ (1 Chr 5:12)

Joel+ (1 Chr 6:36)

Joel+ (1 Chr 7:3)

Joel+ (1 Chr 11:38)

Joel+ (1 Chr 26:22)

Joel+ (1 Chr 27:20)

Joel+ (2 Chr 29:12)

Joel+ (Ezr 10:43)

Joel+ (Neh 11:9)

Joelah (1 Chr 12:7)

Joezer (1 Chr 12:6)

Jogli (Nm 34:22)

Joha+ (1 Chr 8:16)

Joha+ (1 Chr 11:45)

Johanan+ (1 Chr 3:15)

Johanan+ (1 Chr 3:24)

Johanan+ (1 Chr 12:4)

Johanan+ (1 Chr 12:12)

Johanan+ (2 Chr 28:12)

Johanan+ (Ezr 8:12)

Johanan+ (Ezr 10:6)

Johanan+ (Neh 6:18)

John+ (Acts 4:6)

Joiarib+ (Ezr 8:16)

Joiarib+ (Neh 11:5)

Jokim (1 Chr 4:22)

Jona (Jn 1:42)

Jonan (Lk 3:30)

Jonathan+ (Jgs 18:30)

Jonathan+ (1 Chr 27:32)

Jonathan+ (Ezr 8:6)

Jonathan+ (Ezr 10:15)

Jonathan+ (Neh 12:11)

Jonathan+ (Neh 12:14)

Jonathan+ (Neh 12:35)

Jonathan+ (Jer 40:8)

Jorah (Ezr 2:18)

Jorai (1 Chr 5:13)

Joram+ (2 Sm 8:10)

Joram+ (1 Chr 26:25)

Jorim (Lk 3:2)

Jorkoam (1 Chr 2:44)

Josabad (1 Chr 12:4)

Josaphat (Mt 1:8)

Jose (Lk 3:29)

Joseph+ (Nm 13:7)

Joseph+ (Ezr 10:42)

Joseph+ (Neh 12:14)

Joseph+ (Lk 3:24)

Joseph+ (Lk 3:26)

Joseph+ (Lk 3:30)

Joseph+ (Acts 1:23)

Joses+ (Acts 4:36)

Joshah (1 Chr 4:34)

Joshaphat (1 Chr 11:43)

Joshaviah (1 Chr 11:46)

Joshua+ (2 Kgs 23:8)

Josiah+ (Zec 6:10)

Josibiah (1 Chr 4:35)

Josiphiah (Ezr 8:10)

Jotham+ (1 Chr 2:47)

Jozabad+ (1 Chr 12:20)

Jozabad+ (2 Chr 31:13)

Jozabad+ (2 Chr 35:9)

Jozabad+ (Ezr 8:33)

Jozabad+ (Ezr 10:22)

Jozabad+ (Ezr 10:23)

Jozabad+ (Neh 8:7)

Jozabad+ (Neh 11:16)

Jozachar (2 Kgs 12:21)

Jubal (Gn 4:21)

Jucal (Jer 38:1)

Juda+ (Mk 6:3)

Juda+ (Lk 3:26)

Juda+ (Lk 3:30)

Juda+ (Lk 3:33)

Judah+ (Ezr 3:9)

Judah+ (Ezr 10:23)

Judah+ (Neh 11:9)

Judah+ (Neh 12:8)

Judah+ (Neh 12:34)

Judah+ (Neh 12:36)

Judas+ (Mt 13:55)

Judas+ (Acts 5:37)

Judas+ (Acts 9:11)

Jude (Jude 1:1)

Judith* (Gn 26:34)

Julia* (Rom 16:15)

Junia (Rom 16:7)

Jushabhesed (1 Chr 3:20)

Justus+ (Acts 1:23)

Justus+ (Acts 18:7)

Justus+ (Col 4:11)

J: Mentioned Twice

Jaaziah (1 Chr 24:26)

Jachin+ (1 Chr 9:10)

Jacob+ (Mt 1:15)

Jada (1 Chr 2:28)

Jaddua+ (Neh 12:11)

Jahath+ (1 Chr 6:20)

Jahath+ (1 Chr 23:10)

Jahaziel+ (1 Chr 23:19)

Jahleel (Gn 46:14)

Jair+ (Jgs 10:3)

Jairus (Mk 5:22)

Jareb (Hos 5:13)

Jarha (1 Chr 2:34)

Jashobeam+ (1 Chr 11:11)

Jashub+ (Nm 26:24)

Jechonias (Mt 1:11)

Jedaiah+ (Neh 12:7)

Jehiel+ (1 Chr 23:8)

Jehieli (1 Chr 26:21)

Jehoaddan* (2 Kgs 14:2)

Jehoahaz+ (2 Chr 21:17)

Jehoshaphat+ (2 Kgs 9:2)

Jehozabad+ (2 Kgs 12:21)

Jehozadak (1 Chr 6:14)

Jekameam (1 Chr 23:19)

Jemuel (Gn 46:10)

Jerah (Gn 10:26)

Jeremy (Mt 2:17)

Jeriah (1 Chr 23:19)

Jeroham+ (1 Chr 9:12)

Jeshaiah+ (1 Chr 25:3)

Jeshua+ (Ezr 2:6)

Jeshua+ (Ezr 2:36)

Jetheth (Gn 36:40)

Jetur (Gn 25:15)

Jeush+ (1 Chr 23:10)

Jezaniah (Jer 40:8)

Joab+ (Ezr 2:6)

Joanna*+ (Lk 8:3)

Joash+ (1 Kgs 22:26)

Jobab+ (Gn 10:29)

Jochebed* (Ex 6:20)

Joel+ (1 Chr 5:4)

Joel+ (Jl 1:1)

Johanan+ (1 Chr 6:9)

Johanan+ (Neh 12:22)

Jonathan+ (2 Sm 21:21)

Jonathan+ (2 Sm 23:32)

Jonathan+ (1 Chr 2:32)

Jonathan+ (Jer 37:15)

Joseph+ (1 Chr 25:2)

Joses+ (Mt 13:55)

Joshbekashah (1 Chr 25:4)

Joshua+ (1 Sm 6:14)

Josias (Mt 1:10)

Judas+ (Mt 1:2)

Julius (Acts 27:1)

J: Mentioned Three Times

Jabesh (2 Kgs 15:10)

Jabez (1 Chr 4:9)

Jachin+ (Gn 46:10)

Japhia+ (2 Sm 5:15)

Japhlet (1 Chr 7:32)

Jediael+ (1 Chr 7:6)

Jehiel+ (1 Chr 15:18)

Jehonadab (2 Kgs 10:15)

Jeremiah+ (2 Kgs 23:31)

Jeroham+ (1 Sm 1:1)

Jezer (Gn 46:24)

Jezreel+ (Hos 1:4)

Joah+ (1 Chr 6:21)

Joel+ (1 Sm 8:2)

Joel+ (1 Chr 15:7)

Joiarib+ (Neh 11:10)

Jonas+ (Jn 21:15)

Joses+ (Mt 27:56)

Judas+ (Lk 6:16)

Judas+ (Acts 15:22)

K

Kadmiel+ (5)

One of a group of Levites who led a revival among the Israelites in the time of Nehemiah.

First reference Neh 9:4
Last reference Neh 12:24

Kareah (13)
Bald

Father of Johanan and Jonathan, captains of the Israelite forces under Governor Gedaliah, who was placed in authority by King Nebuchadnezzar of Babylon.

First reference Jer 40:8
Last reference Jer 43:5

Kenaz+ (5)

Younger brother of Caleb and father of Othniel, the first judge of Israel after Caleb's death.

First reference Jo 15:17
Last reference 1 Chr 4:13

Keturah* (4)
Perfumed

Abraham's concubine (1 Chr 1:32) and wife (Gn 25:1). He may have married her following Sarah's death, but her children were not part of God's promised line.

First reference Gn 25:1
Last reference 1 Chr 1:33

Kish+ (13)
A bow

A Benjaminite, the father of King Saul. Seeking his

father's donkeys, Saul came to Samuel, who anointed him king. Kish's brother was Abner, Saul's battle commander. Saul and his son Jonathan were buried in Kish's tomb. Same as Cis.

First reference I Sm 9:1
Last reference I Chr 26:28
Key references I Sm 14:50–51; 2 Sm 21:14

Kohath (32)

Allied

A son of Levi. Kohath's family was designated by God to care for the most holy things of the tabernacle.

First reference Gn 46:11
Last reference I Chr 23:12
Key references Nm 4:15; 7:9

Korah⁺ (4)

To make bald

A son of Esau.

First reference Gn 36:5
Last reference I Chr 1:35

Korah⁺ (19)

A descendant of Levi and Kohath who opposed Moses when the prophet said all the Israelites were not holy. Moses commanded Korah and his company to come before the Lord, with their censers filled with incense, and stand in the door of the tabernacle. God warned Moses and Aaron to stand back while He consumed these rebels. Though the prophet and priest prayed for them, God made the earth swallow all 250 men, along with their tents.

First reference Ex 6:21
Last reference 1 Chr 9:19
Key references Nm 16:1–11,
   16–19, 32–35; 26:9–11

Korah[+] (12)

A descendant of Abraham through Jacob's son Levi. Korah's sons are named in the titles of eleven psalms: 42, 44–49, 84–85, and 87–88.

First reference 1 Chr 6:22
Last reference Ps 88 (title)

K: Mentioned Once

Kadmiel+ (Ezr 3:9)

Kallai (Neh 12:20)

Keilah (1 Chr 4:19)

Kelaiah (Ezr 10:23)

Kelita+ (Ezr 10:23)

Kemuel+ (Gn 22:21)

Kemuel+ (Nm 34:24)

Kemuel+ (1 Chr 27:17)

Kenan (1 Chr 1:2)

Kenaz+ (1 Chr 4:15)

Keren-happuch* (Jb 42:14)

Kezia* (Jb 42:14)

Kish+ (2 Chr 29:12)

Kish+ (Est 2:5)

Kishi (1 Chr 6:44)

Kolaiah+ (Neh 11:7)

Kolaiah+ (Jer 29:21)

Korah+ (Gn 36:16)

Korah+ (1 Chr 2:43)

Kore+ (2 Chr 31:14)

Kushaiah (1 Chr 15:17)

K: Mentioned Twice

Kadmiel+ (Ezr 2:40)

Kedar (Gn 25:13)

Kedemah (Gn 25:15)

Kelita+ (Neh 8:7)

Kenaz+ (Gn 36:42)

Keros (Ezr 2:44)

Kish+ (1 Chr 8:30)

Kittim (Gn 10:4)

Koz+ (Ezr 2:61)

Koz+ (Neh 3:4)

K: Mentioned Three Times

Kedar (Gn 25:13)

Kedemah (Gn 25:15)

Kelita+ (Neh 8:7)

Kenaz+ (Gn 36:42)

Keros (Ezr 2:44)

Kish+ (1 Chr 8:30)

Kittim (Gn 10:4)

Koz+ (Ezr 2:61)

Koz+ (Neh 3:4)

L

Laadan+ (6)

A Levite worship leader who was part of David's re-organization of the Levites.

First reference I Chr 23:7
Last reference I Chr 26:21

Laban (55)

To be white or to make bricks

Called Laban the Syrian (Gn 25:20), this brother of Rebekah approved of her marriage to Isaac. When Rebekah's son Esau became angry at his brother, Jacob, for stealing their father's blessing from him, Isaac sent Jacob to Laban. Jacob loved Rachel, Laban's second daughter, and offered to work for him for seven years in order to win her. At the end of that time, Laban tricked Jacob into marrying his first daughter, Leah. Then he offered Rachel to Jacob for another seven years of service. When Jacob wanted to go home, Laban asked him to stay, recognizing that God had blessed him because Jacob was in his camp. Jacob, in turn, tricked Laban into giving him the best of his flocks. Jacob saw the anger of Laban and his sons, and God called him to return home, so he left. Laban pursued Jacob and confronted him for slipping away without warning and taking his household gods. Laban did not find the gods because Rachel, who had taken them, was sitting on them. Laban made a covenant with Jacob. Then, blessing them, he departed.

First reference Gn 24:29
Last reference Gn 46:25
Key references Gn 28:2;
  29:18–28; 30:31–43

Lamech (12)

A descendant of Cain through his son Enoch. Lamech's father was Methuselah, and Lamech was Noah's father. Lamech is the first man whom the Bible records as having more than one wife.

First reference Gn 4:18
Last reference Lk 3:36
Key references Gn 4:19;
  5:28–29

Lazarus (11)

The brother of Mary and Martha, Lazarus was loved by Jesus, who often came to visit the family. When Lazarus became ill, his sisters sent for Jesus, who waited several days before arriving. By the time He appeared in Bethany, Lazarus had died. Jesus promised Martha, "Thy brother shall rise again" (Jn 11:23), and told her He was the resurrection and the life. After weeping at Lazarus's tomb, Jesus had the stone removed from the mouth of this cave then called Lazarus forth. Lazarus walked out, still bound by the grave clothes.

This Lazarus is not to be confused with the beggar named Lazarus in Jesus' parable in Lk 16.

First reference Jn 11:1
Last reference Jn 12:17

Leah (34)
Weary

Laban's tender-eyed daughter who was less beautiful

than her sister, Rachel. Though Jacob loved Rachel and arranged to marry her, Laban insisted that Jacob marry Leah first. He tricked Jacob into marriage with Leah but then allowed him to marry Rachel, too. Leah had four children, while Rachel was barren. When Rachel gave Jacob her maid, Bilhah, to have children with him, and Leah had had no more children, Leah gave her maid, Zilpah, to Jacob, too. But Leah later had two more sons and a daughter. When Jacob returned to his home after serving Laban for many years, he placed Leah in more danger than her sister as they neared Jacob's wronged brother, Esau. Leah's daughter, Dinah, was raped by the prince of Shechem, and Leah's sons Simeon and Levi killed the men of Shechem. Leah was buried at Machpelah with Abraham, Sarah, Isaac, and Rebekah.

First reference Gn 29:16
Last reference Ru 4:11
Key references Gn 29:20–28, 31–35; 30:9, 17–21; 33:1–2; 34:1–2; 49:31

Levi⁺ (16)

Attached

Leah and Jacob's third child. After Dinah was raped by the prince of Shechem, Levi and his brother Simeon attacked the men of the city and killed them. Through Levi's line, God established the priests and Levites, beginning with Aaron and his sons.

First reference Gn 29:34
Last reference Ezr 8:18
Key reference Gn 34:25

Libni+ (4)

White

A descendant of Abraham through Jacob's son Levi.

First reference Ex 6:17
Last reference 1 Chr 6:20

Lot (37)

Abram's nephew, who traveled with him to the Promised Land. Once their grazing area was unable to support all their flocks, Lot chose to move to the plain of the Jordan River and live near the city of Sodom. An alliance of Canaanite kings attacked Sodom and Gomorrah and captured Lot, his people, and his goods. When Abram heard about this, he went to Lot's rescue and regained everything. Lot returned to Sodom, where two angels visited him. Lot offered them his hospitality, but the men of Sodom demanded that he bring the two angels out so they could know them. Instead, Lot offered the men his two virgin daughters, whom they refused. The angels blinded the men and told Lot they were about to destroy the city. Lot tried to gather his extended family, but his sons-in-law would not listen. So Lot took his wife and daughters and left the city. They were warned not to look back, but when his wife did, she was turned into a pillar of salt. After the destruction of the cities of the plain, Lot's daughters lay with their father. The children of these unions became the founders of the Moabites and Ammonites.

First reference Gn 11:27
Last reference 2 Pt 2:7
Key references Gn 13:5–11;
    14:14–16; 19:1–38

Lotan (7)

Covering

A descendant of Seir, who
lived in Esau's "land of
Edom."

First reference Gn 36:20
Last reference I Chr 1:39

L: Mentioned Once

Laadah (1 Chr 4:21)

Laadan⁺ (1 Chr 7:26)

Lael (Nm 3:24)

Lahad (1 Chr 4:2)

Lahmi (1 Chr 20:5)

Lapidoth (Jgs 4:4)

Lebana (Neh 7:48)

Lebanah (Ezr 2:45)

Lebbaeus (Mt 10:3)

Lecah (1 Chr 4:21)

Letushim (Gn 25:3)

Leummim (Gn 25:3)

Levi⁺ (Lk 3:24)

Levi⁺ (Lk 3:29)

Libni⁺ (1 Chr 6:29)

Likhi (1 Chr 7:19)

Linus (2 Tm 4:21)

Lo-ammi (Hos 1:9)

Lois (2 Tm 1:5)

Lucas (Phlm 1:24)

Lucius⁺ (Acts 13:1)

Lucius⁺ (Rom 16:21)

L: Mentioned Twice

Laish (1 Sm 25:44)

Lehabim (Gn 10:13)

Lemuel (Prv 31:1)

Lo-ruhamah (Hos 1:6)

Lud (Gn 10:22)

Ludim (Gn 10:13)

Luke (Col 4:14)

Lydia (Acts 16:14)

L: Mentioned Three Times

Levi⁺ (Mk 2:14)

Lysias (Acts 23:26)

Lysanias (Lk 3:1)

M

Maachah*+ [5]

A daughter of David's son Absalom and King Rehoboam's favorite among his eighteen wives and sixty concubines.

First reference 1 Kgs 15:2
Last reference 2 Chr 11:22

Machir [19]

Salesman

Grandson of Joseph through his son Manasseh and his Syrian concubine. Machir's family took Gilead from the Amorites. Moses gave him the land, and he lived there.

First reference Gn 50:23
Last reference 1 Chr 7:17
Key references Nm 32:39–40;
    1 Chr 7:14

Magdalene* [12]

Woman of Magdala

Surname of Mary (Mt 27:56).

First reference Mt 27:56
Last reference Jn 20:18

Mahalaleel+ [6]

Praise of God

A descendant of Adam through his son Seth.

First reference Gn 5:12
Last reference 1 Chr 1:2

Mahlah* [4]

Sickness

One of Zelophehad's five daughters who received his inheritance because he had no sons. Each had to marry within their tribe, Manasseh.

First reference Nm 26:33
Last reference Jo 17:3

Mahli+ (7)

Sick

A descendant of Abraham through Jacob's son Levi. His father was Merari.

First reference Nm 3:20
Last reference Ezr 8:18

Mahlon (4)

Sick

A son of Naomi and her husband, Elimelech. Mahlon, his father, and his brother died in Moab, forcing Naomi and Mahlon's wife, Ruth, to return to Bethlehem.

First reference Ru 1:2
Last reference Ru 4:10

Manasseh+ (25)

Causing to forget

The elder child of Joseph and Asenath who was adopted, with his brother, Ephraim, by Joseph's father, Jacob. When Jacob blessed the two boys, he gave Ephraim the greater blessing. But he prophesied that both nations that came from the boys would be great.

First reference Gn 41:51
Last reference I Chr 7:17
Key reference Gn 48:17–19

Manasseh+ (24)

Causing to forget

King of Judah and son of King Hezekiah, Manasseh was an evil ruler who erected pagan altars in the temple and led his nation into idolatry. He burned his own sons as offerings to the idols and became involved in witchcraft. The Lord caused the Assyrian army to capture Manasseh and bring him to Babylon. Manasseh repented, and God brought him back to Jerusalem. Manasseh removed the idols from Jerusalem, repaired God's altar, and commanded his nation to follow God.

First reference 2 Kgs 20:21
Last reference Jer 15:4
Key reference 2 Chr 33:1–20

Manoah [18]

Rest

Father of Samson, whose wife was at first barren. The woman received a visit from the angel of the Lord, who told her not to have strong drink or anything unclean, because the child she would bear would be a Nazarite. When Manoah heard this, he prayed that God would send the angel again, so he could know what to do when the child was born. Again the angel appeared to the woman, and she brought her husband to Him. When Manoah received the instructions, he recognized that he had seen God and made an offering to Him.

First reference Jgs 13:2
Last reference Jgs 16:31
Key reference Jgs 13

Mark [5]

Nephew of Barnabas and fellow missionary with Barnabas and Saul. At Pamphylia, Mark left the mission. When his uncle wanted to bring him on a second journey, Paul objected. So

Barnabas took Mark back with him to Cyprus. Mark was the writer of the Gospel that bears his name. Same as Marcus.

First reference Acts 12:12
Last reference 2 Tm 4:11

Martha* (13)

Mistress

Sister of Lazarus and Mary (Luke 10:39). Jesus became friendly with the family when Martha invited Him to her home in Bethany. Martha, encumbered with serving, asked Jesus to tell Mary to help her, but Jesus pointed out that Mary had chosen the better part—listening to His teaching. When their brother became ill, Martha and Mary called for Jesus. While He delayed, Lazarus died. When Jesus reached Bethany, Martha commented, "If thou hadst been here, my brother had not died" (Jn 11:21). Jesus pointed out that He was the resurrection and brought her brother back to life.

First reference Lk 10:38
Last reference Jn 12:2
Key references Lk 10:38–42; Jn 11:1–44

Mary*+ (19)

Jesus' mother, who as a virgin, received the news from an angel that she would bear the Messiah. Mary traveled to Bethlehem with her betrothed, Joseph. Jesus was born there, and there Mary saw the shepherds and kings worship Him. When she and Joseph brought Jesus to the temple, Mary heard Simeon's and Anna's prophecies about her son. When Jesus was twelve years old, the couple brought Him to the temple, did not realize He had not left with their group, and had to return for Him. Mary stood by the cross and saw her son crucified. She was also in the upper room, praying with the disciples after His ascension.

First reference Mt 1:16
Last reference Acts 1:14
Key references Mt 1:18–25;
   Lk 1:26–35; 2; Jn 19:25

Mary*+ [13]

Called Mary Magdelene, she had seven devils cast out of her by Jesus. Mary was present throughout the crucifixion of Jesus. Following His resurrection, she came to the tomb with the other women to anoint His body and saw the angels who reported that Jesus had risen from the dead. She and the other women told the disciples. As Mary wept at the tomb, Jesus appeared to her. She did not recognize Him until He spoke her name.

First reference Mt 27:56
Last reference Jn 20:18
Key references Mk 15:40–41,
   16:9; Lk 24:10–11;
   Jn 20:1–18

Mary*+ [8]

Mary, the mother of James and Joses, was with Mary Magdalene and other women at the crucifixion of Jesus and at the tomb following His resurrection.

First reference Mt 27:56
Last reference Lk 24:10

Mary*+ [11]

The sister of Lazarus and Martha, Mary of Bethany listened at Jesus' feet while her sister became encumbered with household matters. When their brother became ill, Martha and Mary called for Jesus. While He delayed, Lazarus died. Mary saw her brother, Lazarus, resurrected by Jesus and anointed Jesus with spikenard before His death.

First reference Lk 10:39
Last reference Jn 12:3
Key references Lk 10:39–42; Jn 11:28–32; 12:3

Mattaniah+ (7)

A Jewish exile from the tribe of Levi who resettled Jerusalem.

First reference 1 Chr 9:15
Last reference Neh 12:35

Matthew (5)

A tax collector (or publican), also called Levi, who left his tax booth to follow Jesus. Disciple Matthew was in the Upper Room, following Jesus' resurrection, praying. Although Matthew does not list himself as the writer of the Gospel named after him, the early church ascribed it to him. Same as Levi (Mk 2:14).

First reference Mt 9:9
Last reference Acts 1:13

Melchisedec (9)

King of right

King and high priest of Salem who blessed Abram after that faithful man recovered his nephew Lot (Gn 14:18; Heb 7:1). The writer of Hebrews refers to Jesus as high priest "after the order of Melchisedec," since He was not a priest from the line of Levi. Same as Melchizedek.

First reference Heb 5:6
Last reference Heb 7:21

Menahem [8]

Comforter

A king of Israel who usurped the throne from King Shallum. During his ten-year reign, the idolatrous Menahem did evil. To keep his throne, he raised money from the wealthy men of Israel and gave it to Pul, the king of Assyria, as tribute.

First reference 2 Kgs 15:14
Last reference 2 Kgs 15:23

Mephibosheth⁺ [15]

Dispeller of shame

Grandson of King Saul and son of Jonathan. As a child, Mephibosheth was dropped by his nurse and became lame. When David took the throne of Israel, he treated Mephibosheth kindly because of his friendship with Jonathan. When Absalom ousted David from Jerusalem, Mephibosheth's servant Ziba reported that Mephibosheth remained in Jerusalem, confident he would be made king. David gave Mephibosheth's land to Ziba. When David returned to Jerusalem, Mephibosheth claimed that Ziba had deceived him and lied to David. The king ordered the two men to split the land, but Mephibosheth agreed that Ziba should have all, as long as David had returned in peace. Same as Merib-baal.

First reference 2 Sm 4:4
Last reference 2 Sm 21:7
Key references 2 Sm 9:6–10;
16:3–4; 19:24–30

First reference Gn 46:11
Last reference Ezr 8:19
Key references Ex 6:19;
Nm 3:33–37

Meraioth⁺ (4)

Rebellious

Forefather of Ezra (Ezr 7:1) and a descendant of Abraham through Jacob's son Levi.

First reference 1 Chr 6:6
Last reference Ezr 7:3

Merari (39)

Bitter

Levi's third son. His family was in charge of the boards, bars, pillars, sockets, and vessels of the tabernacle, along with the pillars of the court and their sockets, pins, and cords.

Meremoth⁺ (6)

Heights

A priest's son who weighed the valuable utensils that King Artaxerxes of Persia and his officials had given Ezra to take back to Jerusalem's temple.

First reference Ezr 8:33
Last reference Neh 3:21

Merib-baal (4)

Quarreler of Baal

A descendant of Abraham through Jacob's son Benjamin, in the line of King Saul and his son Jonathan. Same as Mephibosheth (2 Sm 4:4).

First reference I Chr 8:34
Last reference I Chr 9:40

Meshach (15)

The Babylonian name for Mishael, one of Daniel's companions in exile. Daniel had King Nebuchadnezzar make Meshach a ruler in Babylon. When some Chaldeans accused Meshach and his friends, fellow Jews and corulers Shadrach and Abed-nego, of not worshipping the king's golden idol, the three faithful Jews were thrown into a furnace. God protected His men, who were not even singed. The king recognized the power of their God and promoted them in his service. Same as Mishael.

First reference Dn 1:7
Last reference Dn 3:30
Key reference Dn 3:16–18

Meshelemiah (4)

Ally of God

A Levite "porter" (doorkeeper) in the house of the Lord.

First reference I Chr 9:21
Last reference I Chr 26:9

Methuselah (6)

Man of a dart

A descendant of Seth who lived for 969 years, the longest-recorded life span in the Bible.

First reference Gn 5:21
Last reference I Chr 1:3

Micah⁺ (18)

Who is like God?

A man of Mt. Ephraim who took eleven hundred shekels from his mother. When he returned them, she had two idols made for him. Micah consecrated one of his sons to be his priest. When a Levite came to his area, Micah hired him as a priest and consecrated him. Some men from Dan stole his idols and took the priest, who went with them willingly. Though Micah and his neighbors tried to recover the items, the Danites were too strong. The thieves set up the idols in Laish, a city they had conquered.

First reference Jgs 17:1
Last reference Jgs 18:27
Key references Jgs 17:1–6, 10–12; 18:17–27

Micah⁺ (4)

Who is like God?

A descendant of Abraham through Jacob's son Benjamin, in the line of King Saul and his son Jonathan.

First reference 1 Chr 8:34
Last reference 1 Chr 9:41

Micaiah (18)

A prophet whom King Ahab of Israel hated because he never prophesied anything good to him. When King Jehoshaphat of Israel asked Ahab for a prophet who would tell the truth, Ahab had Micaiah called. Though Ahab's messenger warned him to give a good message, the prophet would only say what God told him. Micaiah mocked the false prophets' message then told Ahab that if he attacked Ramoth-gilead, his soldiers would be scattered. Micaiah condemned the lying prophets and was struck by one of their number. Micaiah prophesied against him.

First reference 1 Kgs 22:8
Last reference 2 Chr 18:27
Key references 1 Kgs 22:13–
 17; 2 Chr 18:1–16

Michal* (18)

Rivulet

Daughter of King Saul and wife of David. To win her, David had to give Saul a hundred Philistine foreskins; he killed two hundred of the enemy, fulfilling the king's request twice over. When Saul sought to kill David, Michal warned her husband and helped him escape out a window. She told Saul's men that David was sick. Discovered, she claimed David threatened to kill her.

Saul married Michal to Phalti. When David sent for her, after he became king, she was returned to him. But when David danced before the ark, Michal despised and berated him. She had no children.

First reference 1 Sm 14:49
Last reference 1 Chr 15:29
Key references 1 Sm 18:20–
 27; 19:11–12; 25:44

Midian (4)

Brawling, contentious

A son of Abraham by his second wife, Keturah.

First reference Gn 25:2
Last reference 1 Chr 1:33

Milcah* (7)

Queen

Wife of Nahor (Gn 11:26), Abraham's brother. The couple had eight children together. Milcah was Rebekah's grandmother.

First reference Gn 11:29
Last reference Gn 24:47

Milcah* (4)

Queen

One of Zelophehad's five daughters who received his inheritance because he had no sons. Each had to marry within their tribe, Manasseh.

First reference Nm 26:33
Last reference Jo 17:3

Miriam*+ (14)

Rebelliously

Sister of Moses and Aaron and a prophetess of Israel. Miriam led the praises after Israel crossed the Red Sea. She and Aaron objected to Moses' marrying an Ethiopian woman. "Hath the Lord indeed spoken only by Moses?" they asked, seeking acknowledgment of their own prophetic gifts (Nm 12:2). The Lord became angry, confronted them publicly, and made Miriam leprous. Moses prayed for her. God had her stay outside the camp for a week until she was healed. Miriam died in the Desert of Zin.

First reference Ex 15:20
Last reference Mi 6:4
Key references Ex 15:20–21;
   Nm 12:1–15; 20:1

Mishael+ (5)

Who is what God is?

A friend of the prophet Daniel who would not defile himself by eating King Nebuchadnezzar's meat. Along with two other Israelites, he would not worship an idol and was cast into the fiery furnace by the king. Also called Meshach.

First reference Dn 1:6
Last reference Dn 2:17

Mishma (4)

A report, hearing

A descendant of Abraham through Jacob's son Simeon.

First reference Gn 25:14
Last reference 1 Chr 4:26

Mizraim (4)

Upper and Lower Egypt

A descendant of Noah through his son Ham.

First reference Gn 10:6
Last reference 1 Chr 1:11

Mordecai+ (56)

Cousin of Queen Esther, wife of the Persian king Ahasuerus. Though he was an exiled Jew, Mordecai was faithful to his king and warned him of a plot against him by some officers of the king's household. Then Mordecai discovered a plot against the Jews, set up by the king's scheming counselor, Haman. Mordecai warned Esther and encouraged her to confront the king for the good of her people. Before the king and Haman came to the banquet at which Esther intended to reveal Haman's plans, the king discovered Mordecai had never been honored for his role in foiling the plot against him. The king commanded Haman to honor Mordecai by publicly proclaiming his deeds. When Esther revealed Haman's plan against the Jews to her husband, he became angry and commanded that Haman be hanged on the gallows his counselor had prepared for Mordecai. Then he commanded Mordecai to write a law that would defend the Jews against attack and made him first counselor in Haman's place. Mordecai received Haman's entire household as a reward.

First reference Est 2:5
Last reference Est 10:3
Key reference Est 4:13–14

Moses [848]

Drawing out (of the water), rescued

The Old Testament prophet through whom God gave Israel the law. Because Pharaoh commanded that all male newborn Israelites should be killed, Moses' mother placed him in a basket in the Nile River. There he was found by an Egyptian princess, who rescued and raised him. Once grown, Moses killed a man for abusing an Israelite slave and fled to Midian, where he met God in a burning bush. The Lord sent Moses back to Egypt, where his brother, Aaron, became his spokesman. As God's prophet in Egypt, Moses confronted Pharaoh. God visited ten plagues on Egypt because Egypt's ruler would not let Israel go free. After all Egypt's firstborn died, Pharaoh finally sent Israel away. But Egyptian troops followed, planning to recapture them. God parted the Red Sea's waters for His people, but the Egyptians were caught in the returning waves. On the way to the Promised Land, God gave His people the Ten Commandments and other laws. At their goal, ten spies sent into Canaan discouraged Israel from entering their Promised Land. So Moses and his people wandered in the desert for forty years. Moses died on Mt. Nebo, just before Israel finally entered the Promised Land.

First reference Ex 2:10
Last reference Rv 15:3
Key references Ex 3:2–18;
    11:4–10; 12:29–30; 14:21–
    27; 20:1–17; Dt 34:5

Moza⁺ (4)

A descendant of Abraham through Jacob's son Benjamin, in the line of King Saul and his son Jonathan.

First reference 1 Chr 8:36
Last reference 1 Chr 9:43

Mushi (8)

Sensitive

A descendant of Abraham through Jacob's son Levi.

First reference Ex 6:19
Last reference 1 Chr 24:30

M: Mentioned Once

Maacah+ (2 Sm 3:3)

Maacah+ (2 Sm 10:6)

Maachah+ (Gn 22:24)

Maachah+ (1 Kgs 2:39)

Maachah*+ (1 Chr 2:48)

Maachah*+ (1 Chr 3:2)

Maachah+ (1 Chr 11:43)

Maachah+ (1 Chr 27:16)

Maadai (Ezr 10:34)

Maadiah (Neh 12:5)

Maai (Neh 12:36)

Maaseiah+ (2 Chr 23:1)

Maaseiah+ (2 Chr 26:11)

Maaseiah+ (2 Chr 28:7)

Maaseiah+ (2 Chr 34:8)

Maaseiah+ (Ezr 10:18)

Maaseiah+ (Ezr 10:21)

Maaseiah+ (Ezr 10:22)

Maaseiah+ (Ezr 10:30)

Maaseiah+ (Neh 3:23)

Maaseiah+ (Neh 8:4)

Maaseiah+ (Neh 8:7)

Maaseiah+ (Neh 10:25)

Maaseiah+ (Neh 11:5)

Maaseiah+ (Neh 11:7)

Maaseiah+ (Neh 12:41)

Maaseiah+ (Neh 12:42)

Maaseiah+ (Jer 29:21)

Maaseiah+ (Jer 35:4)

Maasiai (1 Chr 9:12)

Maath (Lk 3:26)

Maaz (1 Chr 2:27)

Maaziah+ (1 Chr 24:18)

Maaziah+ (Neh 10:8)

Machbanai (1 Chr 12:13)

Machbenah (1 Chr 2:49)

Machi (Nm 13:15)

Machnadebai (Ezr 10:40)

Madmannah (1 Chr 2:49)

Magbish (Ezr 2:30)

Magor-missabib (Jer 20:3)

Magpiash (Neh 2:10)

Mahalah (1 Chr 7:18)

Mahalaleel+ (Neh 11:4)

Mahalath*+ (Gn 28:9)

Mahalath*+ (2 Chr 11:18)

Mahali (Ex 6:19)

Mahath+ (2 Chr 31:13)

Mahol (1 Kgs 4:31)

Malachi (Mal 1:1)

Malcham (1 Chr 8:9)

Malchiah+ (1 Chr 6:40)

Malchiah+ (Ezr 10:31)

Malchiah+ (Neh 3:14)

Malchiah+ (Neh 3:31)

Malchiah+ (Neh 8:4)

Malchijah+ (1 Chr 9:12)

Malchijah+ (1 Chr 24:9)

Malchijah+ (Ezr 10:25)

Malchijah+ (Neh 3:11)

Malchiram (1 Chr 3:18)

Malchus (Jn 18:10)

Maleleel (Lk 3:37)

Malluch+ (1 Chr 6:44)

Malluch+ (Ezr 10:29)

Malluch+ (Ezr 10:32)

Malluch+ (Neh 10:27)

Manaen (Acts 13:1)

Manasseh+ (Jgs 18:30)

Manasseh+ (Ezr 10:30)

Manasseh+ (Ezr 10:33)

Manasses (Mt 1:10)

Maoch (1 Sm 27:2)

Maon (1 Chr 2:45)

Mara* (Ru 1:20)

Mareshah+ (1 Chr 2:42)

Mareshah+ (1 Chr 4:21)

Marsena (Est 1:14)

Mary*++ (Jn 19:25)

Mary*++ (Acts 12:12)

Mary*++ (Rom 16:6)

Mash (Gn 10:23)

Mathusala (Lk 3:37)

Matri (1 Sm 10:21)

Mattan+ (Jer 38:1)

Mattaniah+ (2 Kgs 24:17)

Mattaniah+ (2 Chr 29:13)

Mattaniah+ (Ezr 10:26)

Mattaniah+ (Ezr 10:27)

Mattaniah+ (Ezr 10:30)

Mattaniah+ (Ezr 10:37)

Mattaniah+ (Neh 13:13)

Mattatha (Lk 3:31)

Mattathah (Ezr 10:33)

Mattathias+ (Ezr 10:37)

Mattathias+ (Neh 12:19)

Mattathias+ (Lk 3:25)

Mattathias+ (Lk 3:26)

Mattenai+ (Ezr 10:33)

Matthan (Mt 1:15)

Matthat+ (Lk 3:24)

Matthat+ (Lk 3:29)

Mattithiah+ (1 Chr 9:31)

Mattithiah+ (Ezr 10:43)

Mattithiah+ (Neh 8:4)

Mebunnai (2 Sm 23:27)

Mehetabeel (Neh 6:10)

Mehir (1 Chr 4:11)

Mehujael (Gn 4:18)

Mehuman (Est 1:10)

Mehunim (Ezr 2:50)

Melatiah (Neh 3:7)

Melchi+ (Lk 3:24)

Melchi+ (Lk 3:28)

Melchiah (Jer 21:1)

Melea (Lk 3:31)

Melicu (Neh 12:14)

Menan (Lk 3:31)

Meonothai (1 Chr 4:14)

Mephibosheth+ (2 Sm 21:8)

Meraiah (Neh 12:12)

Meraioth+ (Neh 12:15)

Meremoth+ (Ezr 10:36)

Meres (Est 1:14)

Merodach-baladan (Is 39:1)

Mesha+ (2 Kgs 3:4)

Mesha+ (1 Chr 2:42)

Mesha+ (1 Chr 8:9)

Meshech+ (1 Chr 1:17)

Meshezabeel+ (Neh 3:4)

Meshillemith (1 Chr 9:12)

Meshillemoth+ (2 Chr 28:12)

Meshillemoth+ (Neh 11:13)

Meshobab (1 Chr 4:34)

Meshullam+ (2 Kgs 22:3)

Meshullam+ (1 Chr 3:19)

Meshullam+ (1 Chr 5:13)

Meshullam+ (1 Chr 8:17)

Meshullam+ (1 Chr 9:7)

Meshullam+ (1 Chr 9:8)

Meshullam+ (1 Chr 9:12)

Meshullam+ (2 Chr 34:12)

Meshullam+ (Ezr 8:16)

Meshullam+ (Ezr 10:15)

Meshullam+ (Ezr 10:29)

Meshullam+ (Neh 3:6)

Meshullam+ (Neh 8:4)

Meshullam+ (Neh 10:7)

Meshullam+ (Neh 10:20)

Meshullam+ (Neh 11:7)

Meshullam+ (Neh 12:16)

Meshullam+ (Neh 12:25)

Meshullemeth*
   (2 Kgs 21:19)

Methusael (Gn 4:18)

Meunim (Neh 7:52)

Miamin+ (Ezr 10:25)

Miamin+ (Neh 12:5)

Mibhar (1 Chr 11:38)

Mibsam+ (1 Chr 4:25)

Micah+ (1 Chr 5:5)

Micah+ (1 Chr 9:15)

Micah+ (1 Chr 23:20)

Micah+ (2 Chr 34:20)

Micha+ (2 Sm 9:12)

Micha+ (Neh 10:11)

Michael+ (Nm 13:13)

Michael+ (1 Chr 5:13)

Michael+ (1 Chr 5:14)

Michael+ (1 Chr 6:40)

Michael+ (1 Chr 7:3)

Michael+ (1 Chr 8:16)

Michael+ (1 Chr 12:20)

Michael+ (1 Chr 27:18)

Michael+ (2 Chr 21:2)

Michael+ (Ezr 8:8)

Michaiah+ (2 Kgs 22:12)

Michaiah*+ (2 Chr 13:12)

Michaiah+ (2 Chr 17:7)

Michri (1 Chr 9:8)

Mijamin+ (1 Chr 24:9)

Mijamin+ (Neh 10:7)

Mikloth+ (1 Chr 27:4)

Milalai (Neh 12:36)

Miniamin+ (2 Chr 31:15)

Miriam*+ (1 Chr 4:17)

Mirma (1 Chr 8:10)

Mishael+ (Neh 8:4)

Misham (1 Chr 8:12)

Mishmannah
    (1 Chr 12:10)

Mispereth (Neh 7:7)

Mizpar (Ezr 2:2)

Mnason (Acts 21:16)

Moab (Gn 19:37)

Moadiah (Neh 12:17)

Molid (1 Chr 2:29)

Moza+ (1 Chr 2:46)

Muppim (Gn 46:21)

M: Mentioned Twice

Maachah*+ (1 Kgs 15:13)

Maachah*+ (1 Chr 7:15)

Maachah*+ (1 Chr 8:29)

Maaseiah+ (1 Chr 15:18)

Maaseiah+ (Jer 32:12)

Madai (Gn 10:2)

Magdiel (Gn 36:43)

Magog (Gn 10:2)

Mahath+ (1 Chr 6:35)

Mahazioth (1 Chr 25:4)

Maher-shalal-hash-baz
  (Is 8:1)

Malchiah+ (Ezr 10:25)

Malchiah+ (Jer 38:1)

Malchijah+ (Neh 10:3)

Mallothi (1 Chr 25:4)

Malluch+ (Neh 10:4)

Mamre (Gn 14:13)

Manahath (Gn 36:23)

Massa (Gn 25:14)

Matred* (Gn 36:39)

Mattan+ (2 Kgs 11:18)

Mattaniah+ (1 Chr 25:4)

Matthias (Acts 1:23)

Mattithiah+ (1 Chr 25:3)

Medad (Nm 11:26)

Medan (Gn 25:2)

Mehetabel* (Gn 36:39)

Melchi-shua (1 Sm 14:49)

Melchizedek (Gn 14:18)

Melech (1 Chr 8:35)

Melzar (Dn 1:11)

Meraioth+ (1 Chr 9:11)

Mered (1 Chr 4:17)

Meremoth+ (Neh 10:5)

Meshech+ (Gn 10:2)

Meshezabeel+ (Neh 10:21)

Meshullam+ (1 Chr 9:11)

Meshullam+ (Neh 12:13)

Mezahab* (Gn 36:39)

Mibsam+ (Gn 25:13)

Mibzar (Gn 36:42)

Micah+ (Jer 26:18)

Micha+ (Neh 11:17)

Michaiah+ (Neh 12:35)

Michaiah+ (Jer 36:11)

Mikneiah (1 Chr 15:18)

Miniamin+ (Neh 12:17)

Mishael+ (Ex 6:22)

Mithredath (Ezr 1:8)

Mordecai+ (Ezr 2:2)

M: Mentioned Three Times

Maaseiah[+] (Jer 21:1)

Machir (2 Sm 9:4)

Maharai (2 Sm 23:28)

Mahli[+] (1 Chr 6:47)

Malchiel (Gn 46:17)

Malchi-shua (1 Chr 8:33)

Marcus (Col 4:10)

Mattithiah[+] (1 Chr 15:18)

Memucan (Est 1:14)

Merab* (1 Sm 14:49)

Meshullam[+] (Neh 3:4)

Michah (1 Chr 24:24)

Mikloth[+] (1 Chr 8:32)

Mizzah (Gn 36:13)

N

Naaman+ (11)

Leprous captain of the Syrian army who came to the prophet Elisha for healing. Angered that Elisha told him to wash seven times in the Jordan River, he had to be persuaded to obey. When he did, he was healed.

First reference 2 Kgs 5:1
Last reference Lk 4:27

Nabal (22)

Dolt

The churlish first husband of Abigail. Nabal refused to give David and his men anything in return for their protection of his lands during David's battles with Saul. Nabal's wife stepped in and generously provided them with food. When her husband heard what she had done, "his heart died within him" (1 Sm 25:37). Ten days later, he died.

First reference 1 Sm 25:3
Last reference 2 Sm 3:3
Key references 1 Sm 25:5–11, 37–38

Naboth (22)

Fruits

Owner of a vineyard that was coveted by King Ahab of Israel. When Naboth refused to trade his inheritance for another vineyard, Ahab became sulky. Discovering her husband in this mood, Queen Jezebel conspired to get Naboth's property. She ordered the leaders of Naboth's town to get two men to accuse Naboth of blasphemy. After the innocent man had been stoned, Ahab took possession of his land.

First reference 1 Kgs 21:1
Last reference 2 Kgs 9:26
Key references 1 Kgs 21:2–4, 7–16

Nadab⁺ (12)

Liberal

A son of Aaron who, along with his brother Abihu, offered strange fire before the Lord. God sent fire from His presence to consume them, and they died.

First reference Ex 6:23
Last reference 1 Chr 24:2
Key reference Nm 3:4

Nadab⁺ (4)

Liberal

Son of Jeroboam, king of Israel, who inherited Jeroboam's throne. Nadab did

evil and made his country sin. Baasha conspired against Nadab and killed him at Gibbethon before usurping his throne.

First reference 1 Kgs 14:20
Last reference 1 Kgs 15:31

Nahash⁺ (4)

A king of the Ammonites. Saul raised an army against Nahash, won, and was made king over Gilgal.

First reference 1 Sm 11:1
Last reference 1 Sm 12:12

Nahash⁺ (4)

Father of a man who brought food and supplies to King David and his soldiers as they fled from the army of David's son Absalom.

First reference 2 Sm 10:2
Last reference 1 Chr 19:2

Nahor⁺ (5)

Snorer

Grandfather of Abram (Abraham).

First reference Gn 11:22
Last reference 1 Chr 1:26

Nahor⁺ (10)

Snorer

Brother of Abram (Abraham) and son of Terah. Nahor married Milcah. When Abram left Haran, Nahor stayed behind. He had eight sons with Milcah and four with his concubine. His son Laban became Jacob's father-in-law. Same as Nachor (Jo 24:2).

First reference Gn 11:26
Last reference Gn 31:53
Key references Gn 22:20; 24:15

Nahshon (9)

Enchanter

Captain and prince of the tribe of Judah, he was appointed by God, through Moses. Nahshon was a forefather of Boaz.

First reference Nm 1:7
Last reference 1 Chr 2:11

Naomi* (21)

Pleasant

Elimelech's wife, Naomi and her family moved to Moab during a famine. Following the deaths of her husband and two sons, Naomi and her daughter-in-law Ruth returned to Bethlehem. Ruth supported them by gleaning fields until Boaz, Elimelech's relative, became their kinsman-redeemer, buying Elimelech's inherited land and marrying Ruth. Naomi became nurse to their son, Obed, who was considered her grandson.

First reference Ru 1:2
Last reference Ru 4:17
Key references Ru 1:6, 20–22; 2:1–2; 4:3–6, 14–17

Naphtali [8]

My wrestling

A son of Jacob and founder of one of Israel's twelve tribes. Naphtali was the second son of Bilhah, Rachel's maid. When his father blessed him, he called Napthali "a hind let loose: he giveth goodly words" (Gn 49:21).

First reference Gn 30:8
Last reference Ez 48:34

Nathan+ [4]

Given

A son of King David, born in Jerusalem.

First reference 2 Sm 5:14
Last reference Lk 3:31

Nathan+ [30]

Given

The prophet who confronted King David about his sin with Bath-sheba. Though Nathan had encouraged David to build the temple, he had to tell the king that his son would build it at God's command. After David sinned with Bath-sheba, the prophet told him a parable that described his sin against her husband, Uriah. As the king became angry about the wrong, Nathan revealed it as

David's own, and the king repented. Nathan warned Bath-sheba when her son Solomon's claim to the throne was endangered by his brother Adonijah. Together the prophet and Bath-sheba told David of the threat.

First reference 2 Sm 7:2
Last reference Ps 51(title)
Key references 2 Sm 7:3–12; 12:1–15; 1 Kings 1:11–14, 23–27

Nathanael [6]

A disciple from Cana who first heard of Jesus from His disciple Philip and wondered, "Can there be any good thing come out of Nazareth?" (Jn 1:46). Jesus described him as an Israelite in whom there was no guile. Quickly Nathanael recognized Jesus as Son of God and King of Israel and followed Him. Probably the same as Bartholomew.

First reference Jn 1:45
Last reference Jn 21:2

Nebat [25]
Regard

Father of King Jeroboam (1 Kgs 11:26). Jeroboam was King Solomon's servant, a mighty man of valor, and king over Israel after Solomon's death and the division of his kingdom.

First reference 1 Kgs 11:26
Last reference 2 Chr 13:6

Nebuchadnezzar [60]

Twice this king of Babylon besieged Jerusalem, took its king, and brought Judah's people into exile. King Jehoiakim of Judah had been Nebuchadnezzar's vassal for three years when he rebelled. Nebuchadnezzar attacked Jerusalem and took him, his family, and his servants, princes, and officers. Leaving the poorest people in the nation's capital, Babylon's king emptied Jerusalem of the treasures of its palace and temple. Zedekiah, made king by Nebuchadnezzar, also rebelled. When his city was starving, the king and his soldiers fled. Nebuchadnezzar pursued, captured Zedekiah, killed his sons before him, put out his eyes, and carried him to Babylon. The prophet Daniel was one of Nebuchadnezzar's captives. He received a vision of the king's dream and interpreted it. Nebuchadnezzar made him a great man in Babylon. When Daniel's three friends, Shadrach, Meshach, and Abed-nego, refused to worship an idol, Nebuchadnezzar had them thrown into a fiery furnace, but they were not consumed. Amazed, the king declared that no one should speak anything amiss about their God and then promoted the three men to higher positions. Daniel prophesied that Nebuchadnezzar would be driven out from among people and eat grass until he recognized the Lord as the supreme God. Same as Nebuchadrezzar.

First reference 2 Kgs 24:1
Last reference Dn 5:18
Key references 2 Kgs 24:1, 10, 12–14; 2 Kgs 25:1, 6–7, 9–10; Dn 2:28–48; 3:13–30; 4:25–36

Nebuchadrezzar (31)

King of Babylon. A variant spelling of *Nebuchadnezzar*.

First reference Jer 21:2
Last reference Ez 30:10
Key references Jer 21:7; 39:1; 52:12; Ez 26:7

Nebuzar-adan (15)

Captain of the guard for King Nebuchadnezzar of Babylon. He burned Jerusalem when Nebuchadnezzar attacked King Zedekiah of Judah. Nebuzar-adan carried the Israelite captives to Babylon. He brought some important prisoners to his king, who killed them. Before he left Israel, Nebuzaradan commanded the captain of the guard there not to harm the prophet Jeremiah, and Jeremiah was freed into Gedaliah's care.

First reference 2 Kgs 25:8
Last reference Jer 52:30
Key references 2 Kgs 25:8–12, 18–21; Jer 39:11–12

Nehemiah+ (5)

Sent at his own request, by the Persian king Artaxerxes, to rebuild Jerusalem, Nehemiah became the governor of Jerusalem. Under his rule, Jerusalem's walls were rebuilt.

First reference Neh 1:1
Last reference Neh 12:47

Ner (16)

Lamp

Grandfather of King Saul and father of Abner, Saul's army commander, who was called Abner son of Ner.

First reference 1 Sm 14:50
Last reference 1 Chr 26:28

Neriah [10]

Light of God

Father of Baruch, the scribe of the prophet Jeremiah.

First reference Jer 32:12
Last reference Jer 51:59

Nethaneel+ [5]

Given of God

Head of the tribe of Issachar during Israel's wandering after the people failed to enter the Promised Land.

First reference Nm 1:8
Last reference Nm 10:15

Nethaniah+ [16]

Given of God

The father of a man named Ishmael, who killed the Judean governor placed over the land by Babylonian king Nebuchadnezzar.

First reference 2 Kgs 25:23
Last reference Jer 41:18
Key reference Jer 41:1–2

Nicodemus [5]

Victorious among his people

A member of the Jewish Sanhedrin who came to Jesus by night to question Him about His miracles. Jesus told Nicodemus that he had to be born again. Nicodemus stood up for Jesus, when the Pharisees wanted to arrest Him, and provided the spices with which Jesus' body was wrapped after His death.

First reference Jn 3:1
Last reference Jn 19:39

Nimrod [4]

A descendant of Noah through his son Ham. Nimrod was "mighty upon the earth" (1 Chr 1:10), and he built the city of Nineveh.

First reference Gn 10:8
Last reference Mi 5:6

Nimshi (5)
Extricated

Father of King Jehu of Israel, whom God anointed to kill off the line of King Ahab of Israel.

First reference 1 Kgs 19:16
Last reference 2 Chr 22:7

Noah⁺ (47)
Rest

The man God chose to build an ark that would save both animals and people. God gave Noah specific building directions. When his boat-building project was finished, he and his family entered the ark and brought in seven of every clean animal and two of the unclean. God caused it to rain for forty days and nights until the world was flooded and everything else on earth was destroyed. For 150 days the ark floated, until the waters abated and the vessel rested on the mountains of Ararat. Noah tested the land by sending out a raven and then a dove. When the dove did not return, he knew that dry land had appeared. God commanded Noah and his family to leave the ark. They went out, and Noah made a sacrifice. Then God promised Noah and his sons that He would never curse the earth by flood again. Same as Noe.

First reference Gn 5:29
Last reference 2 Pt 2:5
Key references Gn 6:8–9,
  14–16; 7:2–5, 24; 8:6–12, 20;
  9:11–17

Noah*+ (4)

Rest

One of Zelophehad's five
daughters who received
his inheritance because he
had no sons. Each had to
marry within their tribe,
which was Manasseh.

First reference Nm 26:33
Last reference Jo 17:3

Noe (5)

Noah

Greek spelling of *Noah*,
used in the New Testament.

First reference Mt 24:37
Last reference Lk 17:27

Nun (29)

Perpetuity

A descendant of Abra-
ham through Joseph's son
Ephraim and father of the
Israelite leader Joshua.
Same as Non.

First reference Ex 33:11
Last reference Neh 8:17

N: Mentioned Once

Naam (1 Chr 4:15)

Naamah*+ (Gn 4:22)

Naaman+ (Gn 46:21)

Naaman+ (1 Chr 8:7)

Naarai (1 Chr 11:37)

Naashon (Ex 6:23)

Nachon (2 Sm 6:6)

Nachor+ (Jo 24:2)

Nachor+ (Lk 3:34)

Nagge (Lk 3:25)

Naham (1 Chr 4:19)

Nahamani (Neh 7:7)

Naharai (1 Chr 11:39)

Nahari (2 Sm 23:37)

Nahash+ (2 Sm 17:25)

Nahath+ (1 Chr 6:26)

Nahath+ (2 Chr 31:13)

Nahbi (Nm 13:14)

Nahum (Na 1:1)

Narcissus (Rom 16:11)

Nathan+ (2 Sm 23:36)

Nathan+ (1 Kgs 4:5)

Nathan+ (1 Kgs 4:5)

Nathan+ (1 Chr 2:36)

Nathan+ (1 Chr 11:38)

Nathan+ (Ezr 8:16)

Nathan+ (Ezr 10:39)

Nathan+ (Zec 12:12)

Nathan-melech (2 Kgs 23:11)

Naum (Lk 3:25)

Neariah+ (1 Chr 4:42)

Nebai (Neh 10:19)

Nebaioth (1 Chr 1:29)

Nebo (Ezr 10:43)

Nebushasban (Jer 39:13)

Nedabiah (1 Chr 3:18)

Nehemiah+ (Neh 3:16)

Nehum (Neh 7:7)

Nehushta* (2 Kgs 24:8)

Nemuel+ (Nm 26:9)

Nepheg+ (Ex 6:21)

Nephishesim (Neh 7:52)

Nephusim (Ezr 2:50)

Nereus (Rom 16:15)

Nergal-sharezer+ (Jer 39:3)

Neri (Lk 3:27)

Nethaneel+ (1 Chr 2:14)

Nethaneel+ (1 Chr 15:24)

Nethaneel+ (1 Chr 24:6)

Nethaneel+ (1 Chr 26:4)

Nethaneel+ (2 Chr 17:7)

Nethaneel+ (2 Chr 35:9)

Nethaneel+ (Ezr 10:22)

Nethaneel+ (Neh 12:21)

Nethaneel+ (Neh 12:36)

Nethaniah+ (2 Chr 17:8)

Nethaniah+ (Jer 36:14)

Nicanor (Acts 6:5)

Nicolas (Acts 6:5)

Niger (Acts 13:1)

Noadiah+ (Ezr 8:33)

Noadiah*+ (Neh 6:14)

Nohah (1 Chr 8:2)

Non (1 Chr 7:27)

Nymphas* (Col 4:15)

N: Mentioned Twice

Nadab+ (1 Chr 2:28)

Nadab+ (1 Chr 8:30)

Naphish (Gn 25:15)

Neariah+ (1 Chr 3:22)

Nehemiah+ (Ezr 2:2)

Nekoda+ (Ezr 2:48)

Nekoda+ (Ezr 2:60)

Nemuel+ (Nm 26:12)

Nergal-sharezer+ (Jer 39:3)

Nethaniah+ (1 Chr 25:2)

Neziah (Ezr 2:54)

Nobah (Nm 32:42)

Nogah (1 Chr 3:7)

N: Mentioned Three Times

Naamah*+ (1 Kgs 14:21)

Naaman+ (Nm 26:40)

Naarah* (1 Chr 4:5)

Naasson (Mt 1:4)

Nahath+ (Gn 36:13)

Nebajoth (Gn 25:13)

Necho (2 Chr 35:20)

Nepheg+ (2 Sm 5:15)

O

Obadiah+ (7)

Serving God

"Governor" of the house-
hold of King Ahab of Is-
rael and a man who feared
God. Obadiah hid one
hundred prophets in a
cave when Queen Jezebel
sought to kill them. Looking for water for Ahab's
cattle, he met Elijah, who
sent him to the king with
the news that he had re-
turned to Israel.

First reference I Kgs 18:3
Last reference I Kgs 18:16

Obed+ (7)

Serving

A descendant of Abraham
through Isaac; father of
Jesse and forebear of Jesus'
earthly father, Joseph.

First reference Ru 4:17
Last reference Lk 3:32

Obed-edom (17)

Worker of Edom

Owner of a house where
the ark of the covenant
was kept for three months
before David brought it to
Jerusalem. God blessed
Obed-edom's household
while it held the ark.

First reference 2 Sm 6:10
Last reference I Chr 15:25

Ocran (5)

Muddler

Father of Pagiel, a chief
of the tribe of Asher who
helped Moses take a cen-
sus of Israel.

First reference Nm 1:13
Last reference Nm 10:26

Og [22]

Round

The Amorite king of Bashan, whom Moses defeated after Israel failed to enter the Promised Land. Israel took sixty cities from Og. News of Og's destruction spread to Rahab and the Gibeonites, who feared Israel's power.

First reference Nm 21:33
Last reference Ps 136:20
Key references Dt 3:1–4;
   Jo 2:10; 9:10

Omri+ [15]

Heaping

Commander of Israel's army under King Elah. After Zimri killed Elah, the people made Omri king. Omri and his army besieged Zimri at Tirzah and took the city. Omri overcame those who supported Tibni for king. He did evil and made Israel sin.

First reference I Kgs 16:16
Last reference Mi 6:16
Key reference I Kgs 16:16–22

Onan [8]

Strong

Second son of Jacob's son Judah and his Canaanite wife. Onan refused to sire a son with his brother's widow, whom he had married, because the boy would be considered his brother's child. God put Onan to death for this.

First reference Gn 38:4
Last reference I Chr 2:3

Oreb [5]

Mosquito

A prince of Midian who was killed by the tribe of

Ephraim when Gideon called the tribe to fight that nation.

First reference Jgs 7:25
Last reference Ps 83:11

Ornan [12]
Strong

The owner of a threshing floor where King David saw the angel of the Lord after he had sinned by taking a census. The angel commanded David to build an altar there, so David tried to buy the land from Ornan. Ornan refused his money, but David insisted and paid him 600 shekels for the land. Same as Araunah.

First reference 1 Chr 21:15
Last reference 2 Chr 3:1

Othniel [6]
Force of God

Caleb's brother, who by capturing Kirjath-sepher won the hand of Caleb's daughter, Achsah, in marriage. Othniel delivered Israel from the king of Mesopotamia and judged Israel for forty years.

First reference Jo 15:17
Last reference 1 Chr 4:13

O: Mentioned Once

Obadiah+ (1 Chr 3:2)

Obadiah+ (1 Chr 7:3)

Obadiah+ (1 Chr 9:16)

Obadiah+ (1 Chr 12:9)

Obadiah+ (1 Chr 27:19)

Obadiah+ (2 Chr 17:7)

Obadiah+ (2 Chr 34:12)

Obadiah+ (Ezr 8:9)

Obadiah+ (Neh 10:5)

Obadiah+ (Neh 12:25)

Obadiah+ (Ob 1:1)

Obal (Gn 10:28)

Obed+ (1 Chr 11:47)

Obed+ (1 Chr 26:7)

Obed+ (2 Chr 23:1)

Obed-edom+ (2 Chr 25:24)

Obil (1 Chr 27:30)

Oded+ (2 Chr 28:9)

Ohel (1 Chr 3:20)

Olympas (Rom 16:15)

Omri+ (1 Chr 7:8)

Omri+ (1 Chr 9:4)

Omri+ (1 Chr 27:18)

On (Nm 16:1)

Ophrah (1 Chr 4:14)

Oren (1 Chr 2:25)

Osee (Rom 9:25)

Othni (1 Chr 26:7)

Ozem+ (1 Chr 2:15)

Ozem+ (1 Chr 2:25)

Ozni (Nm 26:16)

O: Mentioned Twice

Obadiah⁺ (1 Chr 8:38)

Obed⁺ (1 Chr 2:37)

Obed-edom⁺ (1 Chr 15:18)

Oded⁺ (2 Chr 15:1)

Ohad (Gn 46:10)

Onam⁺ (Gn 36:23)

Onam⁺ (1 Chr 2:26)

Onesimus (Col 4:9)

Onesiphorus (2 Tm 1:16)

Ophir (Gn 10:29)

Orpah (Ru 1:4)

Oshea (Nm 13:8)

Ozias (Mt 1:8)

O: Mentioned Three Times

Omar (Gn 36:11)

P

Pagiel (5)
Accident of God

A chief of the tribe of Asher who helped Moses take a census of Israel.

First reference Nm 1:13
Last reference Nm 10:26

Pahath-moab + (4)
Pit of Moab

Father of a man who repaired Jerusalem's walls under Nehemiah. Some of his descendants married "strange" (foreign) women.

First reference Ezr 2:6
Last reference Neh 7:11

Pallu (4)
Distinguished

A descendant of Abraham through Jacob's son Reuben.

First reference Ex 6:14
Last reference 1 Chr 5:3

Pashur+ (5)
Liberation

Forefather of a priest who resettled Jerusalem after the Babylonian Exile.

First reference 1 Chr 9:12
Last reference Neh 11:12

Pashur+ (6)
Liberation

A priest and "chief governor" of the temple who responded to Jeremiah's prophecies by hitting him and putting him in the stocks near the temple.

When Pashur removed him from the stocks, the prophet gave him a new name, Magor-missabib, meaning "afright from around," because he would become a terror to himself and others as God gave Judah over to Babylon.

First reference Jer 20:1
Last reference Jer 38:1

Paul

Little

Latin form of the name *Saul*. God's chosen apostle to the Gentiles, Paul zealously persecuted Christians until he became one himself as he traveled to Damascus and was confronted by Jesus. Scripture begins calling him Paul when he and Barnabas set out on Paul's first missionary journey, to Galatia. The two men disagreed over bringing John Mark on a second missionary venture and split up. Paul brought Silas and Timothy on his next journey and later added Luke to the group. After Paul received a vision, they traveled to Macedonia. The apostle and his disciples made two more missionary journeys to the churches of Asia and Greece. He communicated with the churches through his epistles to the Romans, Corinthians, Galatians, Colossians, and Thessalonians and a letter to Titus. These form part of his contribution to the New Testament. Constrained by the Spirit, Paul went to Jerusalem. In the temple he was rescued from a riot by the Roman tribune, who arrested him. Following a plot to kill him, Paul was sent to Caesarea, where he stayed two years while Felix delayed making a decision on his case. Paul appealed to Caesar but on his way to Rome was shipwrecked. He finally arrived in Rome, where he lived for two years. He may have been released but then rearrested. During his time in prison, he wrote additional epistles that became scripture: Ephesians, probably Philippians, the letters to Timothy, and Philemon. Church tradition records that the emperor Nero martyred Paul. Same as Saul (Acts 7:58).

First reference Acts 13:9
Last reference 2 Pt 3:15
Key references Acts 15:1–21; 17:22–33; 21:27–35; 25:8; 28:30–31

Pedahzur (5)
A rock [God] has ransomed

Father of a chief of the tribe of Benjamin who helped Moses take a census.

First reference Nm 1:10
Last reference Nm 10:23

Pekah (11)
Watch

Captain of King Pekahiah of Israel, Pekah conspired against his king, killed him, and usurped his throne. Pekah was an evil king. The Assyrian king Tiglath-Pileser conquered portions of Israel during Pekah's reign.

First reference 2 Kgs 15:25
Last reference Is 7:1

Peleg (7)

Earthquake

A descendant of Noah through his son Ham. Same as Phalec.

First reference Gn 10:25
Last reference 1 Chr 1:25

Peter (162)

A piece of rock

Jesus' disciple, also called Simon Peter and Simon Bar-Jonah, who was called from his fishing, along with his brother Andrew, to become a fisher of men. The brothers were among Jesus' most intimate disciples. Peter walked on water to meet Jesus after the feeding of the five thousand. He was the first to call Jesus "the Christ." With James and John, he witnessed the transfiguration of Jesus. In the Garden of Gethsemane, Peter fell asleep while Jesus prayed. As Jesus was arrested, Peter cut off the ear of the high priest's servant. While Jesus stood before Caiaphas in an illegal trial, three times Peter denied being His disciple. After the resurrection of Jesus, Peter and John checked the empty tomb. Later Jesus confronted Peter about his love for Him and reconfirmed his ministry. Following the giving of the Great Commission, Peter spoke out boldly in his Pentecost sermon. He healed the lame beggar at the temple gate and refused to stop preaching when the Jewish council arrested him. He had a vision about the acceptance of Gentile believers in the church but later failed to support them. He wrote the books of 1 and 2 Peter. Same as Cephas.

First reference Mt 4:18
Last reference 2 Pt 1:1
Key references Mt 14:28–33;
   16:16; 17:1–8; Jn 18:10;
   20:1–7; 21:15–19; Acts
   2:14–41; 3:1–8; 4:13–20;
   10:1–11:18

Pharaoh-nechoh [4]

The king of Egypt who fought Assyria and King Josiah of Judah. Josiah was killed, and Pharaoh-nechoh made Jehoiakim king in his place. Same as Pharaohnecho.

First reference 2 Kgs 23:29
Last reference 2 Kgs 23:35

Pharez [12]

A grandson of Jacob, born to Jacob's son Judah and Judah's daughter-in-law Tamar. Same as Phares and Perez.

First reference Gn 38:29
Last reference 1 Chr 9:4

Philip+ [16]

Fond of horses

A disciple of Jesus who introduced the soon-to-be-disciple Nathanael to Him. Jesus asked Philip where they could buy bread to feed the five thousand, and Philip was at a loss. In Jerusalem, some Greeks who wanted to see Jesus came to Philip for an introduction. When Jesus told the disciples, "If ye had known me, ye should have known my Father also" (Jn 14:7), Philip wanted Him to show them the Father.

First reference Mt 10:3
Last reference Acts 1:13
Key references Jn 1:43–48;
   6:5–7; 12:21–22; 14:8–9

Philip⁺ (17)

Fond of horses

One of seven men, "full of the Holy Ghost and wisdom," selected to serve needy Christians in Jerusalem while the twelve disciples devoted themselves "to prayer, and to the ministry of the word" (Acts 6:3–4). Philip preached to the Ethiopian eunuch and baptized him. Also called Philip the evangelist.

First reference Acts 6:5
Last reference Acts 21:8
Key references Acts 8:5–8, 26–39

Phinehas⁺ (17)

Mouth of a serpent

Son of the high priest Eleazar and grandson of Aaron. He killed Zimri (Nm 25:14), who brought a Midianite woman before Moses while God was judging those who had fallen into idolatry. Because of Phinehas's act, God turned His wrath from Israel.

First reference Ex 6:25
Last reference Ps 106:30
Key reference Nm 25:6–9

Phinehas⁺ (6)

Mouth of a serpent

Son of the high priest Eli, who honored Phinehas and his brother, Hophni, more than the Lord. The brothers did not know the Lord, misused their priestly office, and disobeyed the law. A man of God prophesied that they would die in the same day. When the Philistines attacked and took the ark of the covenant, both were killed.

First reference I Sm 1:3
Last reference I Sm 14:3

Pilate (56)

Close pressed

Procurator (governor) of Judea before whom Jesus appeared after His trial before the Jewish religious authorities. When Pilate heard Jesus was a Galilean, he sent Jesus to Herod, who had his soldiers mock Him and return Him to Pilate. Pilate questioned Jesus briefly and understood He was innocent. Though Pilate knew envy had spurred the Jewish leaders to condemn Jesus, fearing these leaders, he gave the crowd a choice of prisoners to be released: Jesus or Barabbas. His wife warned him against condemning Jesus, but Pilate still gave Him over to be crucified. Same as Pontius Pilate.

First reference Mt 27:2
Last reference I Tm 6:13
Key references Mt 27:11–26;
  Lk 23:6–11; Jn 18:29–19:15

Pontius Pilate (4)

Pontius, "bridged"; Pilate, "close pressed"

Pilate's family name and first name. Same as Pilate.

First reference Mt 27:2
Last reference I Tm 6:13

Priscilla (5)

Wife of Aquila. This tent-making couple worked with the apostle Paul in their craft and in spreading the gospel. They founded a house church in their home. Same as Prisca.

First reference Acts 18:2
Last reference I Cor 16:19

P: Mentioned Once

Paarai (2 Sm 23:35)

Pahath-moab + (Ezr 8:4)

Pahath-moab + (Neh 10:14)

Palal (Neh 3:25)

Palti (Nm 13:9)

Paltiel (Nm 34:26)

Parmashta (Est 9:9)

Parmenas (Acts 6:5)

Parnach (Nm 34:25)

Parosh+ (Ezr 10:25)

Parosh+ (Neh 3:25)

Parosh+ (Neh 10:14)

Parshan-datha (Est 9:7)

Paruah (1 Kgs 4:17)

Pasach (1 Chr 7:33)

Paseah+ (1 Chr 4:12)

Paseah+ (Ezr 2:49)

Paseah+ (Neh 3:6)

Pashur+ (Neh 10:3)

Patrobas (Rom 16:14)

Paulus (Acts 13:7)

Pedahel (Nm 34:28)

Pedaiah+ (2 Kgs 23:36)

Pedaiah+ (1 Chr 27:20)

Pedaiah+ (Neh 3:25)

Pedaiah+ (Neh 11:7)

Pelaiah+ (1 Chr 3:24)

Pelaiah+ (Neh 8:7)

Pelaiah+ (Neh 10:10)

Pelaliah (Neh 11:12)

Pelatiah+ (1 Chr 3:21)

Pelatiah+ (1 Chr 4:42)

Pelatiah+ (Neh 10:22)

Pelet+ (1 Chr 2:47)

Pelet+ (1 Chr 12:3)

Penuel+ (1 Chr 4:4)

Penuel+ (1 Chr 8:25)

Peresh (1 Chr 7:16)

Perez+ (1 Chr 27:3)

Perida (Neh 7:57)

Persis (Rom 16:12)

Peruda (Ezr 2:55)

Pethahiah+ (1 Chr 24:16)

Pethahiah+ (Ezr 10:23)

Pethahiah+ (Neh 9:5)

Pethahiah+ (Neh 11:24)

Pethuel (Jl 1:1)

Peulthai (1 Chr 26:5)

Phalec (Lk 3:35)

Phallu (Gn 46:9)

Phalti (1 Sm 25:44)

Phaltiel (2 Sm 3:15)

Phanuel (Lk 2:36)

Pharaoh-hophra (Jer 44:30)

Pharaoh-necho (Jer 46:2)

Pharosh (Ezr 8:3)

Phaseah (Neh 7:51)

Phebe (Rom 16:1)

Philemon (Phlm 1:1)

Philetus (2 Tm 2:17)

Philip+ (Lk 3:1)

Philologus (Rom 16:15)

Phinehas+ (Ezr 8:33)

Phlegon (Rom 16:14)

Phuvah (Gn 46:13)

Phygellus (2 Tm 1:15)

Pildash (Gn 22:22)

Pileha (Neh 10:24)

Piltai (Neh 12:17)

Piram (Jo 10:3)

Pispah (1 Chr 7:38)

Poratha (Est 9:8)

Porcius Festus (Acts 24:27)

Prisca (2 Tm 4:19)

Prochorus (Acts 6:5)

Pua (Nm 26:23)

Puah+ (Ex 1:15)

Puah+ (Jgs 10:1)

Puah+ (1 Chr 7:1)

Pudens (2 Tm 4:21)

Put (1 Chr 1:8)

Putiel (Ex 6:25)

P: Mentioned Twice

Padon (Ezr 2:44)

Parosh+ (Ezr 2:3)

Pashur+ (Jer 21:1)

Pedaiah+ (1 Chr 3:18)

Pedaiah+ (Neh 8:4)

Pelatiah+ (Ez 11:1)

Peleth (Nm 16:1)

Perez+ (Neh 11:4)

Phurah (Jgs 7:10)

Phut (Gn 10:6)

Pinon (Gn 36:41)

Pithon (1 Chr 8:35)

Pochereth (Ezr 2:57)

Potiphar (Gn 37:36)

Publius (Acts 28:7)

P: Mentioned Three Times

Pekahiah (2 Kgs 15:22)

Peninnah (1 Sm 1:2)

Phares (Mt 1:3)

Phichol (Gn 21:22)

Potipherah (Gn 41:45)

Pul (2 Kgs 15:19)

Q

Mentioned Once
Quartus (Rom 16:23)

R

Raamah (4)
Mane

A descendant of Noah through his son Ham.

First reference Gn 10:7
Last reference 1 Chr 1:9

Rab-shakeh (16)
Chief butler

An Assyrian field commander sent by King Sennacherib to attack King Hezekiah at Jerusalem. He attempted to get Hezekiah and his people to surrender to Assyria and fight with that nation. Same as Rabshakeh.

First reference 2 Kgs 18:17
Last reference 2 Kgs 19:8

Rabshakeh (16)

Chief butler

A variant spelling of the name of the Assyrian military commander Rab-shakeh.

First reference Is 36:2
Last reference Is 37:8

Rachel* (47)

Ewe

Daughter of Laban and wife of Jacob. When Jacob came to Haran, he fell in love with the beautiful Rachel. He agreed to work for Laban for seven years to win her. But when it was time for the marriage, Laban fooled him by putting her sister, Leah, in Rachel's place. Jacob agreed to work seven more years to gain Rachel and received her as his bride. While Leah had children, Rachel remained barren, so Rachel gave her maid, Bilhah, to Jacob, to bear children for her. Finally God enabled Rachel to conceive, and she bore Joseph. Jacob decided to move his family back to his own homeland. When Laban discovered they had left secretly, he followed, partly in search of the idols Rachel had stolen and partly to make sure all would be well with his daughters. When they planned to meet Jacob's brother, Esau, whom he had wronged, Jacob put Rachel in the safest part of the caravan. As they traveled to Ephrath (Bethlehem), Rachel gave birth to her second son, whom she called Ben-oni, but Jacob renamed him Benjamin. Rachel died following this difficult childbirth and was buried there. Same as Rahel.

First reference Gn 29:6
Last reference Mt 2:18
Key references Gn 29:16–30;
    30:1–8; 31:34; 33:2;
    35:16–19

Rahab* (7)
Proud

A prostitute of Jericho who hid the two spies whom Joshua sent to look over the city before Israel attacked it. When the king of Jericho was warned of their presence, Rahab hid the men on her roof and informed the king they had left. Rahab told the spies that she feared Israel and asked them to be kind to her family. The men promised she and her family would be spared if she hung a scarlet cord

from her window when Israel attacked. When Jericho fell to Joshua's troops, he kept the spies' promise. Same as Rachab.

First reference Jo 2:1
Last reference Jas 2:25

Ram (4)
High

Forefather of Boaz, Jesse, and David.

First reference Ru 4:19
Last reference I Chr 2:10

Rebekah* (30)
Fettering by beauty

When Abraham's servant came to Nahor, seeking a wife for Abraham's son Isaac, Rebekah watered his camels, proving she was God's choice as the bride. She agreed to marry Isaac and traveled to her new home, where Isaac loved and married her. At first barren, when Rebekah conceived, she had the twins Esau and Jacob. Because she loved her second son best, she conspired with Jacob to get him the eldest son's blessing from his father. When Esau discovered what Jacob had done, he became so angry that Rebekah arranged for Jacob to leave before his brother killed him. Same as Rebecca.

First reference Gn 22:23
Last reference Gn 49:31
Key references Gn 24:15–25, 62–67; 25:21–26; 27:5–10, 41–46

Rechab (4)
Rider

A leader of one of the raiding bands controlled by Saul's son Ish-bosheth. Rechab and his brother, Baanah, killed Ish-bosheth. In turn, David had the brothers killed.

First reference 2 Sm 4:2
Last reference 2 Sm 4:9

Rechab (8)
Rider

Father of Jonadab, who commanded his descendants not to drink wine.

First reference 2 Kgs 10:15
Last reference Jer 35:19

Rehabiah (5)

God has enlarged

A descendant of Abraham through Jacob's son Levi, through the line of Moses.

First reference I Chr 23:17
Last reference I Chr 26:25

Rehoboam (50)

A people has enlarged

A son of King Solomon, Rehoboam inherited the kingdom of Israel. But his proud attitude toward his subjects' request for lower taxes made Israel rebel against him and set up Jeroboam as their king. When Rehoboam wanted to fight Jeroboam, God spoke through the prophet Shemiah and ordered Rehoboam not to. Only the southern kingdom of Judah remained under Rehoboam's rule, and he built up its defenses. The priests and Levites sided with Rehoboam, even moving into Judah, because Jeroboam had set up idols in his nation and rejected God's spiritual leaders. But once Rehoboam had established his power, "he forsook the law of the Lord, and all Israel with him" (2 Chr 12:1). In the fifth year of Rehoboam's reign, Shishak, king of Egypt, attacked Jerusalem. When Shemiah told Judah that God had abandoned their nation because it had abandoned Him, its leaders repented. But God did not free them from Shishak's rule, and he looted all the temple treasures. Yet Rehoboam was not destroyed and Judah became somewhat prosperous. Same as Roboam.

First reference 1 Kgs 11:43
Last reference 2 Chr 13:7
Key references 1 Kgs 12:1–24;
    14:25–28; 2 Chr 11:5–14;
    12:1–12

Rehum⁺ (4)

An officer of the Persian king Artaxerxes who joined in opposition to Zerubbabel's rebuilding of the temple in Jerusalem. Rehum wrote a letter to the king calling Jerusalem "a rebellious city" (Ezr 4:15) and causing Artaxerxes to suspend the work.

First reference Ezr 4:8
Last reference Ezr 4:23

Remaliah (11)
God has bedecked

Father of King Pekah of Israel.

First reference 2 Kgs 15:25
Last reference Is 8:6

Reu (5)
Friend

A descendant of Noah through his son Shem. Same as Ragau.

First reference Gn 11:18
Last reference 1 Chr 1:25

Reuben (26)
See ye a son

Jacob and Leah's first son. Reuben slept with his father's concubine Bilhah, and Jacob heard of it. When his brothers wanted to kill Joseph, Reuben balked at it. He was sorrowful when he learned his brothers had sold Joseph as a slave, since he had hoped to return him to their father. When Joseph commanded them to bring Benjamin to Egypt in order to buy food, Reuben offered his sons as hostages to his father. When Jacob blessed his sons, he did not forget Reuben's sin with Bilhah and prophesied that because he was unstable, Reuben would not excel.

First reference Gn 29:32
Last reference 1 Chr 5:3
Key references Gn 37:21–22, 29; 49:3–4

Reuel (7)
Friend of God

A son of Esau.

First reference Gn 36:4
Last reference 1 Chr 1:37

Rezin⁺ (8)
Delight

A king of Syria who attacked Judah during the reigns of kings Jotham and Ahaz. Rezin was killed in battle with King Tiglethpileser's troops after Ahaz asked the Assyrian king to come to his aid.

First reference 2 Kgs 15:37
Last reference Is 9:11

Rizpah* (4)
Hot stone

A concubine of Saul who, after the king's death, was reportedly romanced by Saul's military commander, Abner. When Saul's son Ish-bosheth, king of ten of Israel's tribes, confronted Abner about the liaison with Rizpah, the commander switched his allegiance to David, king of the tribe of Judah. Later, when David ruled all Israel, he allowed men of Gibeon to kill two of Rizpah's sons by Saul in retaliation for an atrocity Saul had committed. The grieving Rizpah spent days outdoors protecting the bodies of her sons from birds and wild animals.

First reference 2 Sm 3:7
Last reference 2 Sm 21:11

Ruth* (13)

Friend

The Moabite daughter-in-law of Naomi, Ruth married Naomi's son Mahlon while the family lived in Moab during a famine. When Ruth's husband, brother-in-law, and father-in-law died, Naomi decided to move back to Bethlehem. Though her daughter-in-law Orpah went back to her family, Ruth refused to leave Naomi. Together they went to Bethlehem, and there Ruth gleaned the barley harvest to provide food for them. Boaz became aware of Ruth and became kinsman-redeemer for her and Naomi. Ruth married Boaz and had a son, Obed, who was considered Naomi's grandson.

First reference Ru 1:4
Last reference Mt 1:5
Key references Ru 1:14–19;
   4:1–10, 13–14

R: Mentioned Once

Raamiah (Neh 7:7)

Rabsaris+ (2 Kgs 18:17)

Rachab* (Mt 1:5)

Raddai (1 Chr 2:14)

Ragau (Lk 3:35)

Raguel (Nm 10:29)

Raham (1 Chr 2:44)

Rahel* (Jer 31:15)

Rakem (1 Chr 7:16)

Ram (Jb 32:2)

Ramiah (Ezr 10:25)

Ramoth (Ezr 10:29)

Rapha+ (1 Chr 8:2)

Rapha+ (1 Chr 8:37)

Raphu (Nm 13:9)

Reaia (1 Chr 5:5)

Reaiah+ (1 Chr 4:2)

Rebecca* (Rom 9:10)

Rechab (Neh 3:14)

Reelaiah (Ezr 2:2)

Regem (1 Chr 2:47)

Regem-melech (Zec 7:2)

Rehob+ (Neh 10:11)

Rehum+ (Neh 3:17)

Rehum+ (Neh 10:25)

Rei (1 Kgs 1:8)

Rephael (1 Chr 26:7)

Rephah (1 Chr 7:25)

Rephaiah+ (1 Chr 3:21)

Rephaiah+ (1 Chr 4:42)

Rephaiah+ (1 Chr 7:2)

Rephaiah+ (1 Chr 9:43)

Rephaiah+ (Neh 3:9)

Resheph (1 Chr 7:25)

Reuel+ (Ex 2:18)

Reuel+ (Nm 2:14)

Reuel+ (1 Chr 9:8)

Reumah* (Gn 22:24)

Rezia (1 Chr 7:39)

Rezon (1 Kgs 11:23)

Rhesa (Lk 3:27)

Rhoda* (Acts 12:13)

Rinnah (1 Chr 4:20)

Roboam (Mt 1:7)

Rohgah (1 Chr 7:34)

Rosh (Gn 46:21)

Rufus+ (Mk 15:21)

Rufus+ (Rom 16:13)

R: Mentioned Twice

Rabmag (Jer 39:3)

Rabsaris⁺ (Jer 39:3)

Ram (1 Chr 2:25)

Reaiah⁺ (Ezr 2:47)

Reba (Nm 31:8)

Rehob⁺ (2 Sm 8:3)

Rehum⁺ (Ezr 2:2)

Rekem⁺ (Nm 31:8)

Rekem⁺ (1 Chr 2:43)

Rezin⁺ (Ezr 2:48)

Ribai (2 Sm 23:29)

Riphath (Gn 10:3)

Romamti-ezer (1 Chr 25:4)

R: Mentioned Three Times

Rimmon (2 Sm 4:2)

S

Salah [6]

Spear

A descendant of Noah through his son Shem. Same as Sala.

First reference Gn 10:24
Last reference Gn 11:15

Salathiel [4]

I have asked God

A descendant of Abraham through Jacob's son Judah, in the line of the nation of Judah's second-to-last king, Jeconiah (also known as Jehoiachin).

First reference 1 Chr 3:17
Last reference Lk 3:27

Salma [4]

Clothing

Father of Boaz and a descendant of Abraham through Jacob's son Judah. He is called "the father of Bethlehem" (1 Chr 2:51). Same as Salmon.

First reference 1 Chr 2:11
Last reference 1 Chr 2:54

Salmon [5]

Clothing

Father of Boaz, who was Ruth's second husband, and a forefather of Jesus. Same as Salma.

First reference Ru 4:20
Last reference Lk 3:32

Samlah (4)

Dress

A king of Edom, "before there reigned any king over the children of Israel" (Gn 36:31).

First reference Gn 36:36
Last reference I Chr 1:48

Samson (39)

Sunlight

The twelfth judge of Israel, from the time of his conception Samson was supposed to follow a Nazarite vow, which meant he could not eat or drink anything from a grapevine, drink alcohol, cut his hair, or eat anything unclean. Samson performed amazing feats of strength. When he married, Samson chose a Philistine woman. God used the union to confront the Philistines, who ruled over Israel. Betrayed by his wife, Samson took out his anger on her people, burning their grain and performing more feats of strength. When he fell in love with Delilah, her fellow Philistines offered her money to find out the source of Samson's strength. Though Samson lied to her several times, he finally admitted that if she shaved his head, he would become weak. She did this, and he lost his strength because God had left him. The Philistines captured Samson, blinded him, and made him a slave. But as his hair grew, his strength returned. Brought to the Philistine temple to perform during their pagan celebration, Samson leaned on the pillars of the temple and brought it down, killing the worshippers and himself.

First reference Jgs 13:24
Last reference Heb 11:32
Key references Jgs 13:13; 14:4;
  16:4–30

Samuel (142)

Heard of God

Prophet and judge of Israel. Samuel was born after his mother, Hannah, petitioned God to give her a child and promised to give him up to God's service in return. After Samuel was weaned, Hannah brought him to the priest Eli to live at the temple and serve the Lord. One night Eli realized that God had spoken to Samuel and encouraged the boy to listen and respond. In his first prophecy, Samuel spoke out against the wickedness of Eli's sons. Samuel led the Israelites to repent of their idolatry, and he judged Israel during his entire life. But when he became old, his sons were not faithful, and the people of Israel asked for a king. Though Samuel warned them against it, Israel insisted on a king, so God had the prophet anoint Saul. Samuel turned his authority over to Saul and encouraged the people to obey him, though their choice of Saul as a leader was evil. When Saul disobeyed God, attacking the Amalekites but not destroying them and their cattle, Samuel informed Saul that God had rejected him as king. Samuel anointed David king in Saul's place. The prophet died and was buried in his home at Ramah. Same as Shemuel.

First reference 1 Sm 1:20
Last reference Heb 11:32
Key references 1 Sm 1:11,

19–20, 24–28; 3:1–18;
7:3–6, 15–17; 10:1, 20–25;
12:1–25; 15:26; 16:13

Sanballat (10)

One of Nehemiah's oppo-
nents as he rebuilt Jeru-
salem, Sanballat plotted
to fight against Jerusalem,
forcing the Israelites to
guard the uncompleted
walls. Sanballat then ac-
cused Nehemiah of fo-
menting a revolt. When
that came to nothing, he
hired a man to report that
men were coming to kill
Nehemiah.

First reference Neh 2:10
Last reference Neh 13:28

Sarah*+ (40)

Female noble

The name God gave Sarai,
wife of Abram (Abraham),
after He promised she
would bear a child. When
she was ninety years old,
God repeated the promise
to give Abraham a son by
her. Sarah heard this and
laughed. A year later she
bore Isaac. When Abra-
ham's son Ishmael—child
of Sarah's maid, Hagar—
mocked Isaac, Sarah feared
for her own son and had
Hagar and Ishmael sent
out of Abraham's camp.
When Sarah died, Abra-
ham bought land from the
Hittites and buried her in
the cave of Machpelah.

First reference Gn 17:15
Last reference Rom 9:9
Key references Gn 18:10–15;
    21:1–10; 23:1–20

Sarai* (17)

Controlling

The barren wife of Abram, Sarai traveled with her husband to Canaan at God's calling. Following a famine, they moved to Egypt, where Abram called her his sister, because he feared he would be killed so that an Egyptian could have her. She was taken by Pharaoh, but God revealed her marriage to him, and he returned her to Abram, sending them away. When Sarai had no children, she gave her maid, Hagar, to Abram to bear children for her. But Hagar despised Sarai and fled. God kept His promise to Abraham that He would give Sarai a son who would be the father of a multitude. He changed her name to Sarah. Same as Sarah.

First reference Gn 11:29
Last reference Gn 17:15
Key references Gn 12:5,
    10–20; 16:1–10; 17:15

Saul+ (367)

Asked

Anointed king of Israel by the prophet Samuel, Saul fought the Philistines throughout his reign. But after the king wrongly made a burnt offering to God at Michmash, Samuel told Saul that because of his sin, his kingdom would not be established forever, and God would seek a man after his own heart. When God ordered Saul to fight the Amalekites and kill all the people and cattle, Saul did not kill their king or cattle. God rejected him as Israel's king, and Samuel

anointed David king. Af-
ter David killed the giant
Goliath, Saul brought him
into his court. Though his
son Jonathan loved David,
Saul became increasingly
jealous of the young man
and sought to kill him.
Eventually David fled the
court and began a series
of battles with Saul. When
Saul gathered an army to
fend off the Philistines,
fearful, he sought out a
witch at Endor. The king
asked her to call up the
dead Samuel, from whom
he received a disconcert-
ing answer. When Saul
went into battle, three of
his sons were killed, and
he seemed to be losing.
Saul's armor bearer re-
fused to kill him, so Saul
fell on his own sword.

First reference 1 Sm 9:2
Last reference Acts 13:21
Key references 1 Sm 10:1,

17–24; 13:8–14; 15:1–3,
8–14, 35; 18:1–2, 5–11;
28:7–19; 31:1–4

Saul⁺ (22)

Asked

A zealous Jew who wit-
nessed the martyrdom of
Stephen and persecuted
Christians. As Saul traveled
to Damascus, planning to
imprison Christians there,
Jesus met him and tem-
porarily blinded him. At
Damascus, God sent Ana-
nias (Acts 9:10) to restore
his sight. After becom-
ing a Christian and be-
ing baptized, Saul began
to preach the message of
Christ in the synagogues.
Learning of a conspiracy to
kill him, he left Damascus
and returned to Jerusalem.
Only Barnabas's testimony
about his preaching made
the disciples believe that

he was not plotting against them. Saul was chosen by the Holy Spirit for a missionary journey. At that time scripture begins to call him Paul. Same as Paul.

First reference Acts 7:58
Last reference Acts 26:14
Key references Acts 8:1, 3;
   9:1–20, 23–27; 13:1–3, 9

Sennacherib (13)

The king of Assyria who attacked and captured Judah's fortified cities during King Hezekiah's reign. Hezekiah paid him tribute to withdraw, but Sennacherib sent his commanders to threaten Jerusalem's people and force them to capitulate. Because the commanders spoke against the Lord, the angel of death killed 185,000 Assyrian soldiers, and Sennacherib withdrew to Nineveh.

First reference 2 Kgs 18:13
Last reference Is 37:37
Key references 2 Chr 32:1,
   9–19; Is 37:36–37

Seraiah+ (5)
God has prevailed

The high priest during King Zedekiah's reign. Seraiah was killed following Nebuchadnezzar's invasion of Jerusalem.

First reference 2 Kgs 25:18
Last reference Jer 52:24

Seraiah+ (4)

A priest who renewed the covenant under Nehemiah.

First reference Ezr 2:2
Last reference Neh 12:12

Serug (5)

Tendril

A descendant of Noah through his son Shem. Serug was the great-grandfather of Abraham. He lived 230 years.

First reference Gn 11:20
Last reference 1 Chr 1:26

Seth (8)

Substituted

Adam and Eve's third son, whom Eve bore after Abel was killed by his brother, Cain. He became a fore-father of Jesus. Same as Sheth (1 Chr 1:1).

First reference Gn 4:25
Last reference Lk 3:38
Key reference Gn 4:25–26

Shadrach

The Babylonian name for Hananiah, one of Daniel's companions in exile. Daniel had King Nebuchadnez-zar make Shadrach a ruler in Babylon. When Chaldeans accused Shadrach and his fellow Jews, Meshach and Abed-nego, of not worshipping the king's golden idol, the three faithful men were thrown into a furnace. God protected them, and they were not even singed. Recognizing the power of their God, the king promoted them in his service.

First reference Dn 1:7
Last reference Dn 3:30
Key reference Dn 3:16–18

Shallum⁺ (4)

Retribution

The fifth-to-last king of the northern kingdom of Israel. Shallum obtained the throne by assassinating King Zechariah. Shallum was himself assassinated only one month later.

First reference 2 Kgs 15:10
Last reference 2 Kgs 15:15

Shallum⁺ (6)

A Jewish exile from the tribe of Levi who resettled Jerusalem.

First reference 1 Chr 9:17
Last reference Neh 7:45

Shaphan⁺ (18)

Rock-rabbit

Scribe for King Josiah of Judah, Shaphan brought the high priest Hilkiah the money the Levites collected to refurbish the temple. The priest reported that he had found the book of the law in the temple. Following the king's orders, Shaphan consulted with Huldah the prophetess.

First reference 2 Kgs 22:3
Last reference Jer 36:12

Shaphan⁺ (10)

Rock-rabbit

Father of Ahikam, who consulted the prophetess Huldah at King Josiah's command.

First reference 2 Kgs 22:12
Last reference Jer 43:6

Shaphat+ [4]

Judge

Father of the prophet Elisha.

First reference I Kgs 19:16
Last reference 2 Kgs 6:31

Shaul+ [4]

Asked

A descendant of Abraham through Jacob's son Simeon. Shaul was born to Simeon and a "Canaanitish" woman.

First reference Gn 46:10
Last reference I Chr 4:24

Shealtiel [9]

I have asked God

Father of Zerubbabel, governor of Judah after the Babylonian Exile.

First reference Ezr 3:2
Last reference Hg 2:23

Sheba+ [8]

An Israelite who rebelled against King David.

First reference 2 Sm 20:1
Last reference 2 Sm 20:22

Shebna+ [8]

Growth

Scribe for King Hezekiah of Judah, Shebna represented Hezekiah and spoke to King Sennacherib's representative, Rabshakeh, when the Assyrians attacked Jerusalem. Afterward, Shebna took a message to the prophet Isaiah.

First reference 2 Kgs 18:18
Last reference Is 37:2

Shechem (14)

Neck

Prince of the city of Shechem who raped Jacob's daughter, Dinah, then wanted to marry her. Dinah's brothers insisted that all males in Shechem be circumcised. While the men recovered, Simeon and Levi attacked the city; killed Shechem, his father, and all the males of the city; and brought Dinah home.

First reference Gn 34:2
Last reference Jgs 9:28
Key references Gn 34:2–7, 11–12, 25–26

Shedeur (5)

Spreader of light

Forefather of a prince of the tribe of Reuben who helped Moses take a census.

First reference Nm 1:5
Last reference Nm 10:18

Shelah⁺ (8)

Request

Son of Jacob's son Judah. Judah refused to marry Shelah to Tamar, the widow of his first two sons.

First reference Gn 38:5
Last reference 1 Chr 4:21

Shelumiel (5)

Peace of God

A man of the tribe of Simeon who helped Aaron take a census.

First reference Nm 1:6
Last reference Nm 10:19

Shem (17)

Name

The eldest son of Noah, Shem joined Noah in the ark. After leaving the ark, Noah became drunk and lay unclothed in his tent. With his brother Japheth, Shem covered their father without looking at him. For this Noah blessed Shem. Same as Sem.

First reference Gn 5:32
Last reference 1 Chr 1:24
Key references Gn 7:13; 9:18, 24–26

Shemaiah⁺ (5)

God has heard

A prophet who told King Rehoboam not to fight Israel when it revolted against him.

First reference 1 Kgs 12:22
Last reference 2 Chr 12:15

Shemaiah⁺ (5)

God has heard

A priest who renewed the covenant under Nehemiah.

First reference Neh 10:8
Last reference Neh 12:35

Shemaiah⁺ (4)

God has heard

A false prophet who opposed the high priest Jehoiada and the prophet Jeremiah.

First reference Jer 29:24
Last reference Jer 29:32

Sherebiah⁺ (5)

God has brought heat

A Levite whom Ezra called to serve in the temple upon his return to Jerusalem. Sherebiah was among a group of Levites who led a revival among the Israelites in the time of Nehemiah.

First reference Ezr 8:18
Last reference Neh 9:5

Sheshan (4)

Lily

A descendant of Abraham through Jacob's son Judah. Sheshan had only daughters and gave one in marriage to his Egyptian servant, Jarha.

First reference 1 Chr 2:31
Last reference 1 Chr 2:35

Sheshbazzar (4)

Another name for Zerubbabel, the leader of exiles who returned from Babylon to Judah.

First reference Ezr 1:8
Last reference Ezr 5:16

Shethar-boznai (4)

A Persian official who objected to the rebuilding of the Jewish temple.

First reference Ezr 5:3
Last reference Ezr 6:13

Shimei⁺ (6)

Famous

A descendant of Abraham through Jacob's son Levi. Same as Shimi.

First reference Nm 3:18
Last reference 1 Chr 23:10

Shimei[+] (18)

Famous

A relative of King Saul who cursed King David when he fled Jerusalem. Later Shimei apologized to David, who pardoned him. But before he died, David warned Solomon about Shimei. Solomon commanded Shimei not to leave Jerusalem, or he would die. When two of Shimei's servants ran away, he left Jerusalem, so Solomon had him killed.

First reference 2 Sm 16:5
Last reference 1 Kgs 2:44
Key references 2 Sm 16:5–8;
    19:18–23; 1 Kgs 2:8–9, 36–46

Shimron (4)

Guardianship

A descendant of Abraham through Jacob's son Issachar. Same as Shimrom.

First reference Gn 46:13
Last reference Jo 19:15

Shimshai (4)

Sunny

A scribe who wrote King Artaxerxes a letter objecting to the rebuilding of Jerusalem. As a result, the king temporarily stopped the rebuilding.

First reference Ezr 4:8
Last reference Ezr 4:23

Shishak (7)

The king of Egypt to whom Jeroboam fled when Solomon discovered he had been anointed king over the northern ten tribes. During the reign of Solomon's son Rehoboam, Shishak attacked Judah, captured Jerusalem, and took the treasures of the temple and palace.

Shobal⁺ (5)

Overflowing

A descendant of Seir, who lived in Esau's "land of Edom."

First reference Gn 36:20
Last reference I Chr 1:40

Sihon (37)

Tempestuous

An Amorite king whom the Israelites defeated when he would not let them pass through his land as they turned back before the Promised Land. Israel conquered Sihon's capital, Heshbon, and all his cities. After killing all his people, they settled there, taking their livestock for themselves. Their success in the conquest of Sihon and his land became a repeated reminder of God's leading as Israel moved into the Promised Land. Rahab and the Gibeonites feared Israel because of this victory.

First reference Nm 21:21
Last reference Jer 48:45
Key references Nm 21:21–25;
   Dt 2:26–35; Jo 2:10;
   Ps 135:10–11

Silas (13)

Sylvan

A prophet chosen by the Jerusalem Council to accompany Paul and Barnabas to the Gentiles. After Barnabas and Paul separated, Paul took Silas on a new journey. Together they were imprisoned in Philippi after Paul freed a slave girl of an evil spirit. They led the jailer and his family to Christ and continued their mission in Greece. Same as Silvanus (2 Cor 1:19).

First reference Acts 15:22
Last reference Acts 18:5
Key references Acts 15:38–41; 16:16–40

Simeon⁺ [13]

Hearing

Second son of Jacob and Leah. With his full brother Levi, Simeon killed the men of Shechem because the prince of that city raped their sister, Dinah. In Egypt, Joseph held Simeon ransom until their nine brothers brought Benjamin to Egypt with them. When Jacob blessed his sons, he remembered Simeon's and Levi's anger at Shechem and cursed them for it.

First reference Gn 29:33
Last reference Ex 6:15
Key references Gn 29:32–33; 34:25; 42:18–20, 24; 49:5–7

Simon⁺ [46]

Hearing

The disciple whom Jesus named Peter, also called Simon Bar-jona. Same as Peter.

First reference Mt 4:18
Last reference 2 Pt 1:1
Key references Mt 16:16–17; Mk 3:16

Simon⁺ [4]

One of Jesus' twelve disciples, called "the Canaanite" and "Zelotes" (the Zealot).

First reference Mt 10:4
Last reference Acts 1:13

Simon⁺ (4)

A sorcerer who became a Christian. Simon offered the apostles money to be able to use the laying on of hands to fill people with the Holy Spirit.

First reference Acts 8:9
Last reference Acts 8:24

Sisera⁺ (19)

Captain under Jabin, king of Canaan. He fought with Barak, Israel's captain, and lost. Sisera fled on foot to the tent of Jael, the wife of Heber the Kenite. She encouraged him to come in then killed him by nailing a tent peg into his temple.

First reference Jgs 4:2
Last reference Ps 83:9
Key reference Jgs 4:13–21

Solomon (306)

Peaceful

Son of King David and Bath-sheba, Solomon was loved by God. Despite the efforts of his half brother Adonijah to take the throne, Solomon became king over Israel with the support of his father, David.

When God came to Solomon in a vision and asked what he wanted, the king requested "an understanding heart" to rule His people (1 Kgs 3:9). Because Solomon asked wisely, God gave him wisdom, understanding, and the wealth and honor he had not requested. The queen of Sheba heard of Solomon and came to ask him hard questions, and he proved his wisdom before her.

Solomon built the Lord's temple with the aid

of Hiram, Tyre's king. At the high point of his reign, Solomon dedicated the temple with a prayer and benediction. Though Solomon loved God, he also worshipped at pagan altars and married many "strange" (foreign) women, including the daughter of Pharaoh. Solomon had seven hundred wives and three hundred concubines. When he was old, his wives turned his heart away from God and he did evil, building pagan altars and worshipping there. So God promised that the throne of all Israel would be taken from his son, who would only rule over Judah.

First reference 2 Sm 5:14
Last reference Acts 7:47
Key references 2 Sm 12:24;
  1 Kgs 3:1–14; 5:1–6; 6:1;
  8:22–61; 10:1–3; 11:1–8,
  11–13

Stephen (7)

Wreathe

A man of the Jewish church, "full of faith and of the Holy Ghost," Stephen was ordained to care for the physical needs of church members. He became involved in a disagreement with Jews who accused him of blasphemy. After witnessing to the Jewish council, Stephen was stoned by an angry mob that included Saul (Acts 7:58).

First reference Acts 6:5
Last reference Acts 22:20

S: Mentioned Once

Sabta (1 Chr 1:9)

Sabtah (Gn 10:7)

Sabtecha (1 Chr 1:9)

Sabtechah (Gn 10:7)

Sacar+ (1 Chr 11:35)

Sacar+ (1 Chr 26:4)

Sadoc (Mt 1:14)

Sala (Lk 3:35)

Sallai+ (Neh 11:8)

Sallai+ (Neh 12:20)

Sallu+ (Neh 12:7)

Salu (Nm 25:14)

Samgar-nebo (Jer 39:3)

Saph (2 Sm 21:18)

Sapphira (Acts 5:1)

Sarah+ (Nm 26:46)

Saraph+ (1 Chr 4:22)

Sargon (Is 20:1)

Sarsechim (Jer 39:3)

Saruch (Lk 3:35)

Sceva (Acts 19:14)

Secundus (Acts 20:4)

Segub+ (1 Kgs 16:34)

Seled (1 Chr 2:30)

Sem (Lk 3:36)

Semachiah (1 Chr 26:7)

Semei (Lk 3:26)

Senuah (Neh 11:9)

Seorim (1 Chr 24:8)

Seraiah+ (2 Sm 8:17)

Seraiah+ (1 Chr 4:35)

Seraiah+ (Neh 11:11)

Seraiah+ (Jer 36:26)

Sergius (Acts 13:7)

Sethur (Nm 13:13)

Shaashgaz (Est 2:14)

Shabbethai+ (Ezr 10:15)

Shabbethai+ (Neh 8:7)

Shabbethai+ (Neh 11:16)

Shachia (1 Chr 8:10)

Shage (1 Chr 11:34)

Shaharaim (1 Chr 8:8)

Shallum+ (1 Chr 4:25)

Shallum+ (1 Chr 7:13)

Shallum+ (2 Chr 28:12)

Shallum+ (Ezr 10:24)

Shallum+ (Ezr 10:42)

Shallum+ (Neh 3:12)

Shallum+ (Jer 32:7)

Shallum+ (Jer 35:4)

Shallun (Neh 3:15)

Shalman (Hos 10:14)

Shama (1 Chr 11:44)

Shamariah (2 Chr 11:19)

Shamed (1 Chr 8:12)

Shamer+ (1 Chr 6:46)

Shamer+ (1 Chr 7:34)

Shamhuth (1 Chr 27:8)

Shamir (1 Chr 24:24)

Shamma (1 Chr 7:37)

Shammah+ (2 Sm 23:25)

Shammai+ (1 Chr 4:17)

Shammoth (1 Chr 11:27)

Shammua+ (Nm 13:4)

Shammua+ (1 Chr 14:4)

Shammua+ (Neh 11:17)

Shammua+ (Neh 12:18)

Shammuah (2 Sm 5:14)

Shamsherai (1 Chr 8:26)

Shapham (1 Chr 5:12)

Shaphan+ (Jer 29:3)

Shaphan+ (Ez 8:11)

Shaphat+ (Nm 13:5)

Shaphat+ (1 Chr 3:22)

Shaphat+ (1 Chr 5:12)

Shaphat+ (1 Chr 27:29)

Sharai (Ezr 10:40)

Sharar (2 Sm 23:33)

Shashai (Ezr 10:40)

Shaul+ (1 Chr 6:24)

Shavsha (1 Chr 18:16)

Sheal (Ezr 10:29)

Shear-jashub (Is 7:3)

Sheba+ (1 Chr 5:13)

Shebaniah+ (1 Chr 15:24)

Shebaniah+ (Neh 10:12)

Sheber (1 Chr 2:48)

Shebna+ (Is 22:15)

Shebuel+ (1 Chr 25:4)

Shecaniah+ (1 Chr 24:11)

Shecaniah+ (2 Chr 31:15)

Shechaniah+ (Ezr 8:3)

Shechaniah+ (Ezr 8:5)

Shechaniah+ (Ezr 10:2)

Shechaniah+ (Neh 3:29)

Shechaniah+ (Neh 6:18)

Shechaniah+ (Neh 12:3)

Shechem (1 Chr 7:19)

Shehariah (1 Chr 8:26)

Shelemiah+ (1 Chr 26:14)

Shelemiah+ (Ezr 10:39)

Shelemiah+ (Ezr 10:41)

Shelemiah+ (Neh 3:30)

Shelemiah+ (Neh 13:13)

Shelemiah+ (Jer 36:14)

Shelemiah+ (Jer 36:26)

Shelemiah+ (Jer 37:13)

Shelesh (1 Chr 7:35)

Shelomi (Nm 34:27)

Shelomith*+ (Lv 24:11)

Shelomith*+ (1 Chr 3:19)

Shelomith+ (1 Chr 23:9)

Shelomith+ (1 Chr 23:18)

Shelomith+ (2 Chr 11:20)

Shelomith+ (Ezr 8:10)

Shelomoth (1 Chr 24:22)

Shema+ (1 Chr 5:8)

Shema+ (1 Chr 8:13)

Shema+ (Neh 8:4)

Shemaah (1 Chr 12:3)

Shemaiah+ (1 Chr 3:22)

Shemaiah+ (1 Chr 4:37)

Shemaiah+ (1 Chr 5:4)

Shemaiah+ (1 Chr 9:16)

Shemaiah+ (1 Chr 24:6)

Shemaiah+ (2 Chr 17:8)

Shemaiah+ (2 Chr 29:14)

Shemaiah+ (2 Chr 31:15)

Shemaiah+ (2 Chr 35:9)

Shemaiah+ (Ezr 8:13)

Shemaiah+ (Ezr 8:16)

Shemaiah+ (Ezr 10:21)

Shemaiah+ (Ezr 10:31)

Shemaiah+ (Neh 3:29)

Shemaiah+ (Neh 6:10)

Shemaiah+ (Neh 12:36)

Shemaiah+ (Neh 12:42)

Shemaiah+ (Jer 26:20)

Shemaiah+ (Jer 36:12)

Shemariah+ (1 Chr 12:5)

Shemariah+ (Ezr 10:32)

Shemariah+ (Ezr 10:41)

Shemeber (Gn 14:2)

Shemer (1 Kgs 16:24)

Shemidah (1 Chr 7:19)

Shemiramoth+
 (2 Chr 17:8)

Shemuel+ (Nm 34:20)

Shemuel+ (1 Chr 6:33)

Shemuel+ (1 Chr 7:2)

Shenazar (1 Chr 3:18)

Shephathiah (1 Chr 9:8)

Shephatiah+ (1 Chr 12:5)

Shephatiah+ (1 Chr 27:16)

Shephatiah+ (2 Chr 21:2)

Shephatiah+ (Ezr 8:8)

Shephatiah+ (Neh 11:4)

Shephatiah+ (Jer 38:1)

Shephi (1 Chr 1:40)

Shepho (Gn 36:23)

Shephuphan (1 Chr 8:5)

Sherah* (1 Chr 7:24)

Sheth+ (Nm 24:17)

Sheth+ (1 Chr 1:1)

Sheresh (1 Chr 7:16)

Sherezer (Zec 7:2)

Shethar (Est 1:14)

Sheva+ (2 Sm 20:25)

Sheva+ (1 Chr 2:49)

Shiloni (Neh 11:5)

Shilshah (1 Chr 7:37)

Shimea+ (1 Chr 3:5)

Shimea+ (1 Chr 6:30)

Shimea+ (1 Chr 6:39)

Shimea+ (1 Chr 20:7)

Shimei+ (1 Kgs 1:8)

Shimei+ (1 Kgs 4:18)

Shimei+ (1 Chr 3:19)

Shimei+ (1 Chr 5:4)

Shimei+ (1 Chr 6:29)

Shimei+ (1 Chr 23:9)

Shimei+ (1 Chr 25:17)

Shimei+ (1 Chr 27:27)

Shimei+ (2 Chr 29:14)

Shimei+ (Ezr 10:23)

Shimei+ (Ezr 10:33)

Shimei+ (Ezr 10:38)

Shimei+ (Est 2:5)

Shimei+ (Zec 12:13)

Shimeah+ (1 Chr 8:32)

Shimeam (1 Chr 9:38)

Shimeon (Ezr 10:31)

Shimhi (1 Chr 8:21)

Shimi (Ex 6:17)

Shimma (1 Chr 2:13)

Shimon (1 Chr 4:20)

Shimrath (1 Chr 8:21)

Shimri+ (1 Chr 4:37)

Shimri+ (1 Chr 11:45)

Shimri+ (2 Chr 29:13)

Shimrith* (2 Chr 24:26)

Shimrom (1 Chr 7:1)

Shinab (Gn 14:2)

Shiphi (1 Chr 4:37)

Shiphrah* (Ex 1:15)

Shiphtan (Nm 34:24)

Shisha (1 Kgs 4:3)

Shitrai (1 Chr 27:29)

Shiza (1 Chr 11:42)

Shobab+ (1 Chr 2:18)

Shobek (Neh 10:24)

Shobi (2 Sm 17:27)

Shoham (1 Chr 24:27)

Shomer+ (2 Kgs 12:21)

Shomer+ (1 Chr 7:32)

Shua*+ (1 Chr 2:3)

Shua*+ (1 Chr 4:11)

Shua*+ (1 Chr 7:32)

Shual (1 Chr 7:36)

Shubael+ (1 Chr 24:20)

Shubael+ (1 Chr 25:20)

Shuham (Nm 26:42)

Shupham (Nm 26:39)

Shuppim+ (1 Chr 26:16)

Shuthelah+ (1 Chr 7:21)

Sia (Neh 7:47)

Siaha (Ezr 2:44)

Sidon (Gn 10:15)

Silvanus+ (1 Pt 5:12)

Simeon+ (Lk 3:30)

Simeon+ (Acts 13:1)

Simeon+ (Acts 15:14)

Simri (1 Chr 26:10)

Sippai (1 Chr 20:4)

Sisamai (1 Chr 2:40)

So (2 Kgs 17:4)

Socho (1 Chr 4:18)

Sodi (Nm 13:10)

Sopater (Acts 20:4)

Sosipater (Rom 16:21)

Sosthenes+ (Acts 18:17)

Sosthenes+ (1 Cor 1:1)

Stachys (Rom 16:9)

Suah (1 Chr 7:36)

Susanna (Lk 8:3)

Susi (Nm 13:11)

Syntyche (Phil 4:2)

S: Mentioned Twice

Salome* (Mk 15:40)

Sara* (Heb 11:1)

Saul⁺ (Gn 36:37)

Seba (Gn 10:7)

Segub⁺ (1 Chr 2:21)

Seir (Gn 36:20)

Serah* (Gn 46:17)

Seraiah⁺ (2 Kgs 25:23)

Seraiah⁺ (1 Chr 4:13)

Sered (Gn 46:14)

Shaaph (1 Chr 2:47)

Shallum⁺ (2 Kgs 22:14)

Shallum⁺ (1 Chr 2:40)

Shallum⁺ (1 Chr 3:15)

Shalmai (Ezr 2:46)

Shalmaneser (2 Kgs 17:3)

Shamgar (Jgs 3:31)

Shammah⁺ (1 Sm 16:9)

Shammah⁺ (2 Sm 23:11)

Shammai⁺ (1 Chr 2:44)

Sharezer (2 Kgs 19:37)

Shashak (1 Chr 8:14)

Shaul⁺ (1 Chr 1:48)

Sheariah (1 Chr 8:38)

Sheba⁺ (Gn 10:7)

Sheba⁺ (Gn 10:28)

Sheba⁺ (Gn 25:3)

Shebaniah⁺ (Neh 10:4)

Shebuel⁺ (1 Chr 23:16)

Shechaniah⁺ (1 Chr 3:21)

Shechem (Nm 26:31)

Shelemiah⁺ (Jer 37:3)

Sheleph (Gn 10:26)

Shema⁺ (1 Chr 2:43)

Shemaiah⁺ (1 Chr 9:14)

Shemaiah⁺ (1 Chr 15:8)

Shemida (Nm 26:32)

Shephatiah⁺ (2 Sm 3:4)

Shephatiah⁺ (Ezr 2:4)

Shephatiah⁺ (Ezr 2:57)

Shilhi (1 Kgs 22:42)

Shillem (Gn 46:24)

Shimei⁺ (1 Chr 4:26)

Shimei⁺ (2 Chr 31:12)

Shimeath* (2 Kgs 12:21)

Shobach (2 Sm 10:16)

Shobai (Ezr 2:42)

Shobal⁺ (1 Chr 2:50)

Shobal⁺ (1 Chr 4:1)

Shophach (1 Chr 19:16)

Shua*⁺ (Gn 38:2)

Shuah⁺ (Gn 25:2)

Shuni (Gn 46:16)

Shuppim+ (1 Chr 7:12)

Sibbecai (1 Chr 11:29)

Sibbechai (2 Sm 21:18)

Simeon+ (Lk 2:25)

Simon+ (Mt 13:55)

Simon+ (Mt 26:6)

Simon+ (Jn 6:71)

Sisera+ (Ezr 2:53)

Sophereth (Ezr 2:55)

Sotai (Ezr 2:55)

S: Mentioned Three Times

Sallu+ (1 Chr 9:7)

Seraiah+ (Jer 51:59)

Shallum+ (1 Chr 6:12)

Shammah+ (Gn 36:13)

Shammai+ (1 Chr 2:28)

Shebaniah+ (Neh 9:4)

Shelah+ (1 Chr 1:18)

Shelomith+ (1 Chr 26:25)

Shemaiah+ (1 Chr 26:4)

Shemiramoth+ (1 Chr 15:18)

Sherebiah+ (Neh 10:12)

Sheshai (Nm 13:22)

Shimeah+ (2 Sm 13:3)

Shobab+ (2 Sm 5:14)

Shuthelah+ (Nm 26:35)

Silvanus+ (2 Cor 1:19)

Simon+ (Mt 27:32)

Simon+ (Lk 7:40)

Simon+ (Acts 9:43)

Stephanas (1 Cor 1:16)

T

Talmon (5)

Oppressive

A Jewish exile from the tribe of Levi who resettled Jerusalem.

First reference 1 Chr 9:17
Last reference Neh 12:25

Tamar*+ (7)

Palm tree

Daughter-in-law of Jacob's son Judah. Tamar married Judah's eldest two sons, whom God killed for wickedness. Judah refused to marry her to his third son, so she pretended to be a harlot, lay with Judah, and had twins by him. Same as Thamar.

First reference Gn 38:6
Last reference 1 Chr 2:4

Tamar*+ (14)

Palm tree

Daughter of King David and half sister of Amnon. Amnon fell in love with her and pretended to be sick so David would send Tamar to him. He raped Tamar and threw her out of his house. Her full brother Absalom heard of this and later had his servants kill Amnon.

First reference 2 Sm 13:1
Last reference 1 Chr 3:9

Tatnai (4)

A governor who objected to the rebuilding of Jerusalem's temple and wrote the Persian king Darius. Darius commanded Tatnai to let the work continue.

First reference Ezr 5:3
Last reference Ezr 6:13

Tema (4)

A descendant of Abraham through Ishmael, Abraham's son with his surrogate wife, Hagar.

First reference Gn 25:15
Last reference 1 Chr 1:30

Teman (5)

South

A "duke of Edom," a leader in the family line of Esau.

First reference Gn 36:11
Last reference 1 Chr 1:53

Terah (11)

Father of Abram (Abraham), Nahor, and Haran. With Abram and Nahor and their families, he left Ur of the Chaldees and headed for Canaan. But when they came to Haran, they stayed there. Terah died in Haran.

First reference Gn 11:24
Last reference 1 Chr 1:26

Thomas (12)

The twin

Jesus' disciple whom people often call "Doubting Thomas." When Jesus wanted to go to Lazarus, courageous Thomas said, "Let us also go, that we may die with him" (Jn 11:16). But after His death, when Jesus appeared to the others, Thomas doubted their story until he saw the Master himself.

First reference Mt 10:3
Last reference Acts 1:13
Key references Jn 11:16;
    20:24–29

Timotheus (18)

Dear to God

The Greek name for Timothy, the apostle Paul's coworker and "son in the faith" (1 Tm 1:2).

First reference Acts 16:1
Last reference 2 Thes 1:1
Key reference 1 Cor 4:17

Timothy (8)

Dear to God

Coworker of the apostle Paul, his name is joined with Paul's in the introductory greetings of 2 Corinthians and Philemon. Paul also wrote two epistles of guidance to this young pastor who was like a son to him. Same as Timotheus.

First reference 2 Cor 1:1
Last reference Heb 13:23
Key references 1 Tm 1:2; 6:20–21

Tirshatha (5)

Title of the governor of Judea, used to describe Nehemiah.

First reference Ezr 2:63
Last reference Neh 10:1

Tirzah (4)

Delightsomeness

One of five daughters of Zelophehad, an Israelite who died during the wilderness wanderings. The women asked Moses if they could inherit their father's property in the Promised Land (a right normally reserved for sons), and God ruled that they should, since Zelophehad had no sons.

First reference Nm 26:33
Last reference Jo 17:3

Titus (14)

The apostle Paul's highly trusted Greek coworker who traveled with him and whom Paul sent to Corinth with a letter of rebuke for the church. Titus had a successful mission, so Paul sent him again to the Corinthians. When Titus was in Crete, Paul wrote him an epistle on church leadership.

First reference 2 Cor 2:13
Last reference Ti 1:4
Key references 2 Cor 7:6–9,
    13–15; Gal 2:1, 3

Tobiah⁺ (13)

An Ammonite who resisted the rebuilding of Jerusalem under Governor Nehemiah. With Sanballat the Horonite he interfered and tried to distract Nehemiah from his work. The two hired a man to warn Nehemiah that he would be killed, and Tobiah sent threatening letters to scare Nehemiah.

First reference Neh 2:10
Last reference Neh 13:8
Key references Neh 4:3, 7–8;
    6:10–12, 17–19

Togarmah (4)

A descendant of Noah through his son Japheth.

First reference Gn 10:3
Last reference Ez 38:6

Tola⁺ (5)

Worm

A descendant of Abraham through Jacob's son Issachar.

First reference Gn 46:13
Last reference 1 Chr 7:2

Tychicus (7)

Fortunate

An Asian coworker of Paul who accompanied him to Macedonia. Paul also sent him on missions to the Ephesians and Colossians and perhaps to Crete.

First reference Acts 20:4
Last reference Ti 3:12

T: Mentioned Once

Tabeal (Is 7:6)

Tabeel (Ezr 4:7)

Tabrimon (1 Kgs 15:18)

Tahan+ (Nm 26:35)

Tahan+ (1 Chr 7:25)

Tahath+ (1 Chr 7:20)

Tahath+ (1 Chr 7:20)

Tahrea (1 Chr 9:41)

Tamah (Neh 7:55)

Tamar*+ (2 Sm 14:27)

Taphath* (1 Kgs 4:11)

Tappuah (1 Chr 2:43)

Tarea (1 Chr 8:35)

Tarshish+ (Est 1:14)

Tebah (Gn 22:24)

Tebaliah (1 Chr 26:11)

Tehinnah (1 Chr 4:12)

Telah (1 Chr 7:25)

Telem (Ezr 10:24)

Temeni (1 Chr 4:6)

Tertius (Rom 16:22)

Thahash (Gn 22:24)

Thamah (Ezr 2:53)

Thamar* (Mt 1:3)

Thara (Lk 3:34)

Tharshish (1 Chr 7:10)

Theudas (Acts 5:36)

Tiberius (Lk 3:1)

Tikvah+ (2 Kgs 22:14)

Tikvah+ (Ezr 10:15)

Tikvath (2 Chr 34:22)

Tilon (1 Chr 4:20)

Timaeus (Mk 10:46)

Timna*+ (Gn 36:12)

Timna+ (1 Chr 1:36)

Timon (Acts 6:5)

Tirhanah (1 Chr 2:48)

Tiria (1 Chr 4:16)

Toah (1 Chr 6:34)

Tob-adonijah (2 Chr 17:8)

Tobijah+ (2 Chr 17:8)

Tohu (1 Sm 1:1)

Tola+ (Jgs 10:1)

Tryphena* (Rom 16:12)

Tryphosa* (Rom 16:12)

Tubal-cain (Gn 4:22)

Tyrannus (Acts 19:9)

T: Mentioned Twice

Tabbaoth (Ezr 2:43)

Tabitha* (Acts 9:36)

Tahath+ (1 Chr 6:24)

Tanhumeth (2 Kgs 25:23)

Tarshish+ (Gn 10:4)

Tartan (2 Kgs 18:17)

Tekoa (1 Chr 2:24)

Teresh (Est 2:21)

Tertullus (Acts 24:1)

Thaddaeus (Mt 10:3)

Theophilus (Lk 1:3)

Tidal (Gn 14:1)

Timna*+ (Gn 36:22)

Timnah (Gn 36:40)

Tiras (Gn 10:2)

Tirhakah (2 Kgs 19:9)

Tobiah+ (Ezr 2:60)

Tobijah+ (Zec 6:10)

Tou (1 Chr 18:9)

Tubal (Gn 10:2)

T: Mentioned Three Times

Tahpenes* (1 Kgs 11:19)

Talmai+ (Nm 13:22)

Talmai+ (2 Sm 3:3)

Tibni (1 Kgs 16:21)

Tiglath-pileser
  (2 Kgs 15:29)

Tilgath-pilneser
  (1 Chr 5:6)

Toi (2 Sm 8:9)

Trophimus (Acts 20:4)

U

Uri+ (6)

Fiery

Father of Bezaleel, a craftsman in the construction of the tabernacle.

First reference Ex 31:2
Last reference 2 Chr 1:5

Uriah+ (26)

Flame of God

Called Uriah the Hittite, he was Bath-sheba's first husband and a warrior in King David's army. When Bath-sheba discovered she was pregnant by the king, David called Uriah home and tried to make him go to his wife, but the faithful soldier would not do so while his fellow soldiers were in the field. So David ordered his commander, Joab, to put Uriah in the heaviest fighting, where he would be killed. After Uriah's death, the prophet Nathan confronted David with this murder and prophesied that Israel would not live in peace during David's reign. Same as Urias.

First reference 2 Sm 11:3
Last reference 1 Chr 11:41
Key references 2 Sm 11:6–17;
    12:9–10

Urijah+ (5)

Flame of God

The priest who followed King Ahaz's command to build a pagan altar as a place of worship. When Ahaz moved the Jewish temple altars and told Urijah how to worship, the priest obeyed him.

First reference 2 Kgs 16:10
Last reference 2 Kgs 16:16

Uzza⁺ [4]

A man who drove the cart in which the ark of the covenant was transported from Kirjath-jearim. When the oxen stumbled, Uzza reached out to steady the ark. God killed him for daring to touch the holy object. Same as Uzzah.

First reference 1 Chr 13:7
Last reference 1 Chr 13:11

Uzzah [4]

Strength

A variant spelling of the name *Uzza*. Same as Uzza (1 Chr 13:7).

First reference 2 Sm 6:3
Last reference 2 Sm 6:8

Uzzi⁺ [4]

Forceful

A descendant of Abraham through Jacob's son Levi and a priest through the line of Aaron.

First reference 1 Chr 6:5
Last reference Ezr 7:4

Uzziah⁺ [23]

Strength of God

Son of Amaziah, king of Judah. As king of Judah, Uzziah obeyed God, and the Lord helped him fight the Philistines and other enemies. The king fortified Jerusalem and built a powerful army. But in his power, Uzziah became proud and wrongly burned incense on the temple's incense altar. Confronted by the priests, he became angry. God immediately made him a leper. Thereafter Uzziah was cut off from the temple, and his son Jotham ruled in his name. Same as Azariah (2 Kgs 14:21).

First reference 2 Kgs 15:13
Last reference Zec 14:5
Key references 2 Chr 26:1–23

Uzziel⁺ (11)

Strength of God

A descendant of Abraham through Jacob's son Levi.

First reference Ex 6:18
Last reference 1 Chr 24:24

U: Mentioned Once

Ucal (Prv 30:1)

Uel (Ezr 10:34)

Ulla (1 Chr 7:39)

Unni⁺ (Neh 12:9)

Ur (1 Chr 11:35)

Urbane (Rom 16:9)

Uri⁺ (1 Kgs 4:19)

Uri⁺ (Ezr 10:24)

Uriah⁺ (Ezr 8:33)

Uriah⁺ (Is 8:2)

Urias (Mt 1:6)

Uriel⁺ (2 Chr 13:2)

Urijah⁺ (Neh 8:4)

Uthai⁺ (1 Chr 9:4)

Uthai⁺ (Ezr 8:14)

Uzai (Neh 3:25)

Uzza⁺ (1 Chr 6:29)

Uzza⁺ (1 Chr 8:7)

Uzzi⁺ (1 Chr 7:7)

Uzzi⁺ (1 Chr 9:8)

Uzzi⁺ (Neh 11:22)

Uzzia (1 Chr 11:44)

Uzziah⁺ (1 Chr 6:24)

Uzziah⁺ (1 Chr 27:25)

Uzziah⁺ (Ezr 10:21)

Uzziah⁺ (Neh 11:4)

Uzziel⁺ (1 Chr 4:42)

Uzziel⁺ (1 Chr 7:7)

Uzziel⁺ (1 Chr 25:4)

Uzziel⁺ (2 Chr 29:14)

Uzziel⁺ (Neh 3:8)

U: Mentioned Twice

Ulam[+] (1 Chr 7:16)

Ulam[+] (1 Chr 8:39)

Unni[+] (1 Chr 15:18)

Urijah[+] (Neh 3:4)

Uz[+] (Gn 10:23)

Uz[+] (Gn 36:28)

Uzal (Gn 10:27)

Uzza[+] (Ezr 2:49)

Uzzi[+] (1 Chr 7:2)

Uzzi[+] (Neh 12:19)

U: Mentioned Three Times

Uriel[+] (1 Chr 6:24)

Urijah[+] (Jer 26:20)

V

Vashti* (10)

Queen of the Persian king Ahasuerus, Vashti refused to appear at his banquet. The king revoked her position and had no more to do with her.

First reference Est 1:9
Last reference Est 2:17

V: Mentioned Once

Vajezatha (Est 9:9)

Vaniah (Ezr 10:36)

Vashni (1 Chr 6:28)

Vophsi (Nm 13:14)

Z

Zacharias+ (9)

A priest who received a vision that his barren wife would bear a child who would be great before the Lord. Because Zacharias doubted, God struck him dumb until the birth of the child. When he agreed with his wife to name the child John, Zacharias could suddenly speak. His son was John the Baptist.

First reference Lk 1:5
Last reference Lk 3:2

Zadok+ (43)

Just

A priest during King David's reign. Zadok and the priest Abiathar consecrated Levites to bring the ark of the covenant into Jerusalem. With Zadok's help, David reorganized the priesthood. As David fled Jerusalem, attacked by his son Absalom, Zadok brought out the ark, planning to go with him. Instead, David left him behind to support him in the city. Following Absalom's death, Zadok helped to persuade Judah to take David back as king. When David was old, his son Adonijah tried to set himself up as king. But Zadok would not support him. Instead, at David's command, he anointed Solomon king. Solomon later made Zadok high priest.

First reference 2 Sm 8:17
Last reference Ez 48:11
Key references 2 Sm 15:24–29; 19:11; 1 Kgs 1:8, 32–39; 2:35; 1 Chr 15:11–12; 24:3

Zalmunna (12)

Shade has been denied

A Midianite king whom Gideon pursued after Zalmunna killed Gideon's brothers at Tabor. Gideon killed Zalmunna.

First reference Jgs 8:5
Last reference Ps 83:11

Zebah (12)

Sacrifice

A Midianite king whom Gideon pursued with three hundred men after Zebah killed Gideon's brothers at Tabor. Gideon killed Zebah.

First reference Jgs 8:5
Last reference Ps 83:11

Zebedee (12)

Giving

Father of Jesus' disciples James and John and a fisherman on the Sea of Galilee. Zebedee's sons worked with him until they left to follow Jesus. James and John are frequently referred to as "the sons of Zebedee."

First reference Mt 4:21
Last reference Jn 21:2

Zebul (6)

Dwelling

Ruler of the city of Shechem under that city's king Abimelech. Zebul encouraged the conspirator Gaal to fight Abimelech's army then pushed him and his men out of the city.

First reference Jgs 9:28
Last reference Jgs 9:41

Zebulun (6)

Habitation

Sixth and last son of Jacob and Leah. Jacob foretold that Zebulun would dwell "at the haven of the sea" (Gn 49:13), bordering on Zidon.

First reference Gn 30:20
Last reference 1 Chr 2:1

Zechariah+ (4)

God has remembered

A Levite, known as "a wise counsellor," who was chosen by lot to guard the west side of the house of the Lord.

First reference 1 Chr 9:21
Last reference 2 Chr 29:1

Zechariah+ (6)

God has remembered

An Old Testament minor prophet who ministered in Jerusalem following the return from exile. Judah prospered under his ministry as the people rebuilt the temple.

First reference Ezr 5:1
Last reference Zec 7:8

Zedekiah+ (4)

Right of God

A false prophet who predicted that King Jehoshaphat of Judah would win over the Syrians. Zedekiah struck and mocked the faithful prophet Micaiah.

First reference 1 Kgs 22:11
Last reference 2 Chr 18:23

Zedekiah⁺ (54)

Originally named Mattaniah, Zedekiah was a brother of King Jehoiachin of Judah. Nebuchadnezzar, king of Babylon, conquered Judah, deposed Jehoiachin, renamed Mattaniah as Zedekiah, and made him king. Like his brother, Zedekiah rebelled against Babylon. Zedekiah did not heed the prophet Jeremiah and imprisoned him. Nebuchadnezzar besieged Jerusalem. When the city no longer had food, Zedekiah and his troops sought to escape. The Chaldean army caught Zedekiah, killed his sons before him, and put out his eyes. They bound him and carried him to Babylon.

First reference 2 Kgs 24:17
Last reference Jer 52:11
Key references 2 Kgs 24:17–20; Jer 39:4–7

Zeeb (6)

Wolf

A Midianite prince captured and killed by the men of Ephraim under Gideon's command.

First reference Jgs 7:25
Last reference Ps 83:11

Zelophehad (11)

United

A descendant of Joseph, through Manasseh, Zelophehad died during the wilderness wanderings that followed Israel's exodus from Egypt. His five daughters asked Moses if they could inherit their father's property in the Promised Land (a right normally reserved for sons). God ruled that they should, since Zelophehad had no sons.

First reference Nm 26:33
Last reference I Chr 7:15

First reference Nm 26:20
Last reference Neh 11:24

Zephaniah⁺ (6)

God has secreted

The second priest in the temple during King Zedekiah's reign. The king sent Zephaniah to the prophet Jeremiah, asking him to pray for Israel. When King Nebuchadnezzar of Babylon captured Jerusalem, Zephaniah was taken to Riblah, where Nebuchadnezzar killed him.

First reference 2 Kgs 25:18
Last reference Jer 52:24

Zerah⁺ (9)

A grandson of Jacob, born to Jacob's son Judah and Judah's daughter-in-law, Tamar.

Zerahiah (4)

God has risen

A descendant of Abraham through Jacob's son Levi and a priest through the line of Aaron.

First reference I Chr 6:6
Last reference Ezr 7:4

Zeresh* (4)

Wife of Haman, the villain of the story of Esther. Zeresh, along with friends, encouraged Haman to build a gallows on which to hang Esther's cousin Mordecai—the gallows that Haman himself would later die on.

First reference Est 5:10
Last reference Est 6:13

Zerubbabel (22)

Descended of Babylon

Governor of Judah, Zerubbabel returned from the Babylonian Exile with many Israelites in his train. He began by rebuilding an altar so Judah could worship for the Feast of Tabernacles. When God spoke through the prophet Haggai, Zerubbabel and the high priest Jeshua obeyed, organizing workers to rebuild the temple. Israel's enemies came to offer their help, but Zerubbabel refused and tried to forestall trouble by telling them that Israel was following the Persian king Cyrus's command. God told the prophet Zechariah that Zerubbabel would finish his task.

First reference I Chr 3:19
Last reference Zec 4:10
Key references Ezr 3:2–5; 3:8; 4:1–3; 5:2; Hg 1:1–2, 12; Zec 4:9

Zeruiah* (26)

Wounded

Sister of King David and mother of David's battle commander, Joab, and his brothers, Abishai and Asahel.

First reference I Sm 26:6
Last reference I Chr 27:24
Key references 2 Sm 2:18; I Chr 2:15–16

Ziba (16)

Station

A servant of King Saul who told King David where Mephibosheth lived after David took the throne. When David fled Jerusalem, during Absalom's attempt to take the throne, Ziba brought him food and the news that Mephibosheth sought to take David's throne. David gave him everything Mephibosheth owned. When David returned to Jerusalem as king, Mephibosheth claimed his servant had lied.

First reference 2 Sm 9:2
Last reference 2 Sm 19:29
Key references 2 Sm 9:2–3;
  16:1–4; 19:24–30

Zibeon (6)

Variegated

A descendant of Seir, who lived in Esau's "land of Edom."

First reference Gn 36:20

Zilpah* (7)

Trickle

Servant of Leah. Leah gave Zilpah to her husband, Jacob, as a wife because she thought her own child-bearing days were ended. Zilpah had two sons, Gad and Asher.

First reference Gn 29:24
Last reference Gn 46:18

Zimri⁺ (8)

Musical

The king of Israel who conspired against King Elah and killed him. After usurping Elah's throne, Zimri killed Elah's male relatives, fulfilling the prophecy of Jehu (1 Kgs 16:1). Zimri reigned for seven days before Israel made Omri king in his place. When the capital was taken, Zimri burned down the king's house with himself inside it.

First reference 1 Kgs 16:9
Last reference 2 Kgs 9:31

Zimri⁺ (4)

A descendant of Abraham through Jacob's son Benjamin, in the line of King Saul and his son Jonathan.

First reference 1 Chr 8:36
Last reference 1 Chr 9:42

Zippor (7)

Little bird

Father of the Moabite king Balak, who consulted the false prophet Balaam.

First reference Nm 22:2
Last reference Jgs 11:25

Zophar (4)

Departing

One of three friends of Job who mourned his losses for a week and then accused him of wrongdoing. God ultimately chastised the three for their criticism of Job, commanding them to sacrifice burnt offerings while Job prayed for them.

First reference Jb 2:11
Last reference Jb 42:9

Zuar (5)

Small

Father of a prince of the tribe of Issachar in Moses' day.

First reference Nm 1:8
Last reference Nm 10:15

Zurishaddai (5)

Rock of the Almighty

Father of a prince of Simeon in Moses' day.

First reference Nm 1:6
Last reference Nm 10:19

Z: Mentioned Once

Zaavan (Gn 36:27)

Zabad[+] (1 Chr 7:21)

Zabad[+] (1 Chr 11:41)

Zabad[+] (2 Chr 24:26)

Zabad[+] (Ezr 10:27)

Zabad[+] (Ezr 10:33)

Zabad[+] (Ezr 10:43)

Zabbai[+] (Ezr 10:28)

Zabbai[+] (Neh 3:20)

Zabbud (Ezr 8:14)

Zabdi[+] (1 Chr 8:19)

Zabdi[+] (1 Chr 27:27)

Zabdi[+] (Neh 11:17)

Zabdiel[+] (1 Chr 27:2)

Zabdiel[+] (Neh 11:14)

Zabud (1 Kgs 4:5)

Zacchur (1 Chr 4:26)

Zaccur[+] (Nm 13:4)

Zaccur[+] (1 Chr 24:27)

Zaccur[+] (Neh 3:2)

Zaccur[+] (Neh 10:12)

Zaccur[+] (Neh 13:13)

Zachariah[+] (2 Kgs 18:2)

Zacher (1 Chr 8:31)

Zadok[+] (1 Chr 12:28)

Zadok[+] (Neh 3:4)

Zadok[+] (Neh 3:29)

Zadok[+] (Neh 10:21)

Zadok[+] (Neh 11:11)

Zadok[+] (Neh 13:13)

Zaham (2 Chr 11:19)

Zalaph (Neh 3:30)

Zalmon (2 Sm 23:28)

Zanoah (1 Chr 4:1)

Zaphnath-paaneah
  (Gn 41:45)

Zara (Mt 1:3)

Zatthu (Neh 10:14)

Zavan (1 Chr 1:42)

Zaza (1 Chr 2:33)

Zebadiah[+] (1 Chr 8:15)

Zebadiah[+] (1 Chr 8:17)

Zebadiah[+] (1 Chr 12:7)

Zebadiah[+] (1 Chr 26:2)

Zebadiah[+] (1 Chr 27:7)

Zebadiah[+] (2 Chr 17:8)

Zebadiah[+] (2 Chr 19:11)

Zebadiah[+] (Ezr 8:8)

Zebadiah[+] (Ezr 10:20)

Zebina (Ezr 10:43)

Zebudah* (2 Kgs 23:36)

Zechariah[+] (1 Chr 5:7)

Zechariah+ (1 Chr 9:37)

Zechariah+ (1 Chr 15:24)

Zechariah+ (1 Chr 24:25)

Zechariah+ (1 Chr 26:11)

Zechariah+ (1 Chr 27:21)

Zechariah+ (2 Chr 17:7)

Zechariah+ (2 Chr 20:14)

Zechariah+ (2 Chr 21:2)

Zechariah+ (2 Chr 24:20)

Zechariah+ (2 Chr 26:5)

Zechariah+ (2 Chr 29:13)

Zechariah+ (2 Chr 34:12)

Zechariah+ (2 Chr 35:8)

Zechariah+ (Ezr 8:3)

Zechariah+ (Ezr 10:26)

Zechariah+ (Neh 8:4)

Zechariah+ (Neh 11:4)

Zechariah+ (Neh 11:5)

Zechariah+ (Neh 11:12)

Zechariah+ (Neh 12:16)

Zechariah+ (Is 8:2)

Zedekiah+ (1 Chr 3:16)

Zedekiah+ (Jer 36:12)

Zemira (1 Chr 7:8)

Zenas (Ti 3:13)

Zephaniah+ (1 Chr 6:36)

Zephaniah+ (Zep 1:1)

Zephi (1 Chr 1:36)

Zephon (Nm 26:15)

Zerah+ (1 Chr 6:21)

Zerah+ (1 Chr 6:41)

Zerah+ (2 Chr 14:9)

Zerahiah (Ezr 8:4)

Zereth (1 Chr 4:7)

Zeri (1 Chr 25:3)

Zeror (1 Sm 9:1)

Zeruah* (1 Kgs 11:26)

Zethan (1 Chr 7:10)

Zethar (Est 1:10)

Zia (1 Chr 5:13)

Zibia (1 Chr 8:9)

Zichri+ (Ex 6:21)

Zichri+ (1 Chr 8:19)

Zichri+ (1 Chr 8:23)

Zichri+ (1 Chr 8:27)

Zichri+ (1 Chr 9:15)

Zichri+ (1 Chr 26:25)

Zichri+ (1 Chr 27:16)

Zichri+ (2 Chr 17:16)

Zichri+ (2 Chr 23:1)

Zichri+ (2 Chr 28:7)

Zichri+ (Neh 11:9)

Zichri+ (Neh 12:17)

Zidkijah (Neh 10:1)

Zidon (1 Chr 1:13)

Ziha+ (Neh 11:21)

Zilthai+ (1 Chr 8:20)

Zilthai+ (1 Chr 12:20)

Zimmah+ (1 Chr 6:20)

Zimmah+ (1 Chr 6:42)

Zimmah+ (2 Chr 29:12)

Zimri+ (Nm 25:14)

Zimri+ (1 Chr 2:6)

Zina (Chr 23:10)

Ziph+ (1 Chr 2:42)

Ziph+ (1 Chr 4:16)

Ziphah (1 Chr 4:16)

Ziphion (Gn 46:16)

Zithri (Ex 6:22)

Ziza+ (1 Chr 4:37)

Ziza+ (2 Chr 11:20)

Zizah (1 Chr 23:11)

Zobebah* (1 Chr 4:8)

Zoheth (1 Chr 4:20)

Zophai (1 Chr 6:26)

Zuriel (Nm 3:35)

Z: Mentioned Twice

Zabad⁺ (1 Chr 2:36)

Zaccai (Ezr 2:9)

Zacharias⁺ (Mt 23:35)

Zadok⁺ (2 Kgs 15:33)

Zarah (Gn 38:30)

Zechariah⁺ (Ezr 8:11)

Zechariah⁺ (Neh 12:35)

Zedekiah⁺ (Jer 29:21)

Zelek (2 Sm 23:37)

Zelotes (Lk 6:15)

Zephaniah⁺ (Zec 6:10)

Zepho (Gn 36:11)

Zerah⁺ (Gn 36:33)

Zerah⁺ (Nm 26:13)

Zetham (1 Chr 23:8)

Zibeon (Gn 36:2)

Zibiah* (2 Kgs 12:1)

Ziha⁺ (Ezr 2:43)

Zimran (Gn 25:2)

Zohar⁺ (Gn 23:8)

Zohar⁺ (Gn 46:10)

Zophah (1 Chr 7:35)

Zuph (1 Sm 1:1)

Zur⁺ (1 Chr 8:30)

Z: Mentioned Three Times

Zabdi⁺ (Jo 7:1)

Zacchaeus (Lk 19:2)

Zaccur⁺ (1 Chr 25:2)

Zachariah⁺ (2 Kgs 14:29)

Zadok⁺ (1 Chr 6:12)

Zattu (Ezr 2:8)

Zechariah⁺ (1 Chr 15:18)

Zerah⁺ (Gn 36:13)

Zillah* (Gn 4:19)

Zipporah* (Ex 2:21)

Zorobabel (Mt 1:12)

Zur⁺ (Nm 25:15)

If you enjoyed

MEN & WOMEN
OF THE **BIBLE**

be sure to look for these other great Bible
resources from Barbour Publishing!

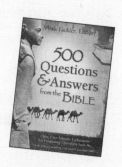
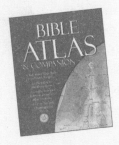